·SUPERMARKET·
HEALTHY

·SUPERMARKET·
HEALTHY

RECIPES & KNOW-HOW FOR
EATING WELL WITHOUT SPENDING A LOT

MELISSA D'ARABIAN

WITH RAQUEL PELZEL

PHOTOGRAPHS BY TINA RUPP

Clarkson Potter/Publishers

New York

Published in the United States by Clarkson Potter/Publishers,
an imprint of the Crown Publishing Group, a division of Random House LLC,
a Penguin Random House Company, New York.
www.crownpublishing.com
www.clarksonpotter.com

CLARKSON POTTER is a trademark and POTTER with colophon is a registered
trademark of Random House LLC.

Library of Congress Cataloging-in-Publication Data
D'Arabian, Melissa.
Supermarket healthy : recipes and know-how for eating well without spending
a lot / Melissa d'Arabian with Raquel Pelzel ; photographs by Tina Rupp.
pages cm
1. Low budget cooking. I. Pelzel, Raquel. II. Title.
TX652.D326 2014
641.5'52—dc23
2014009429

ISBN 978-0-307-98517-0
eBook ISBN 978-0-307-98518-7

Printed in China

Book design by La Tricia Watford
Cover design by La Tricia Watford
Cover photographs by Tina Rupp
Photograph on page 5 by Kristen Vincent

10 9 8 7 6 5 4 3 2 1

First Edition

To Philippe, Valentine, Charlotte, Margaux, and Océane:

You are always my
favorite part of the day.

CONTENTS

HEALTHY EATING EVERY DAY

WHENEVER I WALK INTO A HIGH-END HEALTH food store, I drool. I would love to buy all of my food from those beautifully curated aisles where the oranges are assembled in perfectly aligned pyramids, the lettuces glisten with dewy drops of water, and the endcaps boast cold-pressed juices bursting with vitamins and goodness.

However, just like so many families in America, we have a mortgage, bills, and four kids to budget for. So I made it my job to figure out a way to create food for my family that is just as healthy and good as what is being sold in fancy, premium markets, but that also respects my need to be a smart, price-savvy shopper. That's why I decided to make the focus of my second cookbook, *Supermarket Healthy*, eating well based on using your everyday supermarket to make cost-conscious and consciously minded buying decisions.

Budget living is about spending with purpose and intent and being mindful about how you spend your dollars. Healthful eating is about eating with purpose and intent and being mindful about how you choose the ingredients. In *Supermarket Healthy,* these two paths intersect, and the result is more than 125 recipes that you can feel good about cooking and eating.

I am a big believer in not overspending, and much of my career has been based on my natural inclination to save money. I grew up on a budget, and that savvy coupon-cutting mentality will always course through my veins. I know that I am not alone. I'm not the only one who wants to cook within my budget while still feeling good about the food I buy, eat, and prepare for my family and friends.

Supermarket Healthy celebrates dishes that are as friendly to your waistline as they are to your wallet. Because, lucky for us, the neighborhood grocery store has become a healthy cook's resource for all kinds of key ingredients, from quinoa to organic produce and buzzy superfood items such as omega-rich chia seeds and wild salmon.

I've created every recipe keeping nutrition in mind, but this isn't a diet cookbook and it's not meant to be. Quite simply, this is a cookbook that addresses the fact that when you eat better, you feel better. It is my hope that with this cookbook, you'll also discover that you don't need to spend a lot to feel your best.

Melissa d'Arabian

MAKING SUPERMARKET HEALTHY WORK FOR YOU

Cooking on a budget is empowering. Combine that with eating better, making every bite count, and supplying your body with quality protein, long-lasting carbohydrates for energy, and lots of vitamins and nutrients, and you have a way of cooking that not only feels great but also *is* great!

As I did in my first book, *Ten Dollar Dinners,* I have stocked *Supermarket Healthy* with loads of extra-value features to give you additional buying power at the store.

Strategies

Throughout the book, you'll notice three color-coded strategies that will pop up at the bottom of recipes: Supermarket Strategies, Kitchen Strategies, and Entertaining Strategies.

SUPERMARKET STRATEGIES are ways to make your grocery store work for you. These include buying tips, ways to save, and insights about making choices at the store. These boxes are green.

KITCHEN STRATEGIES are things to keep in mind in your kitchen. These are time-saving tips, make-ahead advice, and at-home swaps so you don't have to run to the store for that *one* ingredient, and advice for how to introduce new flavors to kids. These boxes are blue.

ENTERTAINING STRATEGIES are tactics for serving and stretching food, as well as easy spins on a dish to make it party-friendly. These boxes are orange.

Blueprints

While recipes are wonderful and so important, sometimes it's nice to exercise your creativity and take a recipe off-roading into uncharted territory. A feature in *Supermarket Healthy* is recipe blueprints that show you how to break down a recipe into a sequence of easy-to-follow steps. Think of it as a choose-your-own-adventure recipe. Switch up the ingredients or vary the method ever so slightly, and you have a brand-new recipe.

Nutritionals

Another tool in *Supermarket Healthy* is basic nutritional information that runs with each recipe. While *Supermarket Healthy* isn't a diet cookbook, the nutritional panel should serve as a good resource to help you build a meal, or weekly menus that balance lean meals with slightly more indulgent ones. This book was created with a health-conscious perspective and a focus on good fats, slow-burning complex carbohydrates, ample protein, and lots of vitamins and nutrients.

HOT-BUTTON ISSUES

It seems impossible to write a book about healthy grocery-store eating without considering some hot-button topics such as the importance of eating organically, avoiding genetically modified ingredients (GMOs), and eating gluten-free. As a mom, of course I want the best for my family, but ultimately we all have to decide what is right for our own families and go with it.

Organic

Even if you're on a budget, buying organically grown fruits, vegetables, and grains is totally possible. Just like conventionally grown ingredients, organics go on sale too, so always shop the aisles and compare apples to apples. You can also make a "dirty dozen" list of fruits with the highest traces of pesticide residues and make it a priority to purchase them only when organically grown. Some produce such as bananas have removable peels, so can fall lower on the "buy organic" list. Additionally, you can simply factor in the extra cost of organic ingredients by incorporating one or two meat-free days a week. Meals based on beans and grains are very economical and may provide you with enough wiggle room to purchase organics.

GMOs, Artificial Flavors, and Artificial Sweeteners

In our family, we try to avoid genetically modified ingredients and do our best to abstain from foods made with artificial flavors and sweeteners. When we want to indulge in something sweet, I feel best when I serve my family a treat that is homemade. Of course, I allow my girls to have the occasional crazy-colored cupcake at a friend's birthday party, but when I have the ability to control the ingredients in a recipe, I just prefer to cook with natural and unadulterated products. That doesn't mean I'm a purist, by any means; I still occasionally use white granulated sugar and white flour in my recipes. I just believe in making the less healthy options the exception rather than the rule.

Allergies, Sensitivities, and Restrictions

As a society we are more aware than ever of how food affects our bodies. The result is that people are able to create eating plans that best support their well-being. For instance, in my family alone (including my sister's kids, who live a few houses away from us), we have three vegetarians, a gluten-free eater, and two lactose-intolerant eaters. So I've learned to adapt recipes and to create meals that meet the various needs of all the people around our table.

The recipes in *Supermarket Healthy* naturally lend themselves to this kind of adaptation. If a recipe calls for a tablespoon of butter but is otherwise dairy-free, of course you can use your judgment to substitute olive oil or canola oil for the butter.

To make something gluten-free is a bit trickier. As I was writing this book, I discovered that one of my daughters had a gluten sensitivity—and so began my education in the world of gluten-free ingredients, and how ingredients you'd never even guess could contain trace amounts of gluten (soy sauce, oats). There are many recipes in *Supermarket Healthy* that are gluten-free, or that with a quick adaptation can be made gluten-free (such as by substituting gluten-free pasta for wheat pasta). If you are highly sensitive to gluten or have celiac disease, you will also need to consider cross-contamination risks.

Buying Local

Purchasing produce from a locally based grower is great for the environment, your community, and your health. When food has a shorter distance to travel from the farm to your table, it is fresher, retains more vitamins and nutrients, and doesn't leave as big a carbon footprint on the earth as it would if it were flown in from another continent. I love taking my girls to the farmers' market! I find that when they get to interact with farmers and choose a carrot with dirt still clinging to it or funky-colored vegetables (purple green beans! green cauliflower!), they can better appreciate where food comes from. Additionally, when there is a bumper crop of corn or zucchini, the price per pound at your farmers' market is likely to be competitive with what you would pay at the grocery store. Though even when at a slightly higher price, farmers' markets have good value when you consider the cost per nutrient. The entertainment factor is big for my family, too—we can easily enjoy a few hours at the farmers' market and spend a lot less money than we would if we all went to the movies!

A Few Words: Smart Indulging

I don't think there are any foods that are off-limits in my house. Small quantities of rich cheeses, prime cuts of beef, whole milk, and dessert (I could never give up dessert!) help us feel content and satiated. What's really interesting, however, is if you divide the total quantity of the indulgent ingredient by the number of servings in the recipe, the calories and fat per person are likely negligible because you're consuming only a small portion.

A perfect example is bacon. If you purchase pork bacon, look for leaner center-cut bacon (or chop off the ends of the regular bacon when you get home). If a recipe calls for only a slice or two of bacon, then I'll always choose pork bacon over turkey bacon because I get so much more flavor-bang for the buck, which means I can use less. When all is said and done, one or two slices of bacon in a whole recipe add a ton of flavor while contributing only a few grams of fat (and I feel extra good about buying the nitrate-free version!).

Some other ingredients that I strategically include in my cooking that aren't traditionally seen as "light" are butter, cream, whole milk, chocolate, coconut milk, and even puff pastry. Using these rich ingredients on occasion makes me feel that no sacrifice is needed to eat more healthfully. I can eat a wide variety of foods as long as I do so in moderation and keep portion control in mind.

THE SUPERMARKET HEALTHY PANTRY MUST-HAVES

Here's an overview of a few healthful ingredients that are nice to have on hand to give breakfasts, lunches, and dinners a nutritional boost. I've only included items that you might not have in your pantry. Common denominators like butter, milk, olive oil, and bread crumbs I've left off the list since you probably have them at the ready. If you want a more extensive list, check out my other cookbook, *Ten Dollar Dinners*.

DRY STORAGE
Almond butter

Almond flour
(finely ground raw, skinned almonds that can be purchased or made in the food processor)

Canned fish
(salmon, sardines)

Dried beans and legumes
(black beans, white beans, brown lentils, red lentils)

Grains
(bulgur cracked wheat, long-grain brown rice, instant brown rice, millet, quinoa, wild rice)

Oil
(coconut oil)

Pasta
(buckwheat, rice noodles, seaweed-based noodles, whole wheat)

Seeds
(chia, flax seeds, hemp seeds, pumpkin seeds, sunflower seeds)

Sweeteners
(agave syrup, date sugar)

Umami ingredients
(chili-garlic sauce, fish sauce, soy sauce, Sriracha, tamari sauce, Worcestershire sauce)

Vinegars and cooking wine
(mirin rice wine, rice vinegar, sake, sherry vinegar, vermouth)

White whole wheat flour
(a mild-tasting flour made from a hard white wheat)

Whole wheat panko-style bread crumbs

Whole wheat pastry flour
(a lower-protein whole wheat flour)

REFRIGERATOR
Bold cheeses
(cotija, feta, Parmesan, pecorino, ricotta salata)

Fresh fish
(cod, salmon, shrimp, snapper, tilapia, trout, tuna)

Leafy greens
(hardy greens like kale, spinach, Swiss chard)

Milk
(unsweetened almond milk, unsweetened soy milk)

Milled flax seeds

Miso paste

Raw, unsalted nuts
(almonds, cashews, hazelnuts, pecans, pine nuts, pistachios, walnuts)

Reduced-fat dairy products
(cottage cheese, cream cheese/Neufchâtel), mayonnaise, plain Greek yogurt, sour cream

Smoked trout

FREEZER
Bacon
(pork and turkey)

Chicken
(boneless, skinless breasts)

Edamame
(shelled)

Fish
(cod, salmon, shrimp, snapper, tilapia, trout, tuna)

Fruit
(ripe bananas, blueberries, mangos, peaches, raspberries)

Pork
(tenderloins)

Vegetables
(peas, chopped leaf spinach)

— Chapter 1 —

BREAKFAST

Cinnamon-Oatmeal
Pancakes

Peach Dutch Baby
Pancake

Almond Waffles with
Raspberry-Basil Sauce

Raspberry-Banana
Morning Boost
Smoothie

"Roasted" Banana–
Green Tea Smoothie

Caffeinated Coffee-Oat
Smoothie

Morning Glory Muffins

Easiest Pumpkin Pie–
Chia Pudding

Baked Eggs in
Tomato Sauce

Healthy Breakfast
Benedict

Hot Maple
Multigrain Cereal

Frittata with
Ricotta Salata and
Broccoli Rabe

Kale Breakfast Salad

Cinnamon Popovers
with Cream Cheese
Glaze

Fiber, protein, and complex carbohydrates fuel our bodies with sustainable energy, which is why it's so important to eat breakfasts loaded with good amounts of each. Of course, you can add whole-grain flour to a pancake recipe to increase the nutrients. But there are other things you can do, too, like adding oats to a smoothie, adding vegetables to your eggs, and loading your muffins with flax seeds and grated carrot.

Even when I am making a more treat-type weekend breakfast, like the German-style Peach Dutch Baby Pancake (page 19), I'll always give my kids a high-protein starter, like yogurt or a glass of milk, within the first hour of waking. I find that having something in their bellies before eating the fruit-laden pancakes gives them more even-keeled energy and less of the crazy sugar rush that comes from simple carbs on an empty stomach.

Many of the recipes in this chapter are make-ahead and freezer-friendly; that's because breakfast is the most important meal of the day and it's often the one we're likely to skip or eat on the run. Strategize and make your breakfast ahead of time, so you can throw together a smoothie, pull a chia pudding from the fridge, thaw a healthy muffin, or toast a waffle in no time flat.

CINNAMON-OATMEAL PANCAKES

SERVES 4   **PREPARATION TIME 25 MINUTES**   **COOKING TIME 10 MINUTES**

1 cup old-fashioned rolled oats

1 cup plus 1 tablespoon whole wheat pastry flour

1½ teaspoons baking powder

½ teaspoon baking soda

¾ teaspoon ground cinnamon

½ teaspoon kosher salt

2 large eggs

1½ cups buttermilk (or 1½ cups whole milk plus 2 tablespoons fresh lemon juice)

1 ripe banana, mashed

3 tablespoons lightly packed light brown sugar

1 tablespoon coconut oil, for cooking the pancakes

Maple syrup, sliced bananas, or fresh berries

Pancakes are a staple for many breakfast gatherings. Adding pulsed oats and some whole wheat pastry flour to the batter gives the pancakes fiber and substance, while the buttermilk adds lightness and tang. Coconut oil on the griddle helps the batter cook evenly (without a lot of darker splotches), but you can certainly use vegetable oil instead.

1   Add the oats to a food processor and process them until they are fine and flourlike in texture. Transfer the oat flour to a medium bowl and whisk in the pastry flour, baking powder, baking soda, cinnamon, and salt.

2   To the food processor add the eggs, buttermilk, banana, and brown sugar, processing until the mixture is well blended. While stirring with a wooden spoon, gradually add the buttermilk mixture to the flour mixture until the two are combined. Let the batter rest for 5 minutes at room temperature before making the pancakes. Preheat the oven to 250°F.

3   Melt the coconut oil in a large nonstick skillet set over medium-low heat. Use a ¼-cup measure to portion the batter and add it to the pan. Add three to four ¼-cup measures of batter to the pan (depending how big your pan is), and be sure to leave at least 1 inch between pancakes so they can spread without running into one another.

4   Cook the pancakes until browned on the bottom and some bubbles begin to break around the edges, about 2 minutes. Use a spatula to turn the pancakes over. Cook the other side until browned on the bottom and the center springs back to light pressure, about 2 minutes. Transfer the pancakes to a baking sheet, loosely cover with foil, and place in the oven to keep warm. Repeat with the remaining oil and batter. Serve the pancakes warm with maple syrup, bananas, and/or berries.

PER SERVING: Calories 340 / Protein 14g / Dietary Fiber 7g / Sugars 18g / Total Fat 9g

PEACH DUTCH BABY PANCAKE

SERVES 4   PREPARATION TIME 20 MINUTES   COOKING TIME 25 MINUTES

2 tablespoons unsalted butter

½ cup chopped fresh, frozen, or canned peaches

1 tablespoon lightly packed light brown sugar

1 teaspoon ground cinnamon

¼ teaspoon kosher salt

2 large eggs, plus 1 egg white, at room temperature

½ cup all-purpose flour

2 tablespoons cornstarch

¾ cup 2% milk, warmed

2 tablespoons granulated sugar

2 teaspoons vanilla extract

Confectioners' sugar

If you come to my house on any given Saturday morning, you are likely to see my kids nibbling on some version of a Dutch baby, which is a puffed oven-baked pancake. The real key to a perfect Dutch baby is to have room-temperature ingredients, a hot oven, and a preheated slope-sided pan. For this Dutch baby, I add cooked peaches for a sweet caramel flavor that my family and guests just adore.

1 Preheat the oven to 375°F. Melt the butter in a large oven-safe nonstick skillet (preferably one with sloped sides) over medium-high heat. Pour 1 tablespoon of the melted butter into a small bowl and set aside. Add the peaches, brown sugar, cinnamon, and salt to the remaining butter in the skillet and cook the peaches over medium-high heat until they begin to soften and caramelize, about 3 minutes.

2 Add the eggs, egg white, flour, cornstarch, milk, granulated sugar, vanilla, and reserved melted butter to a blender and blend on medium-high speed until smooth and combined. (If mixing by hand, whisk the eggs and egg white with the milk until the mixture is light yellow and frothy, then whisk in the flour until the mixture is smooth. Add the granulated sugar and vanilla.)

3 Pour the batter over the peaches in the skillet and place the skillet in the oven. Cook until the pancake is puffed in the center and golden brown around the edges, 18 to 22 minutes.

4 Remove the skillet from the oven and let the pancake cool in the pan for 1 minute. Use a spatula to slide the Dutch baby onto a wire rack. Cool for a few more minutes to allow the steam to escape without condensing along the bottom and rendering the pancake soggy. Sprinkle with confectioners' sugar, then slice the pancake into 8 wedges and serve.

PER SERVING: Calories 229 / Protein 7g / Dietary Fiber 1g / Sugars 12g / Total Fat 9g

ALMOND WAFFLES WITH RASPBERRY-BASIL SAUCE

SERVES 6   PREPARATION TIME 15 MINUTES   COOKING TIME 20 MINUTES

FOR THE RASPBERRIES

2 cups (1 pint) fresh or frozen raspberries

1 teaspoon granulated sugar

2 tablespoons fresh orange juice

4 fresh basil leaves, finely chopped

FOR THE WAFFLES

3 tablespoons coconut oil (if solid, microwaved until melted) or vegetable oil

1 large egg, separated, plus 2 large egg whites

3 tablespoons granulated sugar

1 teaspoon vanilla extract

¼ teaspoon almond extract

¾ cup almond flour

1¼ cups unsweetened almond milk (vanilla or plain), plus extra if needed

¼ teaspoon kosher salt

1¼ cups whole wheat pastry flour

2½ teaspoons baking powder

Confectioners' sugar

I love these waffles; they are filling from the protein, fiber, and healthy fats, but they aren't dense thanks to airy whipped egg whites. Raspberry and almond are fantastic flavor companions, offering so much sweetness and richness that I doubt you'll miss butter or syrup. You can even eat the almond waffles without the berries for a portable treat. Just sprinkle with some confectioners' sugar, and pretend you're eating a Parisian gaufre while walking down the Champs-Élysées.

1 To prepare the raspberries: Place the berries in a small bowl and sprinkle with the granulated sugar and orange juice. Set aside for 15 minutes, then stir and gently press on a few berries to extract the juice. Have the basil ready.

2 To make the waffles: Preheat the oven to 300°F. Whisk together the coconut oil, egg yolk, and granulated sugar in a large mixing bowl until smooth, light, and creamy. Whisk in the vanilla and almond extracts and the almond flour, then add the almond milk and salt and whisk until combined.

3 Set a sieve over the almond mixture. To the sieve add the pastry flour and baking powder. Shake the flour mixture through the sieve, then use a wooden spoon to stir it into the almond mixture. (The batter should be thick but pourable; if not pourable, add a few more tablespoons of almond milk.)

4 Heat a waffle iron according to the manufacturer's instructions. Add the egg whites to the bowl of a stand mixer (or a large bowl, if using a hand mixer) and whip on medium-low speed until the whites are foamy. Increase the speed to high and beat until the whites hold firm peaks.

(recipe continues)

5 Using a rubber spatula, fold half of the beaten whites into the almond batter until only a few white streaks remain, then gently fold in the remaining whites just until incorporated and no white streaks remain.

6 Cook the waffles according to the instructions, placing them on a wire rack atop a baking sheet and in the oven to keep warm while you make the rest. Stir the basil into the raspberries and serve the sauce over the waffles with the confectioners' sugar on the side.

PER SERVING: Calories 303 / Protein 9g / Dietary Fiber 8g / Sugars 10g / Total Fat 16g

---

KITCHEN STRATEGY

Freezing Waffles

Waffles are incredibly freezer-friendly. If you plan to freeze a few for later, undercook them slightly, then once they are cool, wrap each one in plastic wrap and store in a resealable freezer bag. Pop in your toaster on a medium-low setting for a golden-brown waffle. You can even serve them for dinner with the panfried chicken on page 190, a drizzle of honey, and a splash of hot sauce.

THREE SMOOTHIES TO START YOUR MORNING RIGHT

MAKES 2 LARGE SMOOTHIES   PREPARATION TIME 5 MINUTES

I make smoothies probably more than anyone I know (my blender is by far the most used kitchen appliance!). I like knowing that I'm getting so much—fiber, good fats, vitamins, antioxidants, complex carbs, and protein—in one easy-to-sip package. Here are a few of my favorites, as well as some tried-and-true techniques and insights.

1¼ cups unsweetened vanilla almond milk, soy milk, or dairy milk

1 peeled and frozen ripe banana, cut into pieces

¼ cup old-fashioned rolled oats

¼ cup peeled, seeded, and finely chopped cucumber

3 tablespoons cooked white beans (homemade, page 81; or canned, rinsed)

¾ cup frozen or fresh raspberries

1 teaspoon vanilla extract

¾ cup ice cubes

Raspberry-Banana Morning Boost Smoothie
COOKING TIME 40 SECONDS

Old-fashioned rolled oats and white beans add body and fiber to this blushing pink smoothie. It's also delicious made with strawberries or blueberries.

1 Add the almond milk to a blender and then add the remaining ingredients in this order: the banana, oats, cucumber, beans, raspberries, vanilla, and ice cubes.

2 Blend on high speed until smooth, 30 to 45 seconds. Divide between glasses and serve.

PER SERVING: Calories 172 / Protein 5g / Dietary Fiber 7g / Sugars 14g / Total Fat 3g

1 medium banana, peeled and cut into quarters

1½ cups unsweetened vanilla soy milk, almond milk, or dairy milk

2 tablespoons milled flax seeds (or hemp seeds)

½ cup frozen kale or spinach (no need to thaw)

2 teaspoons green tea powder

⅛ teaspoon ground cinnamon

1 teaspoon vanilla extract

2 teaspoons pure maple syrup (optional)

¾ cup ice cubes

"Roasted" Banana–Green Tea Smoothie
COOKING TIME 40 SECONDS

This smoothie has a lot of surprises in store. First is the "roasted" banana, which gets microwaved to intensify its natural sweetness. Then, the slightly toasty flavor comes in thanks to green tea powder called matcha. (It's available in Asian markets and some supermarkets, and really pumps up the antioxidants in this blend.) Plus, the gentle caffeine boost is milder with green tea than with coffee. Lastly, flax seeds (or hemp seeds) offer lots of omega-3 fatty acids, and we all know how good for you kale is!

1 Place the banana in a microwave-safe bowl and microwave until it is fragrant and soft, 30 to 40 seconds.

2 Add the soy milk to a blender and then add the remaining ingredients in this order: the flax seeds, frozen kale, green tea powder, cinnamon, vanilla, maple syrup (if using), and ice cubes. Add the hot banana on top of the ice.

3 Blend on high speed until smooth, 30 to 45 seconds. Divide between glasses and serve.

PER SERVING: Calories 154 / Protein 4g / Dietary Fiber 6g / Sugars 15g / Total Fat 6g

KITCHEN STRATEGY

Smoothie on the Run

For even faster morning smoothies, prep your smoothie components in advance and stash them in the freezer in individual freezer bags for a healthy grab-and-blend breakfast. Just add the ice and liquid, then blend and go.

1¼ cups unsweetened vanilla almond milk, soy milk, or dairy milk

1 peeled and frozen ripe banana, broken into chunks

¾ cup cooked oatmeal

2 tablespoons smooth almond butter

1 tablespoon lightly packed light or dark brown sugar

¾ cup frozen coffee ice cubes (or 1 teaspoon instant coffee, plus ¾ cup ice cubes)

Caffeinated Coffee-Oat Smoothie

COOKING TIME 40 SECONDS

This smoothie gives you protein, fiber, antioxidants, and your morning coffee fix all at once. Make the coffee ice cubes in advance (repurpose leftover coffee in ice cube trays), then pop them out of the trays and store in a resealable quart-size freezer bag. The cooked oatmeal offers an extra-creamy texture.

1 Add the almond milk to a blender and then add the remaining ingredients in this order: the banana, oatmeal, almond butter, brown sugar, and coffee ice cubes.

2 Blend on high speed until smooth, 30 to 45 seconds. Divide between glasses and serve.

PER SERVING: Calories 261 / Protein 6g / Dietary Fiber 4g / Sugars 18g / Total Fat 13g

---

BE A SMOOTH(IE) OPERATOR

A few smoothie tips and tricks to keep in mind:

• Berries can substitute for each other; if strawberries are on sale, use them instead of raspberries (and vice versa—don't forget about blueberries, too!).

• A couple spoonfuls of beans increases protein and creaminess without adding a "bean-y" flavor.

• If you have bananas that are past their optimal eating ripeness, they're perfect for freezing and using in smoothies. Peel, halve, and store in a resealable freezer bag.

• Use any dairy or nondairy liquid you like, from reduced-fat milk to almond milk, soy milk, rice milk, or coconut water. I like to use unsweetened versions and then only if needed do I add maple syrup, honey, agave syrup, or brown sugar.

• Always add the liquid to the blender first to create a vortex and ensure easy blending.

• Instead of using plain ice cubes, use frozen cubes made from your favorite fresh juice, coffee, or herbal tea.

MORNING GLORY MUFFINS

MAKES 12 MUFFINS   PREPARATION TIME 20 MINUTES   COOKING TIME 25 MINUTES

Nonstick pan spray

3 medium carrots, peeled

1 cup muesli

¼ cup raw walnut halves

¾ cup whole wheat pastry flour

2 tablespoons milled flax seeds (flaxmeal)

¾ teaspoon baking powder

¼ teaspoon freshly ground nutmeg

¼ teaspoon kosher salt

½ cup coconut oil (if solid, microwaved until melted), at room temperature

½ cup date sugar (or lightly packed light brown sugar)

2 large eggs

⅓ cup skim milk

½ teaspoon vanilla extract

¼ cup large unsweetened coconut flakes

Muffins are a very convenient breakfast item, and it's really easy to make an extra dozen and freeze them for another morning (or even an afternoon snack). They thaw quickly at room temperature, and a healthy muffin plus a glass of milk make a good on-the-go breakfast. Making your own muffins means you can load them with fiber, vitamins, and protein. My shortcut ingredient here is muesli. I spin it in a food processor so its consistency is that of lightly sweetened oat flour. If you don't have muesli, substitute rolled oats and a spoonful of raisins.

1   Preheat the oven to 350°F. Line a 12-cup muffin pan with liners or mist with nonstick pan spray.

2   Fit a food processor with the medium grater attachment and grate the carrots. Transfer the carrots to a medium bowl and replace the grater attachment with the blade attachment.

3   Add the muesli and walnuts to the food processor and pulse until the oats are coarsely ground and the walnuts are roughly chopped. Add the flour, flax seeds, baking powder, nutmeg, and salt and pulse to combine.

4   In a medium bowl, whisk together the coconut oil, sugar, eggs, milk, and vanilla. Pour the egg mixture into the muesli mixture along with the grated carrots and the coconut flakes. Pulse just to combine.

5   Divide the batter evenly among the muffin cups and bake until a toothpick inserted into the center of a muffin comes out clean and the muffins spring back to light pressure, 20 to 22 minutes. Cool for 5 minutes before inverting onto a cooling rack. Serve warm or completely cooled.

PER SERVING: Calories 195 / Protein 4g / Dietary Fiber 3g / Sugars 10g / Total Fat 12g

EASIEST PUMPKIN PIE–CHIA PUDDING

SERVES 4   **PREPARATION TIME** 35 MINUTES (plus 1 hour to set)   **COOKING TIME** NONE

½ cup chia seeds

1 teaspoon pumpkin pie spice

1 cup pumpkin purée (not sweetened pie filling)

⅔ cup light coconut milk (canned or carton)

2 cups unsweetened almond milk or soy milk

1 tablespoon maple syrup or honey, plus more for serving (optional)

¼ cup raw pecan halves, roughly chopped (almonds and cashews work, too)

1 medium banana, peeled and thinly sliced

Chia pudding is so easy, and can be a snack, dessert, or, most often for me, breakfast. I make a batch of chia pudding before I go to bed at night, and it's ready and waiting for me to eat in the morning (this recipe easily scales up or down, too). Adding pumpkin purée makes the pudding extra creamy, and with the pecans and touch of maple syrup or honey, this reminds me of a (healthy) creamy pumpkin pie.

1 Place the chia seeds and pumpkin pie spice in a small plastic container with a lid. Cover and shake to distribute the powder among the seeds.

2 Whisk the pumpkin purée with the coconut milk in a small bowl until smooth. Pour over the chia seeds and add the almond milk and maple syrup. Cover and shake vigorously. Place the pudding in the refrigerator to thicken, shaking it after 30 minutes, and letting it set up for at least 1 hour, or up to several days.

3 Divide the pudding among bowls and serve sprinkled with pecans, bananas, and a drizzle of maple syrup (if using).

PER SERVING: Calories 255 / Protein 8g / Dietary Fiber 14g / Sugars 12g / Total Fat 16g

BAKED EGGS IN TOMATO SAUCE

SERVES 4   **PREPARATION TIME 20 MINUTES**   **COOKING TIME 45 MINUTES**

Nonstick pan spray

1 tablespoon olive oil

2 large garlic cloves, smashed

2 14-ounce cans crushed tomatoes

Pinch of red pepper flakes

½ teaspoon kosher salt, plus extra for seasoning

½ teaspoon ground black pepper, plus extra for seasoning

8 large eggs

½ cup fresh basil leaves, finely chopped

½ cup shredded mozzarella cheese

Crusty loaf of bread (or gluten-free bread), sliced into ½-inch-thick pieces

Baking eggs in a tomato sauce simplifies the preparation of perfectly cooked eggs for a crowd. The eggs are nestled into an aromatic sauce that surrounds the eggs and lets them cook gently to runny-yolk perfection. I like to serve this with a crusty baguette for dipping and scooping up the basil-infused sauce.

1 Preheat the oven to 425°F. Lightly coat a 2-quart baking dish with nonstick pan spray and set aside.

2 Heat the olive oil in a medium saucepan set over medium heat for 30 seconds. Add the smashed garlic and cook, stirring occasionally, until golden, 3 to 4 minutes. Add the crushed tomatoes, red pepper flakes, salt, and pepper. Cover the pan and simmer, stirring occasionally, until the sauce begins to thicken, about 25 minutes. Pour the sauce into the prepared baking dish.

3 Use the rounded part of a spoon to make a small well in the sauce. Break an egg into the well. Repeat, making more wells for the remaining eggs. Sprinkle the eggs with salt and pepper and bake until almost set, about 10 minutes. Remove the baking dish from the oven and sprinkle the basil and mozzarella over the top.

4 Return the baking dish to the oven and bake until the cheese is melted and golden brown, about 4 minutes longer. Spoon into individual bowls and serve immediately with crusty bread.

PER SERVING: Calories 402 / Protein 22g / Dietary Fiber 7g / Sugars 2g / Total Fat 18g

HEALTHY BREAKFAST BENEDICT

SERVES 4   **PREPARATION TIME 15 MINUTES**   **COOKING TIME 15 MINUTES**

**FOR THE CREAMY
BASIL SAUCE**

¼ cup light mayonnaise

2 tablespoons reduced-fat
sour cream

3 tablespoons finely
chopped fresh basil

1 tablespoon finely chopped
fresh chives

½ teaspoon Worcestershire
sauce or vegetarian
Worcestershire sauce
(optional)

¼ teaspoon kosher salt

¼ teaspoon ground black
pepper

FOR THE EGGS

1 tablespoon white vinegar

4 large eggs

2 whole-grain English
muffins, split and toasted

Olive oil mister or nonstick
pan spray

4 slices Canadian bacon

1 cup baby spinach

½ teaspoon kosher salt

½ teaspoon ground black
pepper

If eggs Benedict, a bacon-egg-and-cheese sandwich, and a bacon-y spinach salad were represented by three independent lines intersecting on a graph, this egg Benedict—made with lean Canadian bacon, baby spinach, a poached egg, and a rich herby sauce—would represent the point where all three intersect. A little vinegar in the simmering water helps the egg whites firm up when poaching. For a hint of bacon-y smoke, try sprinkling smoked salt over the egg instead of kosher salt before serving, and for extra richness and nutrients (like vitamin E, vitamin B, and folic acid), blend half an avocado into the basil sauce.

1 To make the creamy basil sauce: Whisk together the mayonnaise, sour cream, basil, chives, Worcestershire sauce (if using), salt, and pepper in a medium bowl.

2 To make the eggs: Fill a medium saucepan two-thirds full with water. Add the vinegar and bring to a bare simmer over medium heat (it should look like fizzy soda water). Crack an egg into a small bowl and tip the bowl so the egg gently slides into the water. Repeat with another egg. Gently simmer for 3½ minutes (raise or reduce the heat as needed) and then use a slotted spoon to transfer the poached eggs to a paper towel–lined plate. Repeat with the remaining 2 eggs.

3 Place 1 English muffin half on each of 4 plates. Lightly mist a large skillet with olive oil or nonstick pan spray and heat over medium-high heat. Add the bacon and cook until browned on both sides, 5 to 6 minutes total.

4 Use a spatula to transfer 1 hot bacon slice to each of the English muffin halves, then immediately top with some of the spinach. Place a poached egg over the spinach and sprinkle with salt and pepper. Drizzle some of the creamy basil sauce over the egg and serve immediately.

PER SERVING: Calories 239 / Protein 15g / Dietary Fiber 3g / Sugars 2g / Total Fat 13g

HOT MAPLE MULTIGRAIN CEREAL

SERVES 4 (the multigrain mix makes 16 servings)   **PREPARATION TIME** 10 MINUTES

COOKING TIME 35 MINUTES

FOR THE GRAIN MIX

1¼ cups steel-cut oats

1¼ cups quinoa, rinsed well under cold water

1¼ cups bulgur

¼ cup whole flax seeds

FOR THE CEREAL

¼ cup sliced almonds

¼ cup maple syrup

1 teaspoon ground cinnamon

1½ cups unsweetened almond or soy milk, or 2% or skim milk

½ teaspoon ground ginger

⅛ teaspoon kosher salt

Why spend big bucks on premixed multigrain breakfast cereal when you can make your own fresher and more interesting version for a fraction of the cost? Make a big batch of the dry grain mix—I like the combination of fortifying oats, fluffy quinoa, wheaty bulgur, and omega-packed flax seeds—then portion it out as needed.

1 To make the grain mix: In a large bowl stir together the oats, quinoa, bulgur, and flax seeds. Transfer to a mason jar or an airtight container.

2 To make the cereal: If using almonds, place them in a medium skillet set over medium heat. Toast the almonds, shaking the pan often, until they are golden, 4 to 5 minutes. Transfer the almonds to a plate and set aside.

3 Add 1 cup of the grain mix to a fine-mesh sieve and rinse under cold, running water. Whisk together the maple syrup with ¼ teaspoon of the cinnamon in a small bowl and set aside.

4 Bring the milk and 1½ cups water to a boil in a sauce-pan set over medium-high heat. Add the rinsed grains, the remaining ¾ teaspoon cinnamon, the ginger, and salt and reduce the heat to medium-low. Simmer gently, stirring occasionally, until the grains are tender and the liquid almost absorbed, 25 to 30 minutes.

5 Divide the cooked grain cereal among serving bowls. Drizzle with cinnamon-maple syrup and serve sprinkled with the toasted almonds.

PER SERVING: Calories 252 / Protein 7g / Dietary Fiber 6g / Sugars 13g / Total Fat 7g

FRITTATA WITH RICOTTA SALATA AND BROCCOLI RABE

SERVES 4   **PREPARATION TIME** 10 MINUTES   **COOKING TIME** 40 MINUTES

¾ pound broccoli rabe, tough ends removed

5 large eggs

3 large egg whites

¼ cup coarsely grated ricotta salata cheese

½ teaspoon kosher salt

½ teaspoon ground black pepper

2 teaspoons olive oil

1 garlic clove, chopped

¼ teaspoon red pepper flakes

2 tablespoons finely grated Parmesan cheese

ENTERTAINING STRATEGY

Fancy Frittatas

Impress your brunch guests by making individual frittatas: simply divide the egg mixture among the greased cups of a 12-cup muffin tin and bake until they are golden and puffed around the edges and the eggs are set, about 25 minutes.

Whole eggs are so delicious, but let's face it—they also have saturated fat and cholesterol. That is why I often replace an egg yolk with an extra egg white, like in this frittata, so that each serving accounts for fewer than two whole eggs per person. Additionally, bulking out the eggs with vegetables allows for fewer eggs to serve more people.

1 Preheat the oven to 325°F. Fill a large bowl with ice water and set aside. Bring a large pot of salted water to a boil and add the broccoli rabe. Cook until the broccoli rabe is al dente and turns bright green, about 3 minutes. Drain the broccoli rabe into a colander, then transfer to the ice water. Once the broccoli rabe is cool, drain it on a kitchen towel, then slice into 1-inch pieces.

2 Whisk together the whole eggs, egg whites, ricotta salata, ¼ teaspoon of the salt, and ¼ teaspoon of the black pepper.

3 Heat the olive oil in a large oven-safe nonstick skillet over medium heat. Add the garlic and cook, stirring, until tender, about 1 minute. Add the chopped broccoli rabe, red pepper flakes, the remaining ¼ teaspoon salt, and the remaining ¼ teaspoon black pepper. Cook, stirring, until fragrant, about 2 minutes. Pour the egg mixture into the skillet and continue to cook, without stirring, until the edges of the frittata start to set, 3 to 4 minutes.

4 Sprinkle the Parmesan cheese over the eggs and place the skillet in the oven. Bake until the frittata has puffed, is firm, and is golden on top, 20 to 25 minutes. Slide it onto a platter and serve the frittata sliced into quarters.

PER SERVING: Calories 178 / Protein 15g / Dietary Fiber 0g / Sugars 2g / Total Fat 11g

frittata (SERVES 4)

Like an omelet, but oh so much easier (no folding, flipping, rolling—or inadvertent scrambles!)

STEP 1: CHOOSE MEAT PREFERENCE.

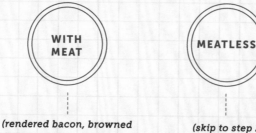

WITH MEAT

MEATLESS

(rendered bacon, browned sausage, chopped deli meat, or rotisserie chicken)

(skip to step 2)

STEP 2: PREP AND CHOP VEGETABLES.

BLANCHED OR ROASTED HARD VEGETABLES

(such as broccoli, broccoli rabe, cauliflower, green beans, or Swiss chard)

RAW SOFT VEGETABLES

(such as bell peppers, eggplant, fennel, mushrooms, tomatoes, or zucchini)

STEP 3: IN AN OVEN-SAFE NONSTICK SKILLET,
sauté the vegetables in a splash of olive oil with

AROMATICS

(chopped onion and garlic)

SALT

PEPPER

RED PEPPER FLAKES (optional)

STEP 4: WHISK TOGETHER

5 EGGS

3 EGG WHITES

SALT

PEPPER

CHOICE OF GRATED CHEESE
(such as fresh mozzarella,
provolone, Gruyère, Monterey
Jack, feta, or mild Cheddar)

STEP 5: POUR THE EGG AND CHEESE MIXTURE
over the vegetables, and top with additional grated cheese

PARMESAN	PECORINO
AGED CHEDDAR	AGED GOUDA

STEP 6: BAKE AT 350°F.
for 10 minutes until set. Let rest and serve warm.

KALE BREAKFAST SALAD

SERVES 4   PREPARATION TIME 20 MINUTES   COOKING TIME 10 MINUTES

FOR THE KALE

¼ cup fresh lemon or orange juice

1 tablespoon pure maple syrup

2 teaspoons balsamic vinegar

½ teaspoon kosher salt

1 bunch kale (preferably Lacinato/dinosaur), ribs removed and leaves stacked and thinly sliced crosswise into ribbons

FOR THE SALAD

Olive oil mister or nonstick pan spray

3 slices turkey bacon

2 tablespoons olive oil

1 tart apple (such as a Granny Smith), cored and cut into bite-size pieces

¼ cup grated Cheddar cheese

4 large eggs

½ teaspoon kosher salt

¼ teaspoon ground black pepper

Salad for breakfast . . . why not? Especially when it's loaded with goodies like Cheddar cheese, crispy bacon, and tart apples. Kale is hearty and so incredibly good for you. To make it a little more tender, massage the greens with the acidic base of the dressing before adding the oil. Hard-boiled egg slices can stand in for fried eggs, especially if you're going for a brunch-time chef's salad look.

1 To dress the kale: Whisk the lemon juice, maple syrup, balsamic vinegar, and salt together in a large bowl. Add the kale ribbons and use your hands to massage the dressing into the kale. Set aside.

2 To prepare the salad: Mist a medium nonstick skillet with olive oil or nonstick pan spray and set it over medium-high heat. Add the bacon and cook until crispy on both sides, 5 to 6 minutes total. Transfer the bacon to a cutting board (don't wash the skillet; you'll use it for the eggs) and chop the slices into rough pieces.

3 Drizzle the olive oil over the kale and toss to combine. Add the apples and cheese and toss to combine, then divide among 4 plates and sprinkle each with the bacon.

4 Crack the eggs into the skillet used for the bacon and cook them over medium heat to your liking, either sunny-side up or over easy. Slide an egg over each salad, sprinkle with salt and pepper, and serve.

PER SERVING: Calories 269 / Protein 13g / Dietary Fiber 2g / Sugars 10g / Total Fat 17g

A Kale Renaissance

There are typically two kinds of kale you'll see in the grocery store or farmers' markets: curly kale and Lacinato (dinosaur) kale. I typically use either in recipes, based on what I find most easily at the market. Curly kale leans toward the hardier side, so if you want a more tender bite for salads, try Lacinato kale. Either way you'll be getting tons of vitamins K, A, and C, as well as lots of fiber.

CINNAMON POPOVERS WITH CREAM CHEESE GLAZE

MAKES 12 POPOVERS   PREPARATION TIME 20 MINUTES   COOKING TIME 40 MINUTES

2 large eggs

2 tablespoons granulated sugar

1 cup 2% milk, warmed, plus 2 tablespoons

1 cup all-purpose flour

1 teaspoon ground cinnamon

½ teaspoon kosher salt

2 tablespoons unsalted butter, melted

¼ cup reduced-fat cream cheese (Neufchâtel), at room temperature

¼ cup confectioners' sugar

My girls love all things related to a cinnamon roll, from the swirling and soft cinnamon-speckled dough to the sticky-sweet icing that slicks the top. One morning, Charlotte was begging me for cinnamon rolls but I didn't have time to make them, so I decided to put the flavors of a cinnamon roll into my trusty quick popover recipe. It couldn't have been easier. These buns satisfy that cinnamon bun itch for both kids and adults.

1 Place a 12-cup muffin tin on the middle rack in the oven and preheat the oven to 400°F.

2 Add the eggs and granulated sugar to a blender jar and mix on medium speed until light yellow. Add the 1 cup warmed milk and blend. Add the flour, cinnamon, and salt and blend until smooth.

3 Use a pastry brush to grease the hot muffin tin generously with the melted butter. Add any remaining butter to the batter and pulse to blend. Pour the batter into the muffin tin, filling the cups about three-quarters full. Bake until the popovers are golden, about 20 minutes. (Do NOT open the oven door!) Turn off the oven, keep the oven door closed, and continue to bake the popovers until golden brown, 10 to 15 minutes.

4 Meanwhile, in a small bowl, whisk the cream cheese with the confectioners' sugar and the remaining 2 tablespoons milk until smooth. Remove the popovers from the oven. Use the tip of a paring knife to poke a tiny slit at the top of each popover (this will allow steam to escape, and will keep your popovers from getting soggy). Brush the popovers with the glaze and serve warm.

PER SERVING (1 popover): Calories 96 / Protein 3g / Dietary Fiber TKg / Sugars 6g / Total Fat 3g

— *Chapter 2* —

SNACKS

Snacking is an important part of my day. Seriously, without smart snacking between breakfast and lunch, and lunch and dinner, I show up to meals way too hungry for my own good! Snacking prevents overeating and is a great way to work in an extra serving or two of high-fiber, high-protein, and vitamin-rich goodness into your routine.

Proactive and purposeful snacking is the key to staving off mindless eating—you know, that handful of pretzels or "just one cookie" from the cookie jar. Instead, have some healthy ready-to-eat dips in the fridge. I include a few options in this chapter that offer lots of nutrition and satisfaction; most are very simple and fast to put together. An assortment of grab-and-go snacks is important, too. From trail mix to mini muffins and protein bars, these are the foods that keep you happily going at a high energy level and a healthy pace throughout the day.

ROASTED PEANUT–CHILE SALSA with CHIPS

SERVES 6   **PREPARATION TIME 30 MINUTES**   **COOKING TIME 25 MINUTES**

FOR THE CHIPS

Olive oil mister or nonstick pan spray

4 6-inch corn tortillas, cut into quarters

¾ teaspoon kosher salt (optional)

FOR THE SALSA

2 Anaheim chiles (or small poblano chiles)

¼ cup unsalted peanuts

1 whole unpeeled garlic clove

¼ cup fresh cilantro leaves

1 teaspoon white vinegar

¼ teaspoon kosher salt

Pinch of ground black pepper

Whipping up a batch of salsa and packing it into a jar takes just minutes and is really worth the effort. I love having a few home-made salsas in the fridge because they make a great healthy snack or turn a plain quick-grilled fish fillet or chicken cutlet into something extra special. This is one of our house favorites—it's crunchy and hearty from the roasted peanuts and mildly spiced from the charred green chiles. Homemade tortilla chips add a special factor to this duo. If you're serving the salsa with store-bought chips, choose ones that are baked instead of fried.

1 To make the chips: Adjust 2 oven racks to the middle and top positions and heat the oven to 450°F. Line a baking sheet with aluminum foil and lightly mist it with olive oil or nonstick pan spray. Spread the tortilla triangles in an even layer (mist with more olive oil or pan spray and sprinkle with salt, if desired) and bake them on the center rack for 4 minutes. Use a spatula to turn the chips over and continue to bake until they are golden and crisp, 4 to 6 minutes longer. Remove the chips from the oven and set aside.

2 To make the salsa: Adjust the oven temperature to broil. Place the chiles on a rimmed baking sheet and broil on the top rack of the oven until all sides of the chiles are charred, using tongs to turn the chiles often, 7 to 8 minutes total (watch the chiles closely, as broiler intensities vary). Transfer the chiles to a medium bowl, cover the bowl with plastic wrap, and set aside until the chiles are cool enough to handle, about 15 minutes. Peel and seed the chiles (don't rinse them) and place them in a blender jar.

3 Heat a medium skillet over high heat for 1 minute. Add the peanuts and garlic, reduce the heat to medium, and cook, shaking the pan often, until the peanuts and garlic are fragrant, about 3 minutes.

4 Add the peanuts to the chiles in the blender (keep the garlic in the skillet). Return the skillet to the heat and continue to cook the garlic until it is soft, using tongs to turn it often, about 3 minutes. Turn off the heat and set aside to cool. Peel the garlic and add it to the blender along with the cilantro, ¾ cup water, and the vinegar, salt, and pepper. Blend until the mixture is completely smooth; taste, and add more salt and pepper if needed.

5 Serve the salsa warm or at room temperature with the chips. (The salsa can be refrigerated in a glass jar or an airtight container for up to 2 weeks.)

PER SERVING: Calories 76 / Protein 2g / Dietary Fiber 2g / Sugars 0g / Total Fat 4g

SMASHED SARDINES on CRACKERS

SERVES 4   **PREPARATION TIME** 10 MINUTES   **COOKING TIME** NONE

1 3.75-ounce tin sardines in oil, well drained

1 teaspoon light mayonnaise

½ scallion (white and light green parts only), finely chopped

1 teaspoon finely chopped fresh thyme leaves

½ teaspoon finely grated lemon zest

1 to 2 teaspoons fresh lemon juice

½ teaspoon sweet paprika

¼ teaspoon ground black pepper

Pinch of kosher salt

12 whole-grain crackers

My sister and I grew up snacking on tinned sardines smashed on crackers. Sardines are one of my secret weapons for heart- and brain-healthy omega-3s. They're incredibly inexpensive, and are one of the most environmentally sustainable seafood choices around. If the sardine flavor is too strong for you, make this with half canned tuna (dolphin-safe) and half tinned sardines.

1   Drain the sardines and turn them out onto a paper towel–lined plate. Blot the sardines with a second paper towel, then transfer to a medium bowl. Add the mayonnaise and use a fork to lightly mash it into the sardines.

2   Add the scallion, thyme, lemon zest, 1 teaspoon of the lemon juice, the paprika, and pepper and stir to combine. Taste and add more lemon juice or a pinch of salt, if needed.

3   Divide the mixture among the crackers and serve immediately.

PER SERVING: Calories 161 / Protein 7g / Dietary Fiber 0g / Sugars 1g / Total Fat 9g

EDAMAME HUMMUS
WITH PITA CHIPS

SERVES 8 **PREPARATION TIME 20 MINUTES** **COOKING TIME 10 MINUTES**

FOR THE PITA CHIPS

Olive oil mister or nonstick pan spray

3 whole wheat pitas, each cut into 8 triangles

1 tablespoon black or white sesame seeds

½ teaspoon kosher salt

FOR THE HUMMUS

2 cups frozen and thawed shelled edamame beans

2 tablespoons fresh lemon juice

1 garlic clove, roughly chopped

¼ teaspoon toasted sesame oil

2 tablespoons canola or olive oil

½ teaspoon kosher salt

¼ teaspoon ground black pepper

Hummus is incredibly versatile. It can serve as an appetizer dip, a condiment, or even a (relatively temperature-flexible) protein boost in another veggie-filled dish (such as the wrap on page 104). The edamame bean (soybean) adds a tiny sweet touch—that and its pretty green color make edamame one of my favorite stand-ins for traditional garbanzo beans. If you can't find black sesame seeds for the chips, use white sesame seeds instead.

1 To make the pita chips: Preheat the oven to 350°F. and line a baking sheet with aluminum foil. Mist the foil with olive oil or nonstick pan spray, place the pita triangles on the foil, and lightly mist with olive oil or nonstick pan spray. Sprinkle with the sesame seeds and salt. Bake the pita until golden and crisp, about 10 minutes. Remove from the oven and set aside.

2 To make the hummus: Add the edamame, lemon juice, garlic, and sesame oil to the bowl of a food processor and pulse until chunky, about five 1-second pulses.

3 Add the canola oil, salt, and pepper to the edamame mixture and process until smooth. Serve immediately with the pita chips or refrigerate in an airtight container for up to 3 days.

PER SERVING: Calories 153 / Protein 7g / Dietary Fiber 4g / Sugars 1g / Total Fat 6g

ROASTED BEET DIP

SERVES 8 TO 10   **PREPARATION TIME** 10 MINUTES   **COOKING TIME** 1 HOUR

3 medium red beets, greens removed (save for another use)

2 unpeeled garlic cloves

2 tablespoons fresh lemon juice

¼ cup plain reduced-fat Greek yogurt

½ teaspoon kosher salt

¼ teaspoon ground black pepper

Crackers, fresh bread, or vegetable sticks

I like keeping an assortment of dips, salsas, and spreads in the fridge. They make an impromptu snack of carrot sticks or a piece of rye crispbread all the more interesting, and they can serve double duty as a spread in wraps and sandwiches, stirred into a salad dressing, or even liquefied with chicken broth or water and used as a sauce. Beets and garlic become extra mellow and sweet when roasted, and after being puréed with lemon juice and yogurt, it transforms into a dip that is creamy, tangy, and kind of addictive.

1   Preheat the oven to 400°F. Completely enclose each beet in a piece of foil, wrapping the edges to securely seal. Add the garlic to a separate piece of foil and wrap so the cloves are completely enclosed.

2   Place the foil packets directly on an oven rack and roast until a paring knife easily slips into the center of the largest beet, about 1 hour. Remove from the oven, carefully open the corners of the foil, and set the beets and garlic aside to cool.

3   Peel the beets and garlic. Roughly chop the beets and add them, along with the garlic, to the bowl of a food processor. Add the lemon juice, yogurt, salt, and pepper and process until smooth.

4   Transfer the dip to a medium bowl and serve with the crackers, fresh bread, or vegetable sticks.

PER SERVING: Calories 18 / Protein 1g / Dietary Fiber 1g / Sugars 2g / Total Fat 1g

WARM WHITE BEAN AND SAGE DIP

SERVES 6   **PREPARATION TIME 15 MINUTES**   **COOKING TIME 10 MINUTES**

2 tablespoons plus
2 teaspoons olive oil

1 garlic clove, very finely
chopped or pressed through
a garlic press

Pinch of red pepper flakes

7 fresh sage leaves

1½ cups cooked cannellini
beans (homemade, page 81;
or canned, rinsed)

½ teaspoon kosher salt

¼ teaspoon ground black
pepper

3 tablespoons low-sodium
chicken broth, vegetable
broth, or water

Sliced baguette, crackers, or
vegetable sticks

*A quick go-to pantry dip is essential—not just for entertaining
but also for life. This warm bean dip comes together in minutes.*

1 Heat 2 teaspoons of the olive oil in a medium nonstick skillet over medium heat for 1 minute. Add the garlic and cook until fragrant, 1 to 2 minutes. Stir in the red pepper flakes and sage, cooking until the sage is crisp but not browned, 2 to 3 minutes. Use tongs to transfer 2 sage leaves to a small paper towel–lined plate.

2 To the skillet add the beans, salt, and pepper and cook until the beans soften, about 3 minutes. Turn off the heat and cool for 5 minutes.

3 Transfer the bean mixture to a food processor. Add the broth and remaining 2 tablespoons olive oil and process until the beans are creamy, about 30 seconds. Scrape the bean dip into a medium bowl.

4 Sprinkle with the reserved sage leaves and serve with a sliced baguette, crackers, or vegetable sticks.

PER SERVING: Calories 120 / Protein 4g / Dietary Fiber 3g / Sugars 2g / Total Fat 6g

KITCHEN STRATEGY

Microwave-Roasted Garlic

Use roasted garlic to add a mellow, toasty quality to any dish that calls for fresh garlic. Combine 12 garlic cloves with 1 tablespoon olive oil and 1 teaspoon water in a microwave-safe dish. Cover the dish with a steamer vent (or plastic wrap—puncture a few times with a fork to let steam escape) and microwave until the garlic is soft, about 1 minute. Set aside to cool, then remove the lid and pop out the garlic from the peels. Submerge in olive oil and refrigerate in a sealed container.

RETHINKING THE CRUDITÉ PLATTER

One of my favorite restaurants is Andrew Weil's True Food Kitchen (with locations throughout the country and a companion cookbook, too!). They serve a crudité platter that sheds new light on this party standby. Gone are uninspired displays of baby carrots and celery sticks, and in their place comes an assortment of bright-colored vegetables, including thick bell pepper strips, tops-on radishes, spears of summer squash, and real carrots in miniature with little bits of their leafy greens still attached. The platter is as beautiful as it is delicious (and healthy).

When I'm serving crudités, in addition to buying the most beautiful and appetizing vegetables I can find (we do eat with our eyes, after all), I pay extra attention to creating a texturally interesting platter. Rather than serving everything raw, it's nice to steam or quick-blanch certain vegetables to give them an extra-tender bite. Cauliflower, broccoli, and green beans are great examples of vegetables that can be less intimidating when cooked than when raw.

To add to the "mix-it-up" factor, I serve crudités with bold-flavored and vibrant-hued dips, like the Roasted Beet (page 49), Warm White Bean and Sage (opposite), and Edamame Hummus (page 48). Add some rye crisps or toasted whole-grain crackers and you have a thoughtful snack that is as welcome for drop-in company as it is for the post-soccer team chow down.

GRILLED ZUCCHINI PIZZA BITES

SERVES 8   **PREPARATION TIME 10 MINUTES**   **COOKING TIME 10 MINUTES**

2 medium zucchini

2 teaspoons olive oil

¼ cup homemade or store-bought marinara sauce

24 pieces of thinly sliced low-fat pepperoni (optional)

4 ounces fresh mozzarella cheese, cut into 24 pieces

½ teaspoon kosher salt

I don't know anyone who can say no to a mini pizza. Here, instead of pizza dough, thinly sliced zucchini rounds provide a healthy base for the marinara sauce and mozzarella. I top each with a small round of pepperoni, which is easily omitted for a lighter, vegetarian snack. These disappear fast, so double the recipe if your crew is extra hungry!

1 Line a rimmed baking sheet with aluminum foil, adjust an oven rack to the upper-middle position, and preheat the broiler to high.

2 Trim the ends from the zucchini and slice each zucchini crosswise into ½- to ¾-inch rounds (you should get about 24 rounds). Heat the olive oil in a large nonstick skillet set over medium-high heat. Add the zucchini and cook until browned on one side (in batches, if needed), 4 to 5 minutes.

3 Transfer the zucchini to the baking sheet, browned side up. Top each zucchini round with ½ teaspoon of the marinara sauce, a pepperoni slice (if using), and a piece of mozzarella. Broil the zucchini until the cheese is melted, 2 to 3 minutes (watch the pizza bites closely, as broiler intensities vary).

4 Remove the zucchini from the oven and transfer to a platter. Sprinkle with the salt and serve warm.

PER SERVING: Calories 74 / Protein 9g / Dietary Fiber 3g / Sugars 1g / Total Fat 5g

ALMOND-CHOCOLATE PANINI

MAKES 2 PANINI   **SERVES** 4   **PREPARATION TIME** 5 MINUTES
COOKING TIME 10 MINUTES

¼ cup almond butter

4 slices whole wheat or
multigrain sandwich bread
(or gluten-free bread)

2 tablespoons semisweet
chocolate chips

Nonstick pan spray

1 tablespoon unsweetened
cocoa powder (optional)

**KITCHEN
STRATEGY**

Nut-Free
Butters

Sunflower butter
made from sun-
flower seeds offers
the rich and creamy
qualities of a nut
butter but is friendly
for those who don't
tolerate nuts. Tahini,
a paste made from
sesame seeds, is a
good alternative,
too, but it isn't quite
as thick as a nut
butter, so it might
not be the best
swap for baking.

*Loaded with protein and healthy fats, almond butter is a nice,
subtle switch from peanut butter, especially in this decadent
warm-chocolate panini. Read the ingredient label before buying
your next jar of almond butter to make sure that minimal heat
processing was used to make the almond butter (more heat
equals more loss of nutrients) and that few to no preservatives,
artificial flavors, or sweeteners were added.*

1 Divide the almond butter between 2 of the bread slices.
Sprinkle 1 tablespoon of the chocolate chips over the top
of each and cover with the remaining 2 bread slices.

2 Lightly coat a large nonstick skillet or grill pan (or
panini press, if using) with nonstick pan spray and heat
over medium heat. Add the sandwiches and cook, pressing down gently on them with the back of a metal spatula to
flatten slightly, until one side is golden brown and crisp, 3 to
5 minutes.

3 Carefully flip the panini and continue to cook until
golden brown on the second side, 3 to 4 minutes more.
Place the cocoa in a fine-mesh sieve (if using) and dust lightly
over the panini. Slice each sandwich into quarters and serve
two triangles per person.

PER SERVING (2 triangles): Calories 198 / Protein 5g / Dietary Fiber 4g /
Sugars 6g / Total Fat 13g

POPCORN TWO WAYS

SERVES 8   **PREPARATION TIME** 5 MINUTES   **COOKING TIME** 10 MINUTES EACH

Low in fat, high in fiber, and with only 31 calories per popped cup, popcorn is a satisfying go-to snack. With a few decadent touches, it becomes something really special. For instance, pop the corn in bacon fat and sprinkle it with the cooked bacon (a couple slices is enough for lots of servings), and the popcorn becomes a salty, savory treat. For sweet cravings, I make what my kids call "chocolate-dipped popcorn," where I toss the popcorn with melted chocolate and confectioners' sugar and a bit of almond butter and coconut oil.

2 slices center-cut bacon

½ teaspoon smoked paprika

½ teaspoon salt

⅓ cup popcorn kernels

Smoky Bacon Popcorn

1 Heat a large heavy-bottomed pot or Dutch oven over medium heat. Add the bacon and cook until crisp, turning the strips midway through cooking, 5 to 7 minutes total. Remove the bacon from the pot, drain on paper towels, and set aside to cool. Turn off the heat and keep the bacon fat in the pot.

2 To a small food processor insert (or using a mini food processor; or a medium bowl, if you don't have a food processor) add the paprika and salt. Working quickly, crumble the cooled bacon into the food processor and pulse with the paprika and salt until the mixture is finely ground and looks like coarse cornmeal. (If you're using a bowl, then place the bacon in a zippered plastic bag and use the bottom of a heavy skillet or a rolling pin to crush the bacon, then add it to the paprika-salt.)

3 Add the popcorn kernels to the bacon fat in the pot and set over high heat. Shake the pot to coat all the kernels with the fat. Once the first kernel pops, cover the pot but leave the lid slightly askew to allow steam to escape (arrange the

(recipe continues)

lid so it sits with the steam venting away from you). Use oven mitts to protect your hands and shake the pot constantly, being careful not to knock off the cover, until the popping slows to 1 to 2 seconds between pops. Immediately turn off the heat and uncover the pot.

4 Transfer the hot popcorn to a brown paper bag and add the bacon salt. Close the bag and vigorously shake to combine. Serve warm.

PER SERVING: Calories 62 / Protein 2g / Dietary Fiber 1g / Sugars 0g / Total Fat 4g

Chocolate-Dipped Popcorn

1 tablespoon coconut oil

¼ cup almond butter

¼ cup semisweet chocolate chips

½ teaspoon table salt

1 teaspoon vanilla extract

¾ cup confectioners' sugar

¼ cup unsweetened cocoa powder

8 cups popped popcorn

1 Fill a medium saucepan with 1 inch of water and bring it to a simmer over medium-high heat. Reduce the heat to low and place a heat-safe bowl on top of the saucepan (the bottom of the bowl shouldn't touch the water).

2 To the bowl add the coconut oil, almond butter, chocolate chips, and salt and stir until smooth. Remove the bowl from the heat and stir in the vanilla.

3 In a separate small bowl, whisk together the confectioners' sugar and cocoa until well combined.

4 Place the popcorn in a large bowl and drizzle with the chocolate mixture. Stir to coat the popcorn (not all the popcorn will be completely coated). Transfer the cocoa-sugar mixture to a fine-mesh sieve and sift half of it over the popcorn. Stir, then sift the remaining cocoa-sugar over the popcorn. Stir again and then serve. (If the chocolate mixture isn't setting up on the popcorn, place the popcorn in the refrigerator for a few minutes to firm up before serving.)

PER SERVING: Calories 172 / Protein 3g / Dietary Fiber 3g / Sugars 14g / Total Fat 9g

LEMON-CHIA MINI MUFFINS

MAKES ABOUT 48 MINI MUFFINS (or 12 standard muffins)
PREPARATION TIME 10 MINUTES　　**COOKING TIME 15 MINUTES**

Nonstick pan spray

2 cups white whole wheat flour

2 teaspoons baking powder

½ teaspoon baking soda

¼ teaspoon kosher salt

½ cup sugar

2 large eggs

¾ cup skim milk

¼ cup coconut oil (if solid, microwaved until melted)

Zest and juice of 2 lemons

¼ teaspoon vanilla extract

3 tablespoons chia seeds

If you compared two standard recipes, one for muffins and the other for cupcakes, I bet you wouldn't notice a giant difference in ingredients! Would you eat a cupcake for breakfast? I sure wouldn't—but these muffins are a different story. White whole wheat flour boosts the fiber content, and chia seeds lend protein, fiber, and omega-3s. Mini muffins are great snacks that can be frozen and kept on hand for on-the-go snacking, or you can bake them into regular-size muffins for company or a breakfast treat (for regular-size muffins, double the nutritional information below).

1 Preheat the oven to 350°F. Use nonstick pan spray to lightly coat the cups of a miniature muffin tin (or standard muffin tin) and set aside.

2 Whisk together the flour, baking powder, baking soda, and salt in a large bowl.

3 In a medium bowl, whisk together the sugar, eggs, milk, coconut oil, lemon zest and juice, and vanilla. Add the sugar-egg mixture to the flour mixture and use a wooden spoon to stir to combine. Gently fold in the chia seeds.

4 Add about 1 tablespoon of batter to each miniature muffin cup. Bake until the muffins are golden and spring back to light pressure, and a toothpick inserted in the center of a muffin comes out clean, 10 to 12 minutes (15 to 18 minutes for standard muffins).

5 Remove the muffins from the tin and set them on a wire rack to cool. Repeat with the remaining muffin batter.

PER SERVING (2 mini muffins): Calories 90 / Protein 2g / Dietary Fiber 2g / Sugars 4g / Total Fat 4g

GO-TO TRAIL MIX

MAKES 3½ **CUPS** (about 8 servings)   **PREPARATION TIME** 3 MINUTES
COOKING TIME NONE

1 cup plain popped popcorn

1 cup low-sugar oat or rice cereal

½ cup raw pecan halves

½ cup raw pumpkin seeds

½ cup mini chocolate chips

There is great power in a tasty trail mix: in one bag, you can pack a sweet-salty treat that is high in protein and fiber and that satisfies a sweet craving. For a healthy and fun snack, I focus on combining low-sugar, high-fiber carbs with some protein and fats for staying power, plus a bit of treat to keep the kids excited (and because life is too short not to have a smidge of chocolate!). Pack these insanely easy and customizable snacks in single-serving containers and keep them in an easy-access spot for quick grab-and-go snacking.

Mix the popcorn, cereal, pecans, pumpkin seeds, and chocolate chips in a large bowl. Divide among 8 resealable snack bags or containers and store for up to 2 weeks.

PER SERVING: Calories 156 / Protein 3g / Dietary Fiber 2g / Sugars 7g / Total Fat 12g

trail mix

Trail mix has come a long way from the M&M, peanut, and raisin variety that I grew up on. Scant portions of cereal that are too small for a breakfast bowl are great mixed for a trail mix. Add pumpkin seeds, sunflower seeds, chocolate chips, and even pretzels or cheese crackers and nuts for protein (shelled pistachios, smoked almonds, and spiced pecans all add a more sophisticated twist) and you have an anytime treat guaranteed to please even the pickiest eaters since you can tailor it to their specific tastes. Homemade trail mix is not only way less expensive than store-bought but also offers lots of room for experimentation.

STEP 1: IN A LARGE MIXING BOWL, COMBINE
crunchy whole grains, high-protein fats, and some sweet treats.
Choose one or more of each to yield the noted amount.

2 CUPS CRUNCHY WHOLE GRAINS

(popcorn, cereal, pretzels, crackers, baked tortilla chips)

1 CUP HIGH-PROTEIN, HIGH-QUALITY FATS (RAW OR TOASTED)

Nuts (pecans, almonds, walnuts, pistachios, cashews, peanuts, hazelnuts)

Seeds (sunflower, pumpkin, hemp, flax, sesame)

½ CUP SWEET TREATS

Dried fruit (raisins, currants, apricots, cherries, pineapple, mango, apples, pears)

White or dark chocolate (chocolate chips, chocolate-covered fruit or nuts)

Yogurt-covered treats (such as pretzels or raisins)

STEP 2: DIVIDE THE TRAIL MIX
into small resealable plastic snack or sandwich bags and
store in an accessible spot for up to a few weeks.

CHOCOLATE PEANUT BUTTER DIP
WITH APPLES

SERVES 12   **PREPARATION TIME 15 MINUTES**   **COOKING TIME NONE**

1 cup natural peanut butter, stirred if the oil has separated

¼ cup coconut oil (if solid, microwaved until melted)

2 tablespoons unsweetened cocoa powder

1 tablespoon honey

Apple slices (I like tart Granny Smith)

One of my biggest health vices is a persistent sweet tooth. So when I absolutely need to eat something sweet, my strategy is to include some protein and fiber with my snack to give it some staying power. This creamy dip (which really is more "fudgy" than "dippy") does the trick and then some. It's rich and filling, plus it keeps in the fridge for several weeks (pack it into a jar and tie with twine for a cute homemade gift!).

1 Place the peanut butter in a medium bowl and use a fork to stir in the coconut oil, cocoa, and honey until well blended. Cover the bowl with plastic wrap and refrigerate for 10 minutes (or up to 3 weeks).

2 Serve a generous scoop of the chilled dip with the sliced apples.

PER SERVING: Calories 180 / Protein 5g / Dietary Fiber 2g / Sugars 3g / Total Fat 15g

CRANBERRY-OATMEAL-FLAX COOKIES

MAKES 15 COOKIES   **PREPARATION TIME 20 MINUTES**   **COOKING TIME 20 MINUTES**

¼ cup sliced almonds

¾ cup old-fashioned rolled oats

½ cup whole wheat pastry flour

¼ cup milled flax seeds (flaxmeal)

¼ teaspoon baking soda

½ teaspoon kosher salt

½ cup (1 stick) unsalted butter, at room temperature

⅓ cup lightly packed light brown sugar

1 teaspoon ground cinnamon

1 teaspoon vanilla extract

1 large egg

½ cup dried cranberries

Nonstick pan spray

A happy blend of savory and sweet, these cookies offer a tri-fecta of almonds, oats, and flax to nourish and curb hunger in a friendly cookie guise. I use whole wheat pastry flour because it's finer than regular whole wheat flour and offers more nutrition than all-purpose flour.

1 Preheat the oven to 350°F. Place the almonds on a rimmed baking sheet and toast in the oven until golden, 3 to 5 minutes. Remove the baking sheet from the oven and transfer the almonds to a large plate to cool.

2 In a medium bowl, whisk together the oats, flour, flaxmeal, baking soda, and salt. Using a stand mixer or hand mixer, cream the butter, brown sugar, cinnamon, and vanilla until airy and light, about 3 minutes. Add the egg and beat until combined. Add the flour mixture to the butter mixture and mix on low speed until just combined. Turn off the mixer and use a wooden spoon to stir in the cranberries and the toasted almonds.

3 Spray a rimmed baking sheet (the one you used for toasting the almonds is fine) with nonstick pan spray, or use parchment paper to line the baking sheet. Scoop rounded tablespoons of dough about 2 inches apart onto the baking sheet. Use your fingers to flatten each ball slightly.

4 Bake the cookies until golden brown, 10 to 12 minutes. Cool on the baking sheet for 15 minutes, then transfer to a wire rack to finish cooling. Repeat with the remaining cookie dough. (The cookies can be stored in an airtight container for up to 5 days.)

PER SERVING (1 cookie): Calories 130 / Protein 2g / Dietary Fiber 2g / Sugars 6g / Total Fat 8g

D'ARABIAN FAMILY PROTEIN BARS

MAKES 10 BARS   **PREPARATION TIME** 10 MINUTES   **COOKING TIME** 30 MINUTES

Olive oil mister or nonstick pan spray

1½ cups old-fashioned rolled oats

2 tablespoons sunflower seeds

3 tablespoons unsweetened shredded coconut

2 tablespoons lightly packed light brown sugar

½ teaspoon ground cinnamon

½ teaspoon kosher salt

3 tablespoons coconut oil (if solid, microwaved until melted)

⅔ cup plain reduced-fat Greek yogurt

⅓ cup almond butter

2 tablespoons honey

½ cup vanilla- or chocolate-flavored whey protein powder

3 tablespoons roasted almonds, roughly chopped

¼ cup dried cranberries

Whether I am traveling or running around town with my four girls, I always feel best when I keep up my protein intake. My kids and husband love when I make homemade protein bars, and of course that is so much cheaper than buying them. Buy protein powder in the bulk aisle of your grocery store. If you are using unflavored protein powder, feel free to add in a bit of cocoa or vanilla extract for extra flavor.

1 Preheat the oven to 350°F. Grease a 9 by 13-inch baking dish with olive oil or nonstick pan spray. Mix the oats, sunflower seeds, coconut, brown sugar, cinnamon, and salt in a large bowl.

2 In another medium bowl, stir together the coconut oil, yogurt, almond butter, and honey. Add the yogurt mixture to the oat mixture and mix until the two are thoroughly combined. Stir in the protein powder, almonds, and cranberries. The mixture will be sticky.

3 Spread the mixture into the prepared dish and bake for 15 minutes. Take the pan out of the oven and let the mixture cool slightly, then slice it crosswise into 10 bars. Carefully remove the bars from the baking dish and use a spatula to transfer them to a parchment paper–lined rimmed baking sheet.

4 Bake until the bars start to turn golden, about 15 minutes longer. Remove the baking sheet from the oven, transfer the bars to a wire rack, and cool completely. (Wrap in aluminum foil or plastic wrap and refrigerate for up to 1 week.)

PER SERVING (1 bar): **Calories 226** / **Protein 9g** / **Dietary Fiber 2g** / **Sugars 9g** / **Total Fat 14g**

— Chapter 3 —

SOUPS AND STEWS

I have the dream of being that mom on the block who just happens to have a kettle of brothy soup simmering on the stove, on the off chance that the neighborhood kids playing kickball in the street want to come in from the cold for a steamy mug of goodness. Word would spread, and perhaps some neighbors would drop by, lured by the savory smells wafting out of our always-open front door. I'd smile warmly (I'm certain I wouldn't be on a work deadline of any sort), and I'd hand them a bowlful of liquid heaven, along with a hunk of crusty bread for dipping.

Turns out, though, that my four girls don't play kickball, and I don't allow them in the street anyway. Also, when the weather turns crisp and cold in the winter, I'm often wearing shorts and a T-shirt because I live in San Diego. Balmy "winters" aside, soup is a year-round affair, even here in Southern California. It makes us feel comforted and cozy, and it is an incredibly healthy and delicious way to get lots of veggies and fiber. Plus, it's often cheap to make! What's not to love?

ALMOST RAW ASPARAGUS SOUP

SERVES 4   **PREPARATION TIME 10 MINUTES**   **COOKING TIME 15 MINUTES**

1½ pounds asparagus, tough ends snapped off

2 teaspoons olive oil

¾ teaspoon kosher salt

¼ teaspoon ground black pepper

¼ cup sliced almonds

1½ cups low-sodium chicken or vegetable broth

Zest of 1 lemon

1 tablespoon finely chopped fresh mint leaves

¼ cup plain nonfat or reduced-fat yogurt

This incredibly quick and simple soup is a wonderful way to highlight asparagus. The asparagus is roasted in the oven just long enough to bring out its sweetness, and then it is puréed until smooth. Lemon zest and mint just seem so right with the asparagus. I like the crunch that toasted almonds add, but of course they can be eliminated for a nut-free version.

1 Preheat the oven to 400°F. Place the asparagus in a baking dish or on a baking sheet and drizzle with 1 teaspoon of the olive oil, the salt, and pepper and roast the asparagus until it is just al dente, about 5 minutes. Remove from the oven and set aside.

2 While the asparagus cools, place the almonds on a clean rimmed baking sheet and toast until lightly browned, 5 to 7 minutes. Transfer the almonds to a plate and set aside.

3 Add the asparagus to a blender along with the chicken broth and 1 cup water and purée until it is very smooth, about 2 minutes. Return the puréed asparagus to a medium saucepan (strain through a fine-mesh sieve if you want an even smoother texture) and stir in the remaining 1 teaspoon olive oil, the lemon zest, and mint. Warm the soup over medium heat.

4 Divide the soup among 4 bowls. Top each with 1 tablespoon of the yogurt and serve sprinkled with the toasted almonds.

PER SERVING: Calories 90 / Protein 5g / Dietary Fiber 3g / Sugars 3g / Total Fat 6g

EASIEST WATERMELON GAZPACHO

SERVES 4   **PREPARATION TIME** 10 MINUTES   **COOKING TIME** NONE

1½ cups low-sodium tomato-based vegetable juice

2 shallots, roughly chopped

2 cups watermelon cubes

1 medium cucumber, peeled, seeded, and roughly chopped

1 to 2 teaspoons finely chopped chipotle chiles in adobo sauce

3 tablespoons red wine vinegar

½ teaspoon kosher salt

¼ teaspoon ground black pepper

¼ cup plain reduced-fat Greek yogurt

1 tablespoon olive oil

2 tablespoons finely chopped fresh dill

4 lime wedges

I'm a huge fan of chilled soups, especially in the summer. They are refreshing and couldn't be easier to make (which means they are perfect for company!). This gazpacho takes advantage of the sweet bounty of watermelon that's available in the summer and combines it with just a bit of smokiness from chipotle chiles in adobo sauce. It has a well-rounded and not-too-sweet foundation of tomato juice; choose a spicy version if you like your gazpacho with more kick. And, instead, if you can get ripe, juicy tomatoes, they are amazing too!

1 To a blender or food processor add the vegetable juice, shallots, watermelon, cucumber, chiles, vinegar, salt, and pepper. Process the mixture until it is well combined but not entirely smooth.

2 Divide the gazpacho among soup bowls and finish each with a dollop of yogurt, a drizzle of olive oil, and some fresh dill. Serve with a lime wedge.

PER SERVING: Calories 97 / Protein 2g / Dietary Fiber 2g / Sugars 11g / Total Fat 4g

---

SUPERMARKET STRATEGY

Any Fruit Gazpacho

Replace the watermelon with nearly any juicy, in-season fruit—peaches, nectarines, cantaloupe, or honeydew—for a twist on the watermelon gazpacho. It goes without saying that ripe tomatoes are always welcome for a classic version as well! Change the fresh herb to any tender one that you have on hand or is plentiful in your garden or market; basil and tarragon are both lovely in gazpacho.

BUTTERNUT SQUASH CHILI

SERVES 4 **PREPARATION TIME 20 MINUTES** **COOKING TIME 1 HOUR**

1 tablespoon extra-virgin olive oil

1 red bell pepper, halved, seeded, and finely chopped

1 medium yellow onion, finely chopped

2 garlic cloves, minced

½ cup dry red wine

3 cups butternut squash cubes, in 1-inch pieces

1½ cups cooked white beans (homemade, page 81; or canned, rinsed), such as Great Northern

1 14-ounce can whole tomatoes with juice, chopped into ½-inch pieces

½ cup store-bought salsa

1 tablespoon chili powder

1 tablespoon ground cumin

2 teaspoons unsweetened cocoa powder

½ teaspoon ground cinnamon

½ teaspoon cayenne pepper (optional)

Kosher salt, if needed

Plain reduced-fat Greek yogurt

1 avocado, halved, pitted, and cut into ½-inch cubes

In the wintertime I crave hearty, "stick to your ribs" food. This chili not only comforts with its warmth but also nourishes with its high nutrient content. Top a bowl of it with some tangy low-fat Greek yogurt and silky cubes of avocado for a bit of satisfying healthy fat. If you'd like to make this chili with lean ground beef, chicken, pork, or turkey, add it in step 2, after the garlic and before the wine. Brown the meat nicely before deglazing the pot.

1 Heat the olive oil in a large soup pot over medium heat for 1 minute. Add the bell pepper and onion and cook, stirring occasionally, until the onion is soft, about 5 minutes.

2 Stir in the garlic and cook until fragrant, about 1 minute more. Pour in the wine, and let the wine bubble for 1 minute, stirring and scraping any browned bits from the bottom of the pot.

3 Add the squash, beans, tomatoes and juice, salsa, 1 cup water, the chili powder, cumin, cocoa, cinnamon, and cayenne, if using. Bring the chili to a simmer, then reduce the heat to medium-low and cook, stirring occasionally, until the squash is tender and the chili begins to thicken, about 45 minutes. (If the soup looks too thick while cooking, just add a little water.) Taste and add salt if needed.

4 Serve with a dollop of Greek yogurt and some avocado cubes.

PER SERVING: Calories 345 / Protein 11g / Dietary Fiber 18g / Sugars 11g / Total Fat 11g

Crisper Drawer Soup

At the end of the week (or as a new Sunday night ritual), open your crisper drawer and plan an odds-and-ends soup. Soup recipes are so forgiving, easily adjusted to whatever ingredients are in the fridge—even if the vegetables are just a shade past their crispest prime.

WHITE BEAN AND ROASTED PEPPER SOUP

SERVES 4 **PREPARATION TIME** 15 MINUTES **COOKING TIME** 20 MINUTES

2 teaspoons olive oil

1 medium yellow onion, coarsely chopped

2 garlic cloves, peeled and smashed

1½ cups coarsely chopped roasted red peppers

1 dried bay leaf

1 teaspoon kosher salt

1 teaspoon ground black pepper

⅛ teaspoon cayenne pepper, plus more to finish

4 cups low-sodium vegetable broth

2 cups cooked navy beans (homemade, page 81; or canned, rinsed)

½ cup plain nonfat Greek yogurt

2 teaspoons fresh lemon juice

When I have last-minute guests in my kitchen, this is the kind of quick meal I often turn to. It's based on pantry standards like onion, garlic, cooked beans (either canned or cooked and frozen; see page 81 for instructions), and jarred roasted red peppers. I often take advantage of the end-of-day baker's rack markdowns on fresh baguettes, and I cut them into halves, then freeze them—they come in so handy for a slapdash, delicious meal. Pop a few sections of bread into a warm oven, and in just about 15 minutes you have fresh bread to serve on the side.

1 Heat the olive oil over medium heat in a large soup pot. Add the onion and garlic and cook, stirring occasionally, until the onion is soft and translucent, about 8 minutes.

2 Stir in the roasted red peppers, bay leaf, salt, black pepper, and cayenne and cook, stirring often, for 2 minutes. Pour in the broth, add the beans, and bring to a boil. Reduce the heat to medium-low and simmer the soup for 10 minutes.

3 Remove and discard the bay leaf. Ladle the soup into a blender and purée in batches until smooth. Return the soup to a clean soup pot and heat until warmed.

4 In a small bowl, combine the yogurt and lemon juice. Ladle the soup into bowls, dollop with the yogurt, and serve sprinkled with a pinch of cayenne.

PER SERVING: Calories 235 / Protein 12g / Dietary Fiber 8g / Sugars 8g / Total Fat 3g

CREAMY CAULIFLOWER "BAKED POTATO" SOUP

SERVES 4   **PREPARATION TIME 20 MINUTES**   **COOKING TIME 30 MINUTES**

2 slices center-cut bacon, finely chopped

1 sweet onion (Maui or Vidalia), finely chopped

1 small head of cauliflower (about 1¼ pounds), cored, trimmed, and divided into small florets

1 medium russet potato, peeled and cut into 1-inch pieces

1 small carrot, finely chopped

2 garlic cloves, very finely chopped or pressed through a garlic press

½ teaspoon kosher salt

¼ teaspoon ground black pepper

2 cups low-sodium chicken broth

¼ cup reduced-fat cream cheese (Neufchâtel)

½ cup plain reduced-fat Greek yogurt

½ cup grated Cheddar cheese

2 scallions (white and light green parts only), finely chopped

There are few soups more decadent than a classic baked potato soup, loaded with cream, Cheddar cheese, and smoky bacon. I make a lighter version by leaving out the cream, subbing cauliflower for most of the potato (using one potato locks in the flavor), and adding a dollop of reduced-fat cream cheese to deliver the creaminess and cheesiness. A stealth addition of one carrot adds a subtle color that makes the soup seem cheesier than it is, since the only Cheddar here is what sits on top of the soup!

1 Add the bacon to a large soup pot set over medium heat and cook until the bacon is crisp, about 7 minutes. Use a slotted spoon to transfer the bacon to a paper towel–lined plate and set aside.

2 Stir the onion into the bacon fat and cook, stirring often, until it is translucent, about 3 minutes. Add the cauliflower, potato, carrot, garlic, salt, and pepper and cook, stirring occasionally, until the vegetables begin to soften, about 5 minutes.

3 Raise the heat to medium-high, add the broth and 1 cup water, and bring the liquid to a boil. Simmer the mixture until the vegetables are very soft, about 13 minutes. Turn off the heat and use a ladle to transfer half the vegetables and liquid to a blender. Add the cream cheese and blend until smooth.

4 Pour the puréed soup into a large bowl or clean saucepan. Blend the second half of the soup until it is smooth and add it to the first batch. Heat the soup over medium heat until it is warmed through. Divide among soup bowls and serve topped with a dollop of yogurt and some of the grated cheese, bacon, and scallion.

PER SERVING: Calories 180 / Protein 10g / Dietary Fiber 3g / Sugars 6g / Total Fat 9g

KITCHEN STRATEGY

Efficiently Freezing Soup

Freeze large batches of soup for a healthy in-a-pinch meal. Put the soups in gallon-size resealable freezer bags (or use quart-size bags for individual servings). Try to get as much air out of the bag as possible and then seal. Freeze flat on a baking sheet or plate and then, once they are completely frozen, stack one on top of another (don't forget to use a permanent marker to label the soup).

MISO-WONTON SOUP

SERVES 6   PREPARATION TIME 1 HOUR   COOKING TIME 30 MINUTES

FOR THE WONTONS

8 ounces boneless, skinless chicken breast, chopped into 1-inch pieces

1 small bunch baby bok choy, or 3 or 4 large ribs of bok choy

¼ cup finely chopped fresh chives (or scallion tops)

3 garlic cloves, roughly chopped

1 ½-inch piece of fresh ginger, peeled and roughly chopped

1 tablespoon low-sodium soy sauce

2 teaspoons toasted sesame oil

1 teaspoon cornstarch

40 wonton wrappers (about ¾ of a 12-ounce package)

FOR THE MISO SOUP

8 cups low-sodium store-bought or homemade chicken broth

2 to 4 tablespoons miso paste (preferably white)

¼ cup fresh cilantro leaves

If you're a lover of wonton soup, then you absolutely have to try making your own. For this wonton filling, boneless chicken breasts (or ground—see the Kitchen Strategy on page 78), sesame oil, chives, garlic, and ginger are pulsed together in a food processor in less than 10 seconds. The soup comes together in minutes, too. The real "work" is in filling the wontons, but the investment in time really pays off. For an extra flavor dimension, add ground pork or even pulse some raw shrimp into the filling. The wontons are also superchic when served without the soup, accompanied by a quick pantry dipping sauce made from soy sauce, a splash of rice vinegar, and a drop of toasted sesame oil.

1 To make the wontons: Line a medium plate with plastic wrap and place the chicken pieces on top. Set the chicken in the freezer to chill for 20 to 30 minutes.

2 Meanwhile, place the bok choy on a cutting board and separate the leafy tops from the white stalks. Slice the stalks on the bias into ¼-inch-thin pieces and set aside. Roughly chop the green tops and set aside.

3 Use a food processor to pulse the chilled chicken into a rough chop. Add the bok choy greens, chives, garlic, ginger, soy sauce, sesame oil, and cornstarch. Continue to pulse until the mixture is well combined and still somewhat rough, about eight 1-second pulses.

4 Fill a small bowl with cold water and line a baking sheet with a piece of parchment paper. Place 8 wonton wrappers on a work surface and put about 1 heaping teaspoon of the chicken mixture in the center of each wrapper. Use your finger to moisten two adjoining edges of the wonton wrapper with the water. Fold the top over to meet the bottom and

(recipe continues)

press the edges to seal. Wet one corner of the triangle with water, then gently fold the other corner around and press to create the wonton. Repeat with the remaining wonton wrappers, placing the wontons on the prepared baking sheet as they are filled. Continue to fill and shape the wontons, 8 at a time (so the wrappers don't dry out) until they are all filled, using a sheet of parchment paper to separate the layers of wontons, if needed.

5 To make the soup: Add the chicken broth to a large saucepan and bring it to a simmer. Whisk in 2 tablespoons of the miso and taste; for a stronger miso flavor, add up to 2 more tablespoons of the miso. Reduce the heat to low and add the bok choy stalks.

6 Bring a medium pot of salted water to a boil. Add 6 to 8 wontons (don't overcrowd the pot or they will stick together) and cook until the wrappers are transparent and the filling feels firm, about 3 minutes. Use a slotted spoon to transfer the cooked wontons to a bowl. Repeat with the remaining wontons, adding about 6 to each bowl.

7 Divide the broth among the bowls of wontons, sprinkle with cilantro leaves, and serve.

PER SERVING: Calories 254 / Protein 18g / Dietary Fiber 1g / Sugars 2g / Total Fat 3g

KITCHEN STRATEGY

DIY Ground Chicken
Boneless, skinless chicken breasts are a staple in my fridge and freezer, while ground chicken is not. That's why when I make chicken meatballs or chicken-filled wontons, I just pulse the raw, semi-frozen chicken in the food processor (pulsing keeps it from getting gummy in the processor) instead of making a special trip to the store. That said, of course you can use ground chicken rather than do it yourself. If that's the case, combine the ingredients for whatever you're making in a large bowl rather than in the food processor.

LENTIL SOUP WITH TURKEY SAUSAGE AND CHARD

SERVES 6   **PREPARATION TIME 15 MINUTES**   **COOKING TIME 55 MINUTES**

2 tablespoons olive oil

2 turkey sausage links (brown-and-serve style, not raw sausage), sliced into bite-size pieces

1 medium red onion, finely chopped

2 garlic cloves, very finely chopped or pressed through a garlic press

1½ teaspoons ground cumin

¾ teaspoon dried oregano

¾ teaspoon dried thyme

½ teaspoon dried sage

2½ teaspoons kosher salt

½ teaspoon ground black pepper

1½ cups brown lentils, well rinsed

1 bunch Swiss chard, ribs removed and leaves cut into thin ribbons

1 lemon, halved

Lentils are affordable, shelf stable, delicious, relatively quick cooking (especially when compared with dried beans), and require no pre-soaking. Their most winning trait, however, is their nutritional value: they offer generous amounts of fiber and protein, with hardly a trace of fat. I love this steaming soup on a cold afternoon. Or, if I have just a little left over, I ladle it over small pasta for a lentil version of chili-mac.

1 Heat the olive oil over medium-high heat in a large pot. Add the sausage and cook, stirring often, until it browns, 4 to 5 minutes. Use a slotted spoon to transfer the sausage to a medium bowl and set aside.

2 Add the onion to the pot and cook until softened, 3 to 4 minutes. Stir in the garlic, cumin, oregano, thyme, sage, ½ teaspoon of the salt, and the pepper and continue to cook until the garlic is fragrant, about 30 seconds.

3 Stir in the lentils, then add 8 cups water. Raise the heat to high and bring the water to a boil. Reduce the heat to medium-low, and place the cover on the pot so it sits slightly askew. Cook the lentils, stirring occasionally, until they are just shy of being tender and are still a little hard in the center, 25 to 30 minutes.

4 Return the sausage to the pot along with any accumulated juices. Stir in the remaining 2 teaspoons salt, then stir in the chard ribbons. Continue to cook until the lentils and the chard are tender, about 10 minutes longer. Squeeze the juice from the lemon halves into the soup and serve.

PER SERVING: Calories 252 / Protein 17g / Dietary Fiber 17g / Sugars 5g / Total Fat 7g

TUSCAN RIBOLLITA WITH KALE AND CANNELLINI BEANS

SERVES 8   **PREPARATION TIME** 20 MINUTES   **COOKING TIME** 1 HOUR, 10 MINUTES

2 tablespoons olive oil

2 medium carrots, finely chopped

2 celery stalks, finely chopped

1 medium yellow onion, finely chopped

½ fennel bulb, cored and finely chopped

2 garlic cloves, very finely chopped or pressed through a garlic press

3 fresh thyme sprigs

½ teaspoon red pepper flakes

1 15-ounce can low-sodium crushed tomatoes

8 cups low-sodium vegetable broth

1 teaspoon kosher salt

½ teaspoon ground black pepper

2 cups cooked cannellini beans (homemade, page 81; or canned, rinsed)

1 bunch Lacinato kale, stems removed and leaves coarsely chopped

¼ cup finely grated Parmesan cheese

4 cups bite-size pieces whole wheat bread

½ lemon, cut into wedges

This hearty, wintry meal offers protein, vitamins, and fiber in one tidy vegetarian package (leave out the Parmesan cheese to make it vegan). The combination of kale and cannellini beans is traditional, but you can also use Swiss chard, spinach, or escarole in combination with any of your favorite beans.

1 Heat 1 tablespoon of the olive oil over medium heat in a large soup pot. Add the carrots, celery, onion, fennel, and garlic and cook, stirring occasionally, until the vegetables are soft and the onion is translucent, 15 to 20 minutes.

2 Add the thyme sprigs and red pepper flakes and cook, stirring often, for 1 minute, then stir in the tomatoes and bring to a simmer. Pour in the broth and add the salt and pepper. Stir in the beans and kale, and bring to a boil. Reduce the heat to medium-low and gently simmer until the kale is tender, 15 to 20 minutes.

3 Stir the bread into the soup and continue to simmer, stirring occasionally, until the soup thickens and the bread is mostly broken down, 20 to 25 minutes. Ladle the soup into bowls and serve warm with a drizzle of the remaining 1 tablespoon olive oil, some of the grated Parmesan cheese, and a lemon wedge.

PER SERVING: Calories 274 / Protein 12g / Dietary Fiber 10g / Sugars 9g / Total Fat 7g

KITCHEN STRATEGY

Turn Leftover Soup into Ribollita
Any soup can become ribollita in a snap: simply add some broth to bulk it out if need be, mix in stale or day-old bread, and add some cooked beans.

MAKE AHEAD AND FREEZE BEANS

A 1-pound bag of dried beans yields the same quantity after cooking as four to five cans of beans—and costs only a buck! Cooking dried beans is a cinch, too. Here's how to do it on the stovetop or in a slow cooker:

1. Soak the beans overnight (if using a slow cooker, soaking isn't necessary, but it's a step I prefer so the beans are easier to digest).

2. Simmer the beans gently (don't boil) until they are just tender, 1 to 1½ hours (if using a slow cooker, aim for 4 to 5 hours on high or 8 to 10 hours on low).

3. Taste 4 to 5 beans to make sure they are all tender and cooked through. Different varieties of beans can take longer or less

time to cook; additionally, older beans can take 1 to 2 hours longer than fresher ones, so timing can vary quite a bit.

4. Once the beans are cool, divide them into quart-size freezer bags (some people like to freeze cooked beans in the liquid, but I always drain mine before freezing). Usually, packages of 1½ to 2 cups of beans is a good measure (that's about how much is in a can of beans). Then label the bags and freeze.

5. When needed, remove the bag from the freezer and add the frozen beans to a soup or stew, or thaw them first if they aren't going to be heated (such as if you're using them to make hummus or in a salad).

Making Soup Kid-Friendly

Start with a soup recipe that incorporates their favorite vegetable or fun noodle shape. Try offering soup mix-ins, like herbs, seasoned yogurts, and pesto (see page 175), or serve different kinds of crackers with the soup to make the meal more customizable (kids love to mix and match). Once they like soup in general, try new varieties such as a Vietnamese noodle soup (see opposite) or Creamy Cauliflower "Baked Potato" Soup (page 74). Don't forget that leftovers make great Thermos lunches!

PORK AND RICE NOODLE PHO

SERVES 4   **PREPARATION TIME** 25 MINUTES   **COOKING TIME** 1 HOUR, 30 MINUTES

1 pork tenderloin (about
1 pound)

1 pound pork or beef bones
(optional)

2 teaspoons canola oil

3 garlic cloves, smashed

2 medium carrots, roughly
chopped

2 celery stalks, roughly
chopped

1 medium yellow onion,
peeled and roughly chopped

1 2-inch piece of fresh
ginger, sliced into ¼-inch-
thick pieces

1 bunch fresh cilantro, stems
and leaves separated

1½ teaspoons kosher salt

1 dried bay leaf

¼ teaspoon coriander seeds

1 star anise

8 ounces dried rice
vermicelli noodles

2 limes, quartered

½ cup bean sprouts

1 fresh red chile (such as
Fresno or red jalapeño),
thinly sliced

A giant, steaming bowl of Vietnamese pho is a soup that keeps on giving: there is the deep rich broth, the springy noodles, the tender pork, the bite of fresh herbs, and the sharpness of spicy chiles. In my version, I create a rich stock using pork or beef bones (ask the butcher at your supermarket's meat counter for the bones—they should be pretty cheap to buy) and half a pork tenderloin. The rest of the pork tenderloin is added with the noodles and cooks up in just 10 minutes.

1 Thinly slice half the pork tenderloin and coarsely chop the rest. Add the pork bones (if using) to a large soup pot set over medium-high heat, and brown them, stirring occasionally, for 8 to 10 minutes. Remove the bones from the pot and set aside.

2 Add the canola oil to the pot and heat until shimmering, about 30 seconds, then stir in the smashed garlic and cook until golden and fragrant, about 2 minutes. Add the carrots, celery, onion, and ginger and cook, stirring occasionally, until they begin to brown, about 5 minutes.

3 Stir in the chopped pork and cilantro stems, 1 teaspoon of the salt, the bay leaf, coriander seeds, and star anise. Pour in 10 cups of water, return the bones to the pot, and bring to a boil. Reduce the heat to medium-low and simmer for 1 hour.

4 Strain the broth through a fine-mesh sieve into a clean large pot. Return it to a boil, then add the thinly sliced pork and the rice vermicelli. Cook until the pork is tender and the noodles are cooked through, about 10 minutes.

5 Season the soup with the remaining ½ teaspoon salt. Ladle into bowls and serve with the lime quarters, bean sprouts, cilantro leaves, and chile.

PER SERVING: Calories 306 / Protein 16g / Dietary Fiber 1g / Sugars 1g / Total Fat 4g

CHICKEN-CHILE POZOLE

SERVES 4 **PREPARATION TIME** 10 MINUTES (plus 30 minutes to soak chiles)
COOKING TIME 25 MINUTES

2 dried New Mexico red chiles (or Guajillo chiles, for more heat), stems discarded

1½ cups boiling water

2 garlic cloves, peeled

½ medium white onion, coarsely chopped

2 teaspoons fresh oregano leaves

Juice of 1 lime, plus 1 lime cut into wedges

1 teaspoon kosher salt

4 cups low-sodium chicken broth

2 15-ounce cans white hominy, rinsed and drained

1½ pounds cooked white meat chicken or pork, shredded

½ avocado, pitted and diced

3 radishes, thinly sliced

1 cup fresh cilantro leaves

My family got turned on to pozole thanks to a friend of one of my daughter's who always brings pozole for school potlucks. This brothy Mexican soup is chock-full of hominy, mild dried chiles, and shredded chicken or pork. Philippe and our girls (well, at least two of the four!) go crazy for it. Shredded chicken (either left over from an earlier dinner or off of a rotisserie chicken) and mild New Mexico dried red chiles make this soup weeknight and kid-friendly. If you want a spicier version, try adding a dried chipotle chile (or two) to the mix.

1 Place the dried chiles in a medium bowl and cover with the boiling water. Cover the bowl with plastic wrap and set the chiles aside to soak for 30 minutes, turning them occasionally to make sure they are completely submerged.

2 Transfer the chiles and their soaking liquid to a blender. Add the garlic, onion, oregano, lime juice, and ½ teaspoon of the salt, and purée.

3 Pour the chile mixture into a large soup pot and bring to a simmer over medium-high heat. Reduce the heat to medium-low and simmer, stirring occasionally, until the sauce is thick, 15 to 20 minutes.

4 Stir in the broth and return the mixture to a simmer. Stir in the hominy and the chicken. Season with the remaining ½ teaspoon salt and continue to cook until the chicken and hominy are warmed through, 7 to 10 minutes.

5 Divide the pozole among 4 soup bowls and sprinkle with the avocado, radish slices, and cilantro. Serve with a lime wedge.

PER SERVING: Calories 463 / Protein 57g / Dietary Fiber 9g / Sugars 1g / Total Fat 11g

— *Chapter 4* —

SALADS, WRAPS, AND SANDWICHES

There's a reason why salads and sandwiches belong in the same chapter. Think about it—a sandwich really is just a salad between bread slices (or rolled in a wrap), right? The recipes in this chapter offer versatile, speedy, healthy, and, above all, tasty ways to get in your five servings of vegetables a day.

Stretching out a small amount of protein is smart, not just for your wallet but for your health, too. Making salad at home means you can control all of the ingredients going into the bowl (that's right, 2,000-calorie restaurant salad, I'm looking at you!). Eating a healthy salad or vegetable-heavy sandwich is a good habit to adopt. Use these recipes as guidelines, swapping out one light mayo for another low-fat yogurt sauce, or kale for spinach, or avocado for nuts. Salads and sandwiches are incredibly forgiving when it comes to following a recipe. Use what you have and interpret the ingredients as you like.

SOUTHWEST CHICKEN SALAD WITH SMOKED PAPRIKA VINAIGRETTE

SERVES 4 **PREPARATION TIME** 25 MINUTES **COOKING TIME** 20 MINUTES

FOR THE CHICKEN AND CORN

2 boneless, skinless chicken breasts

1½ teaspoons olive oil

Kosher salt and ground black pepper

1½ cups fresh corn kernels

FOR THE SMOKED PAPRIKA VINAIGRETTE

3 tablespoons red wine vinegar

1 garlic clove, finely minced

1 teaspoon kosher salt

½ teaspoon smoked paprika

½ teaspoon dried oregano

Ground black pepper

¼ cup olive oil

FOR THE SALAD

1 cup cherry tomatoes, halved

3 scallions (green parts only), finely chopped

1 cup cooked black beans (homemade, page 81; or canned, rinsed)

4 medium carrots, peeled and grated on the large-hole side of a box grater

1½ cups baby spinach

There is something incredibly comforting about this chicken, corn, black bean, and smoky paprika salad, as it brings the wonderful flavors of barbecue to the table in a lean package. The salad is chock-full of veggies and protein, and the starchy corn adds sweetness and crunch. Without the chicken, this salad makes a great side dish for tacos or beans and rice.

1 To make the chicken and corn: Heat a gas or charcoal grill to medium-high heat. Set the chicken on a cutting board and coat both pieces evenly with the olive oil. Season the chicken with 1 teaspoon of salt and ½ teaspoon of pepper and grill until cooked through, about 7 minutes on each side. Transfer to a plate, tent with foil, and set aside for 10 minutes before chopping into bite-size pieces.

2 Bring a medium saucepan of water to a boil. Add 1 teaspoon of salt and the corn. Cook until the corn is al dente, 3 to 4 minutes. Drain in a colander, transfer to a medium bowl, and set aside.

3 To make the dressing: In a medium bowl, whisk together the vinegar, garlic, 1 teaspoon salt, paprika, oregano, ½ teaspoon pepper, and olive oil.

4 To assemble the salad: In a large bowl, combine the chicken, corn, tomatoes, scallions, beans, carrots, and spinach and toss to combine. Pour the dressing over the salad, toss, and serve.

PER SERVING: Calories 365 / Protein 21g / Dietary Fiber 9g / Sugars 6g / Total Fat 19g

SALMON AND HERBED BEAN SALAD

SERVES 4   **PREPARATION TIME** 30 MINUTES   **COOKING TIME** NONE

FOR THE DRESSING

1 cup plain reduced-fat Greek yogurt

1 teaspoon finely grated lemon zest

1 tablespoon fresh lemon juice

2 teaspoons finely chopped fresh mint leaves

Kosher salt and ground black pepper

FOR THE SALAD

2 cups finely chopped fresh flat-leaf parsley

½ cup chopped fresh mint

¾ cup halved cherry tomatoes

½ seedless cucumber, peeled and chopped into ¼-inch pieces

2 cups cooked white beans (homemade, page 81; or canned, rinsed)

3 tablespoons fresh lemon juice

2 tablespoons olive oil

¾ teaspoon kosher salt

¼ teaspoon ground black pepper

4 cups baby greens

1 cup canned salmon, large bones removed

Canned salmon is an often overlooked protein: it keeps for ages in the pantry and it's inexpensive, easy to use, fast, and doesn't even require turning on the oven. Just like fresh salmon, canned salmon is loaded with omega-rich fats, which are linked to heart and brain health (plus it has even more calcium than fresh salmon!), which is why I try to make a salmon-centered recipe at least once a week for my family. Of course, this would be great with canned tuna, too.

1 To make the dressing: Whisk together the yogurt, lemon zest and juice, mint, salt, pepper, and 1 tablespoon water. Set aside.

2 To make the salad: Stir the parsley, mint, tomatoes, cucumber, and beans together in a medium bowl. In a small bowl, whisk together the lemon juice, olive oil, salt, and pepper until it is thick and creamy. Pour the dressing over the beans and toss to combine.

3 Divide the baby greens among 4 plates and top with the beans. Flake the salmon over the top, and serve drizzled with the yogurt dressing.

PER SERVING: Calories 334 / Protein 26g / Dietary Fiber 8g / Sugars 8g / Total Fat 12g

ENTERTAINING STRATEGY

Quick Roast Salmon

A gorgeous piece of wild salmon can give a simple salad or bean side dish instant appeal. Drizzle a few 4-ounce pieces with olive oil and sprinkle with salt and pepper, then roast on a baking sheet at 375°F until it flakes at the edges and gives to light pressure, 7 to 8 minutes.

KALE AND WHITE BEAN CAESAR

SERVES 4   PREPARATION TIME 10 MINUTES   COOKING TIME NONE

FOR THE CAESAR DRESSING

1 teaspoon Dijon mustard

Juice of 1 lemon

1 small garlic clove, very finely chopped or pressed through a garlic press

2 tablespoons olive oil

Pinch of red pepper flakes

½ teaspoon kosher salt

⅛ teaspoon ground black pepper

FOR THE SALAD

1¼ cups cooked white beans (homemade, page 81; or canned, rinsed)

4 cups trimmed and sliced kale (tough ribs removed and leaves stacked and thinly sliced crosswise into ribbons)

½ cup grated Parmesan cheese

In this salad, I layer white beans with a garlicky Caesar-style dressing in a mason jar. On top of the beans I add the kale ribbons and then top it all with Parmesan cheese. I'll often make a few different kinds of salads and pack them in individual servings (see the "Salad-in-a-Jar" Blueprint on page 94). Isn't it great when "fast food" is healthy too?

1 To make the dressing: In a small bowl, whisk together the mustard, lemon juice, and garlic. While whisking, slowly drizzle in the olive oil. Add the red pepper flakes, salt, and black pepper. (Add 1 to 2 tablespoons of water if needed.)

2 To make the salad: Divide the beans among 4 mason jars and top with the dressing. Add the kale and then top with the Parmesan cheese. Cover tightly and refrigerate. Shake to dress the salad before serving.

PER SERVING: Calories 287 / Protein 12g / Dietary Fiber 5g / Sugars 5g / Total Fat 18g

salad-in-a-jar

Stashing a few ready-to-go salads packed in mason jars is a smart way to ensure you always have a healthy meal or snack on the go whenever the need arises: for work lunches, picnics, even soccer practice. Prepare several jarred salads over the weekend to have them at the ready for the beginning of the week (though some ingredients like kale, raw cauliflower, and broccoli keep nicely for three-plus days). Tip: Use a coupon to load up on mason jars at your local craft store.

TOPPINGS

CHEESE
(grated Parmesan, shredded Gouda, blue cheese crumbles)

NUTS
(toasted chopped hazelnuts, candied pecans, slivered raw almonds)

SEEDS
(toasted pumpkin seeds, sunflower seeds, sesame seeds)

LEAFY GREENS

SPINACH, CHOPPED KALE, TORN LETTUCE, ARUGULA

VEGGIES, BEANS, GRAINS, MEAT

RAW OR COOKED VEGETABLES, COOKED BEANS OR LEGUMES, COOKED PASTA OR GRAINS, COOKED MEAT

DRESSING

CREAMY
miso, page 96; Thousand Island, page 103; yogurt, page 91

VINAIGRETTE
Dijon, page 95; smoked paprika, page 89; Caesar, page 93

TWIST ON THE LID AND REFRIGERATE.
Do not shake until you're ready to eat the salad.
Note that salads with cooked pasta or meat should be eaten within 2 days.

SPINACH, GRAPE, AND FETA SALAD

SERVES 4   **PREPARATION TIME** 10 MINUTES   **COOKING TIME** NONE

FOR THE DIJON VINAIGRETTE

1 teaspoon Dijon mustard

2 tablespoons red wine vinegar

2 tablespoons olive oil

¼ teaspoon kosher salt

⅛ teaspoon ground black pepper

FOR THE SALAD

4 cups baby spinach

1 cup red grapes, halved

⅓ cup crumbled feta cheese

2 tablespoons sliced skin-on almonds

2 scallions (light green and dark green parts only), finely chopped

Baby spinach has an ideal texture for a salad—it's tender but just firm enough, meaning it can hold up better than more delicate leaf lettuces. Grapes and tangy feta work beautifully in this salad, and a handful of almonds lends crunch, protein, and the powerful antioxidant vitamin E. In this Dijon vinaigrette, red wine vinegar adds extra body and a robust flavor.

1 To make the vinaigrette: In a small bowl, whisk together the mustard and vinegar. While whisking, slowly drizzle in the olive oil. Whisk in the salt and pepper. (Add 1 to 2 tablespoons of water if needed.)

2 To make the salad: In a large bowl, toss together the spinach, grapes, feta, almonds, and scallions. Pour the dressing over the salad, toss to combine, and serve.

PER SERVING: Calories 238 / Protein 4g / Dietary Fiber 2g / Sugars 8g / Total Fat 20g

KITCHEN STRATEGY

Getting Kids to Love Salad

I find that separating all of the components of a salad into small bowls encourages kids to create the salads they will most enjoy. Place a piece of chicken, seared shrimp, or any protein you're using on a platter and surround it with bowls of mix-ins—baby spinach, tender lettuces, toasted nuts, roasted vegetables, raw vegetables, fruits, and even dried fruits. Accompany these with a small dish of dressing and a spoon for drizzling it on the salads. Giving children a bit of control over their meals gets them more excited about eating and encourages healthier food choices.

GARLIC-CHILI SHRIMP AND MISO GARDEN SALAD

SERVES 4   **PREPARATION TIME** 20 MINUTES   **COOKING TIME** 3 MINUTES

FOR THE SHRIMP

2 teaspoons chili-garlic sauce (such as Huy Fong)

2 teaspoons honey

½ pound peeled and deveined medium shrimp (20–24 per pound)

FOR THE MISO DRESSING

2 teaspoons miso paste (preferably white)

Juice of 1 lime

1 teaspoon grated fresh ginger

Pinch of kosher salt

1 tablespoon canola oil

2 teaspoons toasted sesame oil

FOR THE SALAD

6 cups baby greens

2 medium carrots, ends trimmed and shaved into ribbons using a vegetable peeler

1 medium cucumber, thinly sliced on the bias

All it takes are a couple of interesting ingredients—in this case, Vietnamese chili-garlic sauce and miso paste—to turn an ordinary garden salad into a unique main course. If you can't find chili-garlic sauce (often in the international aisle of most supermarkets), use one teaspoon of your favorite hot sauce (such as Sriracha) instead.

1 To make the shrimp: Adjust an oven rack to the top position and preheat the broiler to high. In a medium bowl, whisk together the chili-garlic sauce and honey. Add the shrimp and toss to combine. Place the shrimp on an aluminum foil–lined baking sheet and broil until the edges brown and the shrimp begin to curl, 2 to 3 minutes (watch the shrimp closely, as broiler intensities vary). Transfer the shrimp to a plate and set aside.

2 To make the dressing: Whisk the miso, lime juice, ginger, and salt together in a small bowl. Add the canola oil and sesame oil, and whisk to combine. Taste and add a splash of water to thin the dressing, if needed.

3 To make the salad: Toss together the baby greens, carrot ribbons, and cucumber slices. Add the miso dressing and toss to combine. Divide among 4 plates and serve each with a few shrimp on top.

PER SERVING: Calories 179 / Protein 14g / Dietary Fiber 4g / Sugars 8g / Total Fat 8g

Giving Salad Extra Curb Appeal

A modest amount of indulgence lends a simple green salad a lofty air while keeping your budget, calories, and fat intake in check. Try some of these fancy salad toppers: black sesame seeds, candied or spiced nuts, shaved ribbons of hard cheese, crumbled high-quality blue cheese, marinated artichoke hearts, chopped avocado, grilled or roasted asparagus, poached shrimp, flaked crabmeat, smoked trout, and prosciutto slivers. Many of these are shelf stable, meaning they keep in the fridge for a month (or more) or in a pantry for several months. When you spot them on sale, buy extra for a special indulgence!

CAULIFLOWER AND CHICKPEA SALAD WITH SMOKED TROUT AND OLIVES

SERVES 4   **PREPARATION TIME 15 MINUTES**   **COOKING TIME NONE**

½ medium cauliflower, crumbled into very small florets (about 1½ cups)

1 cup cooked chickpeas (homemade, page 81; or canned, rinsed)

1 3-ounce can smoked rainbow trout, drained, skin removed, and flaked

12 pitted Kalamata olives, thinly sliced (about ¼ cup)

1 tablespoon roughly chopped fresh marjoram

Juice of ½ lemon

½ teaspoon kosher salt

Satisfying and so incredibly healthy, this salad is a true pantry standby. Cauliflower keeps fresh in the fridge for weeks, so I always like to have a head on hand. The smoked trout adds a luscious smoky taste, but if you don't have any in the cupboard, swap it for canned tuna or canned salmon. Nix the fish for a vegan salad, and add more chickpeas plus some sunflower seeds and sliced skin-on almonds or pecans to make up the protein.

Stir together the cauliflower florets, chickpeas, trout, olives, marjoram, lemon juice, and salt in a large bowl. Divide among plates and serve.

PER SERVING: Calories 150 / Protein 9g / Dietary Fiber 9g / Sugars 2g / Total Fat 5g

---

CAULIFLOWER POWER

Are you using cauliflower to its full potential? An excellent source of vitamin C and vitamin K (which helps with inflammation), cauliflower is also a good source of antioxidants—all the more reason to get more into your daily routine.

EAT IT RAW Cauliflower is great raw, not just as a crudité with dip but also in salads. It's so nice and crunchy that I often use it as a carb-free replacement for bread crumbs.

BLANCH IT If crunchy isn't your thing, blanch the florets in salted boiling water for a couple minutes until they are al dente, then shock in ice water. Drain and refrigerate for use in salads or to quickly brown in a hot skillet.

ROAST IT Drizzle cauliflower with olive oil and roast on a baking sheet with a sprig or two of fresh rosemary or thyme (chopped bacon adds a ton of flavor, too—use less olive oil if using bacon). Once the cauliflower becomes browned and tender, cool it, then refrigerate to add to salads, sandwiches, pasta, or rice.

WINTRY PORK TENDERLOIN, QUINOA, AND GRAPEFRUIT SALAD

SERVES 4   **PREPARATION TIME 15 MINUTES** (plus time to marinate the tenderloin)
COOKING TIME 20 MINUTES

FOR THE TENDERLOIN

¼ cup Dijon mustard

2 garlic cloves, very finely chopped or pressed through a garlic press

2 teaspoons finely chopped fresh thyme

1 teaspoon finely chopped fresh rosemary

½ teaspoon kosher salt

¼ teaspoon ground black pepper

1 pork tenderloin (about 1 pound)

FOR THE SALAD

1 grapefruit

3 cups baby spinach or mixed lettuces

1 cup cooked quinoa (or brown rice)

1 small fennel bulb, cored and thinly sliced or shaved using a mandoline

½ avocado, cut into bite-size pieces

2 scallions, chopped

I love a main dish salad where you get everything on one plate: complex carbs, protein, vitamins, and antioxidants. It's one-stop shopping for your body. Here, Dijon-and-herb-marinated pork tenderloin pairs perfectly with earthy quinoa, juicy grapefruit, fennel, avocado, and a mound of spinach.

1 To marinate the tenderloin: Whisk together the mustard, garlic, thyme, rosemary, salt, and pepper in a small bowl. Coat the pork tenderloin with the mustard rub, then place in an airtight container or resealable plastic bag and refrigerate for at least 30 minutes, or up to 12 hours.

2 Preheat the oven to 400°F. Remove the tenderloin from the container and place it on an aluminum foil–lined rimmed baking sheet, and roast until its internal temperature registers between 150° and 155°F., 15 to 20 minutes. Remove the tenderloin from the oven, loosely tent with foil, and set aside to rest for 10 minutes before slicing crosswise into thin pieces.

3 To make the salad: Slice off the top and bottom from the grapefruit so it stands upright. Working top to bottom, slice away the rind and white pith, exposing the fruit. Holding the fruit over a bowl to catch the juices (save the juices for making the vinaigrette), use a sharp knife to slice between the membranes of the grapefruit to release the grapefruit segments. Cut the segments in half and set aside.

4 Arrange the spinach on a large platter. Top with the quinoa, then the fennel, and lay on the tenderloin slices. Arrange the grapefruit, avocado, and scallions over the top.

FOR THE VINAIGRETTE

1 teaspoon Dijon mustard

2 tablespoons white wine vinegar

¼ teaspoon kosher salt

¼ teaspoon ground black pepper

2 tablespoons olive oil

5 To make the vinaigrette: In a medium bowl, whisk together the mustard, vinegar, reserved grapefruit juice, salt, and pepper. (Add 1 to 2 tablespoons of water if needed.) Whisk in the olive oil until the dressing is creamy, then drizzle it over the salad and serve.

PER SERVING: Calories 399 / Protein 27g / Dietary Fiber 7g / Sugars 5g / Total Fat 22g

---

KITCHEN STRATEGY

Two Ways to Big Batch It

1. Buy extra protein, cook it now, eat it later. When a staple protein, such as boneless chicken breasts or pork loin, is on sale, I usually buy extra. Then, when I am preparing the chicken or pork for dinner, I cook double the amount I want at that time. The extra cooked meat can easily transform a modest side dish into a meal substantial enough for lunch or dinner tomorrow, or even for later in the week.
2. Make a big batch of plain rice or quinoa or beans and keep it in your fridge for up to a week. Then stir in roasted vegetables or dried fruit or toasted nuts and seeds for a whole new side dish that takes just minutes to make.

POMEGRANATE SQUASH, APPLES, AND ARUGULA

SERVES 4   **PREPARATION TIME** 15 MINUTES   **COOKING TIME** 40 MINUTES

1¼ pounds butternut squash, cut into 1-inch cubes (about 3¼ cups)

1 large red onion, halved, each half sliced lengthwise into quarters (8 pieces total)

1½ tablespoons plus 2 teaspoons olive oil

1 teaspoon plus a pinch of kosher salt

1 large red apple, halved, cored, and cut into ½-inch pieces

1 tablespoon fresh lemon juice

2 cups arugula

3 tablespoons pomegranate seeds

This stunner of a side dish is so pretty on a holiday-decked table, yet it is simple enough to make for a midweek supper. The pomegranate seeds and arugula add wonderful contrasts of sweet, sour, bitter, juicy, and crunchy.

1 Preheat the oven to 400°F. In a large bowl, toss together the squash, red onion, 1½ tablespoons of the olive oil, and 1 teaspoon of the salt. Turn the mixture out onto a rimmed baking sheet and roast for 20 minutes.

2 Remove the baking sheet from the oven. Add the apple to the squash and use a wooden spoon or spatula to stir it around, turning over the squash and onion pieces so the other sides can brown. Return the baking sheet to the oven and roast until the apple is tender, about 20 minutes longer.

3 Whisk the lemon juice, remaining 2 teaspoons olive oil, and a pinch of salt in a medium bowl. Add the arugula, toss to combine, and turn out onto a platter. Arrange the roasted vegetables over the arugula and serve sprinkled with the pomegranate seeds.

PER SERVING: Calories 212 / Protein 3g / Dietary Fiber 9g / Sugars 15g / Total Fat 8g

PROVENÇAL VEGETABLE WRAP

SERVES 4   **PREPARATION TIME** 25 MINUTES (plus 30 minutes to marinate)
COOKING TIME 12 MINUTES

1½ tablespoons olive oil

Zest and juice of 1 lemon

2 garlic cloves, very finely chopped or pressed through a garlic press

½ teaspoon dried oregano

¾ teaspoon kosher salt

½ teaspoon ground black pepper, plus a pinch as needed

1 medium red bell pepper, halved, seeded, and thinly sliced

½ medium red onion, thinly sliced

½ medium eggplant, sliced crosswise into ½-inch-thick slices

1 medium zucchini, sliced into ½-inch-thick rounds

4 9- to 10-inch low-fat whole wheat or whole-grain wraps or tortillas

¾ cup hummus (homemade, page 48, or store-bought)

I travel often for work, which means I have become an expert at making my own airplane food. It's a such a great feeling to pull out a homemade snack when on a long flight, and for me, that means making a veggie wrap. It's tasty and satisfying, but not too heavy. Marinated veggies cooked just until tender stay the perfect consistency through hours of cab rides and airport security (and as a side note, you can even double the batch so you have the fixings for a super-fast pasta dinner upon your return!).

1 Whisk together 1 tablespoon of the olive oil, the lemon zest and juice, garlic, oregano, ½ teaspoon of the salt, and the black pepper in a medium bowl. Add half the marinade to another medium bowl. To one bowl add the bell pepper and onion; to the other bowl add the eggplant and zucchini. Let the vegetables marinate at room temperature for 30 minutes.

2 Heat the remaining ½ tablespoon olive oil in a heavy-bottomed large skillet over medium-high heat. Add the bell pepper and onion and cook, stirring occasionally, until crisp-tender, about 8 minutes. Stir in the eggplant and zucchini and cook, stirring occasionally, until just tender, 5 to 7 minutes more. Season with the remaining ¼ teaspoon salt and a pinch of black pepper.

3 In a dry skillet or microwave, warm the tortillas until pliable. Set a tortilla on a cutting board and spread 3 tablespoons of the hummus down the center of the tortilla. Divide one-quarter of the vegetable mixture evenly over the surface of each tortilla, then tightly roll the wraps, tucking in the ends like a burrito. Arrange the wraps seam side down, then slice in half on the bias and serve.

PER SERVING: Calories 389 / Protein 12g / Dietary Fiber 8g / Sugars 5g / Total Fat 15g

TURKEY REUBEN WRAP

SERVES 4   **PREPARATION TIME 10 MINUTES**   **COOKING TIME 3 MINUTES**

FOR THE DRESSING

1 tablespoon coarsely ground black pepper

2 teaspoons coriander seeds

2 teaspoons yellow mustard seeds

¼ cup plain nonfat yogurt

1 tablespoon ketchup

2 teaspoons yellow mustard

Squeeze of fresh lemon juice

½ dill pickle, finely chopped (about 2 tablespoons)

FOR THE WRAPS

4 9- to 10-inch whole wheat or whole-grain wraps

12 slices turkey deli meat

4 slices Swiss cheese, halved

1 cup sauerkraut

Cheesy, saucy, and stacked with tangy sauerkraut, a Reuben sandwich is one of the great masterpieces of the deli counter. Whittle down the calories and fat using turkey deli meat instead of corned beef (pastrami-style if available) and nonfat plain yogurt in the dressing in place of mayonnaise. Spices like toasted coriander seeds, black pepper, and yellow mustard seeds give the sauce that unmatched pastrami taste.

1   To make the dressing: Place the pepper, coriander seeds, and mustard seeds in a small skillet and toast over medium heat, shaking the pan often, until the mustard seeds pop and the coriander smells fragrant, 1 to 2 minutes. Transfer to a spice grinder and pulverize until coarsely ground.

2   Add the spices to a small bowl and whisk in the yogurt, ketchup, mustard, and lemon juice. Then stir in the chopped pickle and set aside.

3   To make the wraps: Preheat the broiler to high. Place the wraps on a parchment paper–lined baking sheet. Cover each wrap with 3 slices of the turkey, slightly overlapping the turkey, if needed. Lay the cheese over the turkey, then place the open-faced wraps under the broiler until the cheese melts, 30 seconds to 1 minute (watch the cheese closely, as broiler intensities vary).

4   Remove the wraps from the oven and drizzle the dressing over each wrap. Divide the sauerkraut among the wraps and roll them, tucking in the ends as with a burrito. Arrange seam side down, then slice in half on the bias and serve hot.

PER SERVING: Calories 265 / Protein 15g / Dietary Fiber 4g / Sugars 1g / Total Fat 10g

ARTICHOKE, RED PEPPER, AND MUSHROOM MELTS

SERVES 4 **PREPARATION TIME** 20 MINUTES **COOKING TIME** 2 MINUTES

¼ cup reduced-fat cream cheese (Neufchâtel)

¼ teaspoon garlic powder

¾ cup canned artichoke hearts, drained and chopped

¾ cup jarred roasted red peppers, drained and chopped

4 ounces white button mushrooms, finely chopped

2 scallions (green parts only), finely chopped

¼ cup shredded sharp Cheddar cheese

½ teaspoon herbes de Provence or dried oregano

¼ teaspoon kosher salt

¼ teaspoon ground black pepper

Olive oil mister or nonstick pan spray

4 crusty bread slices (such as sourdough), lightly toasted

3 tablespoons chopped pecans

While living and working abroad in France during my pre-mom days, I became obsessed with French tartines, which are open-faced sandwiches. Usually served on a large single slice of crusty country bread, tartines are often capped with a golden brown, molten layer of melted cheese, such as in the most famous tartine of all, the croque monsieur. Here, my much healthier version stacks roasted red peppers, mushrooms, and artichoke hearts onto a cream cheese and Cheddar base. The result is a really cheesy sandwich that tastes a whole lot more sinful than it really is.

1 Mix the cream cheese and garlic powder in a medium bowl. Add the artichokes, red peppers, and mushrooms and stir to combine, then stir in the scallions, Cheddar, herbs, salt, and black pepper.

2 Adjust an oven rack to the upper-middle position and preheat the broiler to high. Line a rimmed baking sheet with aluminum foil and mist with olive oil or nonstick pan spray. Spread some of the cream cheese–vegetable mixture over each slice of toasted bread and place on the prepared baking sheet.

3 Broil the sandwiches until the cheese begins to bubble and melt, 1 to 2 minutes (watch the sandwiches closely, as broiler intensities vary). Remove the baking sheet from the oven and sprinkle some pecans over each sandwich. Serve hot.

PER SERVING: Calories 310 / Protein 10g / Dietary Fiber 4g / Sugars 2g / Total Fat 12g

make a melt

Good news: Melts aren't just for tuna any-more! You can easily capture the flavors of your favorite diner-style melt with this flex-ible plug-and-play strategy. And remember, a little cheese goes a long way.

STEP 1: CHOOSE BREAD.

(BREAD)　　　(WRAP)

STEP 2: ADD MAIN INGREDIENT.

DELI MEAT　　　**COOKED OR CANNED FISH**　　　**RAW OR ROASTED VEGETABLES**

STEP 3: ADD MELT-FRIENDLY CHEESE

(Havarti, jalapeño Monterey Jack, mozzarella, muenster, Swiss)
and broil until melted.

STEP 4: TOP WITH HOMEMADE OR JARRED PICKLED VEGETABLES.

*(cucumbers, red cabbage, peppers, beets, tomatoes;
see page 117 for a quick-pickled onion method)*

STEP 5: TOP WITH DRESSING.

*(Thousand Island dressing, page 105, is a versatile choice.
Some other options include low-fat mayo mixed with Sriracha or pesto,
Caesar dressing, page 93, or hummus)*

App the Wrap

Turn any of the wraps on pages 104, 105, and 109 into an appetizer by replacing the whole-grain or whole wheat wrap with a rice paper circle (the wrappers used for summer rolls in Southeast Asian restaurants). Simply soak each rice paper in warm water until it begins to soften, about 15 seconds. Place it on a kitchen towel while repeating with the other wraps. Fill, slice on the bias (or into bite-size pieces), and serve!

VIETNAMESE CHICKEN-KALE WRAP

SERVES 4   **PREPARATION TIME** 20 MINUTES   **COOKING TIME** NONE

FOR THE CHICKEN SALAD

2 tablespoons light mayonnaise

2 teaspoons Sriracha sauce

½ teaspoon kosher salt

2 cups finely chopped cooked chicken

1 jalapeño pepper, seeded and finely chopped

FOR THE VEGETABLE MIXTURE

1 tablespoon plus 1 teaspoon fish sauce

1 tablespoon rice vinegar

Juice of 2 limes

2 medium carrots, ends trimmed and shaved into ribbons using a vegetable peeler

1 4-inch piece of daikon, peeled and shaved into ribbons using a vegetable peeler

2 teaspoons canola oil

6 kale leaves, ribs removed and leaves stacked, rolled, and sliced into thin ribbons

FOR THE WRAPS

4 9- to 10-inch low-fat whole wheat or whole-grain wraps or tortillas

½ cup fresh cilantro leaves

A Vietnamese bánh mì *sandwich is a study in sandwich perfection, with each bite offering something sweet, savory, salty, spicy, herby, crunchy, chewy, creamy, and crisp. Usually it's made with a combination of pork and pâté, but I use a lightened version of chicken salad instead. To bulk up the wrap a bit, I add a kale topping to the usual pickled carrot and daikon accompaniment.*

1 To make the chicken salad: Whisk together the mayonnaise, Sriracha, and salt. Add the chicken and jalapeño, and stir to combine.

2 To make the vegetable mixture: Whisk the fish sauce, vinegar, and lime juice in a medium bowl. Pour half the mixture into a small bowl. To the mixture in the small bowl add the carrot and daikon ribbons, and toss to combine. In the medium bowl, whisk in the oil, then add the kale, using your hands to massage it with the dressing.

3 To make the wraps: Place the wraps on a cutting board. Divide the kale (leaving any liquid in the bowl) among the wraps and place down the center of each wrap. Top each with about ½ cup of the chicken salad, a handful of the carrot and daikon ribbons, and some cilantro. Roll the wraps, tucking in the ends like a burrito. Arrange the wraps seam side down, then slice each wrap in half on the bias and serve.

PER SERVING: Calories 302 / Protein 27g / Dietary Fiber 2g / Sugars 3g / Total Fat 9g

FRIED GREEN TOMATO, BACON, AND SPINACH SANDWICH

SERVES 4   PREPARATION TIME 15 MINUTES   COOKING TIME 20 MINUTES

FOR THE LEMON-GARLIC MAYO

3 tablespoons light mayonnaise

1 tablespoon finely chopped fresh basil

1 tablespoon finely grated lemon zest

¼ teaspoon garlic powder

½ teaspoon kosher salt

¼ teaspoon ground black pepper

FOR THE SANDWICH

1 to 2 large green tomatoes, sliced crosswise into four ½-inch-thick rounds, each about the width of the English muffin

½ teaspoon kosher salt

¼ teaspoon ground black pepper

½ cup medium or fine yellow cornmeal

8 slices turkey bacon

1 teaspoon olive oil

4 whole wheat English muffins, split and toasted

1 cup baby spinach or baby mixed greens

Fried green tomatoes: I love how those three words conjure much excitement and hungry anticipation! English muffins work so nicely with tomatoes—not only are they about the same width, but all those nooks in the muffin are perfect for catching juices from the crunchy cornmeal-fried tomato and the garlicky lemon mayo. If you can't find green tomatoes (which are really just under-ripe red ones, not to be confused with some varieties of heirloom tomatoes or tomatillos), use very pale and hard red tomatoes and just cook them a minute or two less. For a vegetarian version, use avocado slices instead of bacon. Sprinkling the avocados with a little smoked salt or smoked paprika adds savory umami flavor.

1 To make the lemon-garlic mayo: Whisk together the mayonnaise, basil, lemon zest, garlic powder, salt, and pepper in a small bowl. Cover the bowl with plastic wrap and refrigerate.

2 To make the sandwich: Season both sides of each tomato slice with the salt and pepper. Place the cornmeal in a small bowl and dredge each tomato slice in it, coating the slices on both sides with an even layer of cornmeal (press it on to make it adhere, if needed). Set aside.

3 Place the bacon in a large nonstick skillet set over medium-high heat and cook, turning the bacon frequently, until it is crisp and browned, 6 to 8 minutes. Transfer the bacon to a paper towel–lined plate and set aside.

4 Add the olive oil to the skillet, then place the cornmeal-coated tomato slices in the pan and cook until both sides are golden but the tomato is still firm, 6 to 8 minutes total.

5 Spread the mayo on both the tops and bottoms of the English muffins. Place a fried tomato slice on the bottom muffin half, top with 2 bacon slices, and finish each with ¼ cup of the baby spinach. Cover with the top muffin half and serve.

PER SERVING: Calories 338 / Protein 13g / Dietary Fiber 7g / Sugars 5g / Total Fat 13g

— Chapter 5 —

VEGGIE MAINS

I've amped up my vegetable-centric main dishes since I moved down the street from my sister's family—home of three vegetarians. Whenever we have big family meals, I always have a protein-rich and substantially vegetable-driven plate on the table. Roasted squash, mushrooms, ever-adaptable eggplant, and beans and legumes are many of my trusty friends when it comes to offering healthy and nutritious meals that leave out the meat. Even nonvegetarians appreciate a substantial meatless plate, one that places vegetables, grains, and beans at center stage.

Since meat usually is the most expensive component of a meal, going meatless at least one day a week is also excellent relief for your wallet. The challenge is to create a meat-free meal that leaves meat lovers satisfied. I believe the key is in offering lots of flavor and texture contrasts. If you make each bite interesting, people find it impossible to resist going back for more.

SUMMER SQUASH AND MUSHROOM TACOS

SERVES 4   **PREPARATION TIME 20 MINUTES**   **COOKING TIME 25 MINUTES**

FOR THE ROASTED VEGETABLES

1 medium yellow summer squash, cut into 1-inch cubes

1 medium zucchini, cut into 1-inch cubes

2 portobello mushroom caps, cut into 1-inch cubes

1 medium yellow onion, halved and thinly sliced

1 tablespoon olive oil

Kosher salt and ground black pepper

FOR THE KALE TOPPING

1 tablespoon olive oil

2 garlic cloves, finely chopped

Pinch of red pepper flakes

1 bunch curly kale, tough ribs removed and leaves roughly chopped

¼ cup low-sodium vegetable broth

2 tablespoons apple cider vinegar

Kosher salt and ground black pepper

FOR THE TACOS

8 6-inch corn tortillas, warmed

½ cup crumbled cotija cheese

A tempting picture of a squash taco on the side of a food truck inspired me to create my version of the vegetarian taco. Meaty roasted mushrooms, sweet roasted squash, and a caramelized roasted onion make up the bulk of this taco, with spicy-tangy braised kale as a topper. I often make the components ahead of time, so that for dinner all I have to do is warm up the tortillas.

1 To make the roasted vegetables: Preheat the oven to 400°F. On a rimmed baking sheet arrange the squash, zucchini, mushrooms, and onion. Drizzle with the olive oil, then toss to combine, adding ½ teaspoon of salt and ¼ teaspoon of pepper. Roast the vegetables until just tender, about 10 minutes.

2 To make the kale topping: In a large skillet, combine the olive oil, garlic, and red pepper flakes and cook until the garlic is fragrant, about 1 minute. Add the kale and cook, stirring occasionally, until it wilts, 2 to 3 minutes. Pour in the broth, cover the skillet, and cook the kale until tender, about 8 minutes. Stir in the vinegar, ¼ teaspoon of salt, and ¼ teaspoon of black pepper. Turn off the heat and set aside.

3 To assemble the tacos: Place the tortillas on a work surface and add some of the vegetable filling and kale topping. Sprinkle each with cotija cheese, fold, and serve.

PER SERVING: Calories 278 / Protein 9g / Dietary Fiber 7g / Sugars 6g / Total Fat 11g

SALSA TIPS, TRICKS, AND SHORTCUTS

Homemade salsa is a real treat, but if you don't have time to make a batch, just add a freshly prepared ingredient to perk up your favorite store-bought brand. Here are some ideas to get you going.

To jarred salsa verde (tomatillo salsa), tomato salsa, or pico de gallo, add:

• Charred corn kernels (char under the broiler or on a grill)

• Fresh cilantro or basil

• Chopped cucumber

• Chopped ripe peaches or nectarines

• Halved grape tomatoes or quartered cherry tomatoes

• Chopped cabbage kimchi

• Diced pineapple

• Finely chopped charred jalapeño peppers

• Roasted red peppers

Instead of making the from-scratch tomatillo sauce opposite, blend a jar of store-bought tomatillo salsa (check the ingredient label to make sure it's not packed with salt) with the cilantro and broth. Since jarred salsa can already be fairly loose, start by adding half the broth, then blend in more for a thinner consistency, if needed. This is a great strategy for freshening up a jar of tomato salsa, too. Fresh herbs like cilantro and basil, fresh jalapeño peppers, or red Fresno chiles, chopped scallions, cucumbers, ripe tomatoes, grilled corn, and a squeeze of lemon or lime juice work wonders!

P.S.: Even just a squeeze of fresh lime or lemon juice can make a big difference!

RED CABBAGE–STUFFED ENCHILADAS VERDE

SERVES 4   **PREPARATION TIME** 40 MINUTES   **COOKING TIME** 1 HOUR

FOR THE PICKLED RED ONION

½ cup red wine vinegar

2 teaspoons sugar

1 teaspoon kosher salt

½ large red onion, thinly sliced

FOR THE TOMATILLO SAUCE

1¼ pounds tomatillos, husks removed and rinsed

4 garlic cloves, peeled

1 medium red onion, halved and thinly sliced

1 jalapeño pepper, quartered lengthwise (remove seeds for less heat)

1½ teaspoons canola oil

1 teaspoon kosher salt

2 cups fresh cilantro leaves

1¼ cups low-sodium vegetable or chicken broth, warmed

(ingredients continue)

Most enchiladas are weighted down with loads of cheese, but not these. By using crumbly, salty cotija Mexican cheese as an accent sprinkled over the finished enchiladas, you still get the satisfaction that comes from its richness while curbing the fat count. And instead of a stuffing of cheese or meat, this caramelized red cabbage cooked with cumin and coriander provides a complexly flavored and nutritious filling. These are also excellent stuffed with the squash and mushroom taco filling on page 115.

1   To pickle the red onion: Heat the vinegar, sugar, and salt together in a small saucepan over medium heat, stirring often, until the sugar and salt are dissolved, 2 to 3 minutes. Add the onion, stir to combine, turn off the heat, and set aside. Once the onion cools, refrigerate in an airtight container (the pickled onions are best served chilled).

2   To make the tomatillo sauce: Preheat the oven to 400°F. On a rimmed baking sheet, arrange the tomatillos, garlic, onion, jalapeño, canola oil, and salt. Toss to combine and roast until the tomatillos are golden and juicy, 20 to 25 minutes. Remove from the oven, cool for 10 minutes, then transfer to a blender. Add the cilantro and broth and purée. Leave the oven on.

3   To make the cabbage filling: To a large nonstick skillet add the canola oil, cumin seeds, coriander, cinnamon stick, black pepper, and red pepper flakes. Cook over medium heat, stirring often, until the cumin seeds are golden and fragrant, about 1 minute. Add the onion and cook, stirring occasionally, until it softens and the edges begin to brown,

(recipe continues)

FOR THE CABBAGE FILLING

1 tablespoon canola oil

1 teaspoon cumin seeds

1 teaspoon ground coriander

1 cinnamon stick

¼ teaspoon ground black pepper

¼ teaspoon red pepper flakes

½ large red onion, thinly sliced

½ small red cabbage, halved and thinly sliced crosswise (3½ cups)

½ teaspoon kosher salt

Juice of 1 lime

FOR ASSEMBLING THE ENCHILADAS

Eight 6-inch corn tortillas, warmed

¼ cup crumbled cotija cheese (or ricotta salata or feta; optional)

2 tablespoons roughly chopped fresh cilantro leaves

2 to 3 minutes. Stir in the cabbage and salt and cook, stirring occasionally, until the cabbage is completely wilted, 5 to 8 minutes. Stir in the lime juice and a splash of water, stirring and scraping up any browned bits from the bottom of the skillet. (Remove and discard the cinnamon stick.)

4 To assemble the enchiladas: Pour ½ cup of the tomatillo sauce into the bottom of an 8- or 9-inch square baking dish. Place a warm tortilla on a work surface and add ¼ cup of the cabbage filling, then roll to enclose. Set the tortilla in the pan with the seam side down. Repeat with the remaining tortillas and cabbage. Spoon some of the remaining tomatillo sauce over the tortillas, using the back of a spoon to spread it evenly. (Make sure the enchiladas are well coated with sauce to keep them moist during baking.) Bake the enchiladas until they are warmed through, about 20 minutes. Remove the enchiladas from the oven and sprinkle with the crumbled cheese (if using) and cilantro. Serve hot with drained, pickled red onions on the side.

PER SERVING: Calories 290 / Protein 8g / Dietary Fiber 9g / Sugars 10g / Total Fat 10g

ACORN SQUASH "FONDUE"

SERVES 4   **PREPARATION TIME** 10 MINUTES   **COOKING TIME** 1 HOUR, 10 MINUTES

2 acorn squash, halved, seeded, and fibers removed

½ teaspoon kosher salt

¼ teaspoon ground black pepper

1 tablespoon Dijon mustard

1 large garlic clove, very finely chopped or pressed through a garlic press

½ cup shredded Gruyère cheese

2 slices white whole wheat bread, lightly toasted and cut into ½-inch cubes

¾ cup whole milk

Pear slices (optional)

On special occasions my husband and I used to visit our favorite fondue restaurant near our apartment in Paris (the restaurant was aptly named Pain, Vin, Fromage, or "Bread, Wine, Cheese"). As a way to share that Parisian fondue magic with my family, I've given it a much healthier twist by making it in an acorn squash! The squash both contains the cheese-bread filling and blends with it, providing a wonderfully creamy sweetness. Plus, it's just so pretty to serve this "fondue" in the squash halves. Offer it to your guests on a holiday or special occasion.

1 Preheat the oven to 350°F. Sprinkle the squash halves with the salt and pepper, then use a basting brush to coat the squash with the mustard. Sprinkle the garlic in the squash halves, spreading it around as best you can.

2 Divide half the cheese among the 4 squash halves (1 tablespoon each) and then top with the bread cubes. Sprinkle on the remaining cheese and then pour the milk over the bread, dividing it evenly among the squash halves. Gently press the bread cubes into the milk to make sure they are all saturated.

3 Place the squash halves in a baking dish or on a rimmed baking sheet and cover tightly with foil. Bake for 40 minutes, then remove the foil and continue to bake until the filling is golden brown and the squash is tender, about 30 minutes more.

4 Serve one squash half to each person, with pear slices on the side for dipping, if desired. Be sure everyone scoops up some of the filling and squash in each bite.

PER SERVING: Calories 206 / Protein 9g / Dietary Fiber 4g / Sugars 8g / Total Fat 7g

RED LENTILS AND QUINOA

SERVES 6   PREPARATION TIME 10 MINUTES   COOKING TIME 40 MINUTES

FOR THE LENTILS

1 teaspoon olive oil

1 medium red onion, finely chopped

1 garlic clove, very finely chopped or pressed through a garlic press

1 1-inch piece of fresh ginger, peeled and finely grated

½ teaspoon kosher salt

¼ teaspoon red pepper flakes

¼ teaspoon ground black pepper

⅛ teaspoon ground cardamom

1 cup red lentils, rinsed well

FOR THE QUINOA

1 teaspoon olive oil

1 garlic clove, very finely chopped or pressed through a garlic press

1 cup red quinoa, rinsed well under cold water

½ teaspoon kosher salt

¼ cup finely chopped fresh flat-leaf parsley

Lentils are a real superfood: one cup of cooked lentils offers 18 grams of protein and 16 grams of fiber—wow! They are easy to buy and store in the pantry, they have a very long shelf life (they're best used within a year of purchasing), and they are incredibly economical. In this recipe, red lentils are cooked until soft and saucelike, and then they are spooned over fluffy quinoa. If you're looking for a change of pace from beans and rice, you've found it.

1 To make the lentils: Heat the olive oil in a medium sauce-pan over medium heat. Add the onion and garlic and cook, stirring often, until the onion is soft, about 7 minutes.

2 Stir in the ginger, salt, red pepper flakes, black pepper, and cardamom and cook for 1 minute. Add the lentils and 2 cups water to the saucepan. Increase the heat to high and bring the lentils to a boil. Reduce the heat to medium-low, cover the saucepan, and simmer the lentils until they are very soft and have somewhat lost their shape, about 30 minutes.

3 To make the quinoa: Heat the olive oil in a medium saucepan or medium pot over medium heat. Add the garlic and quinoa and cook, stirring often, until the quinoa is lightly toasted, about 5 minutes.

4 Stir in 1½ cups water and the salt, increase the heat to high, and bring the quinoa to a boil. Reduce the heat to medium-low, cover, and simmer until the liquid is completely absorbed and the quinoa uncoils, about 20 minutes. Fluff the quinoa with a fork.

5 Serve the lentils over the quinoa, sprinkled with parsley.

PER SERVING: Calories 237 / Protein 12g / Dietary Fiber 7g / Sugars 3g / Total Fat 3g

BROWN RICE WITH SPINACH, CASHEWS, AND SUNFLOWER SEEDS

SERVES 6   PREPARATION TIME 10 MINUTES   COOKING TIME NONE

2 cups cooked long-grain brown rice, cold or at room temperature

1½ tablespoons olive oil

2 tablespoons fresh lemon juice, plus more if needed

1 teaspoon grainy Dijon mustard

1 teaspoon kosher salt, plus more if needed

½ teaspoon ground black pepper, plus more if needed

2 scallions (white and light green parts only), thinly sliced

½ cup roasted cashews, roughly chopped

¼ cup toasted sunflower seeds

4 cups loosely packed baby spinach leaves, coarsely chopped

Brown rice is a staple in my pantry; it's an inexpensive way to round out a plate whether you're serving chicken breasts, vegetables, or a stir-fry. I usually make extra rice (cook once; eat twice!) and turn the leftovers into a second dish, like this one. Keep in the fridge for those busy days when family members are coming and going on their own schedules. Nuts and seeds are healthy sources of protein and fat, which will give everyone steady energy. If you're hosting meat eaters, serve this with some grilled chicken or lean steak on the side.

1 Place the rice in a medium bowl and use a fork to fluff it.

2 Whisk together the olive oil, lemon juice, mustard, salt, and pepper in a small bowl. Pour over the rice and stir to combine.

3 Stir in the scallions, cashews, and sunflower seeds. Taste and add more salt or pepper and lemon juice, if needed.

PER SERVING: Calories 215 / Protein 5g / Dietary Fiber 3g / Sugars 1g / Total Fat 12g

ROASTED ZUCCHINI LASAGNA

SERVES 6   **PREPARATION TIME 35 MINUTES**   **COOKING TIME 40 MINUTES**

FOR THE VEGETABLES

3 8-inch-long zucchini
(about 2¾ pounds), ends
removed and zucchini sliced
lengthwise into ¼-inch-thick
strips (you should have 15 to
20 strips)

4 teaspoons olive oil

1 teaspoon kosher salt

2 medium red bell peppers,
halved, seeded, and thinly
sliced

1 large red onion, halved
and thinly sliced

FOR THE TOFU-RICOTTA FILLING

8 ounces firm tofu, crumbled
(about 1 cup)

½ cup part-skim ricotta
cheese

Zest of 1 lemon (juice
the lemon for the tomato
topping)

2 garlic cloves, very finely
chopped or pressed through
a garlic press

½ teaspoon kosher salt

¼ teaspoon ground black
pepper

¼ cup finely chopped fresh
basil leaves

(ingredients continue)

In this play on lasagna, strips of zucchini stand in for the lasagna noodles and a fresh tomato salad is piled on top of the casserole in place of the tomato sauce. I also use tofu and part-skim ricotta as a way to bump up the protein content without losing all the decadence that comes with the cheese. This is exactly the kind of dish I love making in the summer, when vegetables are cheap and plentiful. Any kind of roasted vegetable can be layered into the mix too, so use what you have on hand—I've added sweet summer corn, chopped spinach, and sautéed mushrooms.

1   To make the vegetables: Preheat the oven to 400°F. Line a rimmed baking sheet with parchment paper and add the zucchini, 2 teaspoons of the olive oil, and ½ teaspoon of the salt. Toss to combine, then lay the zucchini strips flat. On another rimmed baking sheet (or a large baking dish), place the bell peppers and onion, the remaining 2 teaspoons olive oil, and the remaining ½ teaspoon salt. Roast the vegetables until the ends are lightly browned, about 20 minutes, turning over the zucchini strips and stirring the peppers and onion midway through roasting. Set aside the vegetables to cool. Leave the oven on.

2   To make the tofu-ricotta filling: In a medium bowl, stir together the tofu, ricotta, lemon zest, garlic, salt, and pepper. Then stir in the chopped basil.

3   To make the tomato topping: In a small bowl, stir together the chopped tomatoes, lemon juice, salt, and pepper.

(recipe continues)

FOR THE TOMATO TOPPING

2 ripe medium tomatoes, cored and finely chopped

Juice of 1 lemon

½ teaspoon kosher salt

¼ teaspoon ground black pepper

FOR ASSEMBLING THE LASAGNA

2 teaspoons olive oil

2 tablespoons finely grated pecorino cheese

4 To assemble the lasagna: Spread the olive oil in an 8-inch square baking dish. Layer in about 6 strips of zucchini, overlapping them slightly. Dollop the zucchini with half of the tofu-ricotta mixture, then sprinkle with half the roasted peppers and onion. Add another layer of zucchini, slightly pressing down on the zucchini to compact the mixture. Repeat once, finishing the lasagna with a third layer of zucchini.

5 Cover the zucchini with the tomato topping and sprinkle with the pecorino cheese. Bake for 15 minutes, then turn the oven to broil and continue to cook the lasagna until the tomato topping starts to brown around the edges, 4 to 5 minutes longer (watch the topping closely, as broiler intensities vary). Remove from the oven and cool for 15 minutes before slicing and serving.

PER SERVING: Calories 181 / Protein 11g / Dietary Fiber 4g / Sugars 6g / Total Fat 11g

ENTERTAINING STRATEGY

A Rainbow of Tomatoes

Heirloom tomatoes seem to come in every shade of the rainbow—green, yellow, pink, purple, red, even striped. When tomatoes are plentiful and in season, try using these less-common varieties of tomatoes (some of my favorite heirlooms are Green Zebra, Cherokee Purple, and Brandywine); the different shades will make for a showstopping presentation.

EGGPLANT MEATBALLS WITH MARINARA SAUCE

SERVES 4 (16 meatballs)   **PREPARATION TIME 25 MINUTES**
COOKING TIME 1 HOUR, 10 MINUTES (plus 20 minutes to cool)

1 large eggplant (about 12 ounces)

1 large egg, lightly beaten

½ cup cooked white beans, such as cannellini or navy (homemade, page 81; or canned, rinsed), smashed with a fork

1 large garlic clove, very finely chopped or pressed through a garlic press

½ cup finely chopped fresh basil leaves or flat-leaf parsley

½ cup finely grated Parmesan cheese, plus extra for sprinkling (optional)

¾ teaspoon kosher salt

½ teaspoon ground black pepper

1 cup panko-style bread crumbs (preferably whole wheat)

Olive oil mister or nonstick pan spray

2 cups marinara sauce (homemade or store-bought)

Who says meatballs have to have meat? After roasting, eggplant takes on a meaty, hearty flavor that is an excellent foundation for "meatballs." I have one more twist up my sleeve, though: I add some smashed white beans for texture and an extra boost of protein. Pair these meatballs with your favorite marinara sauce.

1 Preheat the oven to 375°F. Line a rimmed baking sheet with aluminum foil and place the eggplant on top. Use a fork to prick the eggplant 4 times, then place the eggplant in the oven and roast it until it has completely collapsed and a paring knife easily slips into the center, 40 to 50 minutes. Cool the eggplant for 20 minutes. Leave the oven on.

2 Slice the eggplant in half lengthwise and use a spoon to scoop out the flesh (discard the skin). Place the roasted eggplant in a medium bowl and stir in the egg and beans. Add the garlic, basil, ½ cup Parmesan cheese, the salt, and pepper and stir to combine, then mix in the bread crumbs.

3 Again, line the rimmed baking sheet with a sheet of aluminum foil and lightly mist it with olive oil or nonstick pan spray. Shape the eggplant mixture into balls about the size of a golf ball (you should get about 16). Place them on the prepared baking sheet and lightly mist the top of the balls with spray. Bake the eggplant balls until they are golden-brown and firm, about 20 minutes.

4 While the meatballs cook, warm the marinara sauce in a small saucepan. Remove the meatballs from the oven, sprinkle with a little extra Parmesan, if desired, and serve with the marinara sauce.

PER SERVING: Calories 304 / Protein 14g / Dietary Fiber 10g / Sugars 14g / Total Fat 11g

SWEET POTATO–MILLET BURGERS

MAKES 4 BURGERS   **PREPARATION TIME** 25 MINUTES   **COOKING TIME** 50 MINUTES

1 small sweet potato (about 6 ounces), peeled and chopped into ½-inch pieces

1½ teaspoons kosher salt

½ cup millet

½ cup cooked chickpeas (homemade, page 81; or canned, rinsed), smashed with a fork

About ¾ cup whole wheat bread crumbs

1 4-ounce can roasted green chiles (preferably Hatch New Mexico chiles; optional)

1 small shallot, very finely chopped

1 teaspoon ground cumin

1 teaspoon sweet paprika

¾ teaspoon onion powder

1 large egg

¼ cup cornmeal

Olive oil mister or nonstick pan spray

4 whole wheat burger buns, lightly toasted

Favorite burger toppings, such as raw onion, tomato slices, and lettuce

Let's be honest here: a vegetable and grain–based burger is never going to really taste like a good old-fashioned beef burger. It can, however, be delicious in its own right. In this burger, millet is the nutrient powerhouse, while the sweet potatoes add body and the green chiles, cumin, and paprika add a Southwestern kick. Millet is extremely good for you, offering fiber, iron, and the B vitamins that are so important for vegetarians. These burgers are excellent reheated for lunch or even wrapped in plastic and stashed in the freezer for a rainy-day meal. I've included options for both pan-searing the burgers and oven baking; baking is a little simpler, though it yields a less caramelized burger.

1 Bring 1½ cups water to a boil in a small saucepan. Add the sweet potato and ¾ teaspoon of the salt, reduce the heat to medium-low, and cook for 10 minutes. Add the millet and the chickpeas, reduce the heat to low, and cook, covered and stirring occasionally, until the millet is tender and absorbs all of the water, about 20 minutes (add more water, if needed). Turn off the heat and transfer the mixture to a medium bowl, letting it cool slightly.

2 Stir in ½ cup of the bread crumbs, all the chiles (if using), the shallot, cumin, paprika, onion powder, and the remaining ¾ teaspoon salt. Shape the mixture into 4 patties, pressing them so they are about ½ inch thick (they will be very soft). Place the patties on a plate and refrigerate for 30 minutes.

3 Lightly beat the egg in a medium bowl. In another medium bowl, stir together the remaining ¼ cup bread crumbs with the cornmeal. Place 1 chilled patty in the beaten egg, turning it over to coat the other side. Dip the patty in the cornmeal–bread crumb mixture, and sprinkle the mixture over the top of the patty, lightly pressing it on. Repeat with the remaining 3 patties.

4 If you're pan-searing the veggie burgers, heat a large nonstick skillet over medium heat. Mist the skillet with olive oil or nonstick pan spray, then add the patties, cooking until they are golden brown, 3 to 4 minutes. Flip the patties (they will be somewhat soft) and cook on the other side until golden brown, 3 to 4 minutes longer.

5 If you're baking the burgers, preheat the oven to 375°F. Generously mist an aluminum foil–lined baking sheet with spray. Bake the patties until they are browned, about 20 minutes, using a spatula to flip them midway through the baking. For an extra-browned crust, turn the oven to broil and move the patties to the top rack and broil for 30 seconds before serving.

6 Serve each burger on a bun and with your favorite toppings.

PER SERVING: Calories 349 / Protein 11g / Dietary Fiber 8g / Sugars 5g / Total Fat 6g

SUPERMARKET STRATEGY

Pantry Veggie Burgers
If you can't find millet at your market, don't worry. In place of millet, use 1 cup of cooked quinoa, brown rice, or bulgur. And instead of the sweet potato, you can use any mashed, thick vegetable—plain canned pumpkin works great, as do mashed roasted carrots or puréed rutabaga.

PORTOBELLO *STEAK-FRITES* WITH SWEET POTATOES

SERVES 4   **PREPARATION TIME** 40 MINUTES (plus 20 minutes to soak the mushrooms)
COOKING TIME 50 MINUTES

2 medium sweet potatoes

2 tablespoons plus 2½ teaspoons olive oil

Juice of 1 lemon

¾ teaspoon kosher salt

¾ teaspoon ground black pepper

4 4- to 5-inch-wide portobello mushroom caps, cleaned

2 teaspoons flaky sea salt

¼ teaspoon smoked paprika

1 tablespoon cornstarch

1½ medium shallots, halved and thinly sliced

Eating steak-frites *in Parisian cafés is one of my most delicious and treasured culinary memories of my time spent living abroad. In this vegetarian take on* steak-frites, *I replace the steak with succulent portobello mushrooms and the customary thin, crisp fries with oven-browned sweet potatoes.* Steak-frites *usually arrives tableside with a knob of shallot butter melting over the meat. As a nod to that tradition, I serve the vegetable composition with shallots crisped in a little olive oil instead.*

1 Fill a large bowl with ice cubes and water. Use a knife to trim a long, thin slice off one side of each sweet potato (slice the piece lengthwise). Then turn the potato over and repeat on the other side, so each potato has two straight sides. Slice the potatoes lengthwise into ½-inch-thick planks, stack the planks, then slice lengthwise into ½-inch sticks. Add the sweet potato sticks to the ice water and set aside for 20 minutes.

2 Whisk together 1 tablespoon of the olive oil, half the lemon juice, ½ teaspoon of the kosher salt, and ¼ teaspoon of the pepper in a large, shallow dish. Brush the mushroom caps with the marinade, then place the caps rounded side down in the remaining marinade. Leave at room temperature to marinate for 20 minutes.

3 Adjust an oven rack to the upper-middle position and preheat the oven to 450°F. Line a baking sheet with aluminum foil. Mix ½ teaspoon of the sea salt and the smoked paprika in a small bowl. Drain the potatoes, turn them out onto a cutting board, and pat them dry. Add the cornstarch to a

(recipe continues)

resealable plastic bag along with the potatoes, seal the bag, and shake to coat the potatoes with the cornstarch.

4 Turn the potatoes out onto the prepared baking sheet, drizzle with 1 tablespoon of the olive oil, and use your hands to gently turn and toss the potatoes in the oil. Spread the sticks into a single layer, then sprinkle with the paprika salt and roast for 20 minutes. Use a spatula or tongs to turn the fries and continue to roast until lightly browned, about 15 minutes more.

5 While the potatoes roast, heat a large oven-safe grill pan or skillet over high heat for about 2 minutes. Add ½ teaspoon of the olive oil and place the mushrooms rounded side down in the pan. Cook until grill marks form, 4 to 5 minutes, then transfer the pan to the oven and continue roasting until the mushrooms are browned and tender, 10 to 15 minutes.

6 Add the remaining 2 teaspoons oil to a small skillet set over medium heat. Add the shallots, the remaining ¼ teaspoon kosher salt, and the remaining ½ teaspoon pepper and cook, stirring often, until the shallots soften and brown around the edges, 4 to 5 minutes. Set a portobello mushroom on each plate along with some fries. Drizzle each mushroom cap with some shallots and shallot oil, sprinkle with the remaining flaky sea salt, and serve.

PER SERVING: Calories 189 / Protein 3g / Dietary Fiber 3g / Sugars 8g / Total Fat 10g

KITCHEN STRATEGY

Do You Need to Salt Eggplant?

If you're using Globe eggplants—the most common one you'll see in the supermarket—people say you should always salt the sliced or chopped eggplant and let it sit for 20 minutes to draw out the bitterness that comes from the seeds. You know what? I never do this, and no one has ever turned down my Cheesy Eggplant Parm (opposite). If you are very sensitive to bitterness, try Chinese or Japanese eggplants, which have fewer seeds.

CHEESY EGGPLANT PARMESAN

SERVES 6 **PREPARATION TIME** 10 MINUTES **COOKING TIME** 1 HOUR, 5 MINUTES

Olive oil mister or nonstick pan spray

1 large or 2 small eggplants, sliced crosswise into ¾-inch-thick rounds

1 teaspoon ground black pepper

1½ cups low-fat cottage cheese

1 large egg white

½ cup finely grated Parmesan cheese

2 cups jarred low-sodium and low-fat or fat-free marinara sauce

½ cup shredded part-skim mozzarella cheese

Just because a dish is vegetarian, that doesn't mean it's healthy. Case in point: eggplant Parmesan. Usually this classic Italian casserole is oozing with melted mozzarella and Parmesan cheese and is thickly stacked with breaded and panfried slices of eggplant. In my healthy version, the eggplant is pan-seared in a nonstick skillet without bread crumbs and then layered with low-fat cottage cheese and Parmesan.

1 Heat a large nonstick skillet over medium-high heat. Lightly coat the skillet with olive oil or nonstick pan spray and add some of the eggplant slices (as many as will fit in a single layer). Season with some pepper and cook the eggplant until lightly browned, about 6 minutes. Turn over the eggplant, sprinkle with some more pepper, reduce the heat to medium, and cook until the eggplant is soft and cooked through, about 6 minutes longer. Repeat with the remaining eggplant slices and remaining pepper, adding more pan spray to the skillet as needed.

2 Preheat the oven to 350°F. Use a food processor to pulse the cottage cheese until it is semi-smooth. Transfer the cottage cheese to a medium bowl and stir in the egg white and ¼ cup of the Parmesan cheese.

3 Lightly coat a 3-quart baking dish with nonstick pan spray. Add half the eggplant slices. Top with the cottage cheese and the remaining eggplant slices, followed by the marinara sauce. Sprinkle with the mozzarella and then the remaining ¼ cup Parmesan cheese. Bake until hot and bubbling, 30 to 40 minutes. Cool the eggplant Parmesan for 15 minutes before slicing and serving.

PER SERVING: Calories 160 / Protein 15g / Dietary Fiber 3g / Sugars 7g / Total Fat 5g

BAKED FALAFEL WITH TANGY YOGURT SAUCE

SERVES 4   **PREPARATION TIME 30 MINUTES** (plus 30 minutes to chill)
COOKING TIME 20 MINUTES

FOR THE FALAFEL

1½ cups cooked chickpeas (homemade, page 81; or canned, rinsed)

2 scallions (white and light green parts only), thinly sliced

½ cup frozen chopped spinach, thawed, with extra liquid squeezed out

¼ cup finely chopped fresh cilantro leaves

1 large egg white

2 teaspoons finely grated lemon zest

1 garlic clove, very finely chopped or pressed through a garlic press

1 teaspoon ground coriander

1 teaspoon ground cumin

½ teaspoon cayenne pepper

Splash of hot sauce (optional)

1 teaspoon baking powder

½ teaspoon kosher salt

¼ teaspoon ground black pepper

½ cup white whole wheat flour (or whole wheat pastry flour)

Olive oil mister or nonstick pan spray

Made with chickpeas and a handful of fresh cilantro, Middle Eastern falafel has long been the vegetarian's answer for a substantial meal. The problem is that falafel is almost always fried, meaning that all that goodness is buffered by the effects of deep frying. In this version, I bake the falafel patties on a wire rack so air circulates around them, eliminating the need to flip midbaking. Some frozen spinach gives them a vibrant color while adding iron and B vitamins, too.

1 To make the falafel: Use a food processor to pulse the chickpeas until they are roughly chopped, three or four 1-second pulses. Add the scallions, spinach, cilantro, egg white, lemon zest, garlic, coriander, cumin, cayenne, and hot sauce (if using), and pulse to combine. The mixture should be coarse without any large chunks, but not completely smooth.

2 Transfer the chickpea mixture to a medium bowl and stir in the baking powder, salt, black pepper, and ¼ cup of the flour (the mixture should be very sticky but hold together when pressed—if too wet and loose, stir in 1 tablespoon of flour). Refrigerate for 30 minutes.

3 To make the yogurt sauce: Line a medium plate with a paper towel. Set the grated cucumber on the towel and blot the cucumber with another paper towel. Transfer the cucumber to a medium bowl and add the yogurt, lemon juice, garlic powder, salt, and pepper. Drizzle the olive oil over the top of the sauce.

FOR THE YOGURT SAUCE

½ medium cucumber, peeled, seeded, and grated

¾ cup plain reduced-fat Greek yogurt

Juice of ½ lemon

¼ teaspoon garlic powder

¼ teaspoon kosher salt

¼ teaspoon ground black pepper

1 teaspoon olive oil

4 Preheat the oven to 400°F. Add the remaining ¼ cup flour to a large plate and use a ¼-cup measuring cup to scoop out the chickpea mixture from the bowl, making 8 mounds. Roll each mound in the flour, then gently press between your palms into a patty. Repeat with the remaining mixture for 8 patties total. Lightly mist both sides of each patty with olive oil or nonstick pan spray.

5 Line a rimmed baking sheet with a baking rack and mist the baking rack with olive oil or nonstick pan spray. Set the patties on the rack and bake until they are golden and cooked through, about 20 minutes. Serve the falafel with the yogurt dipping sauce.

PER SERVING: Calories 226 / Protein 11g / Dietary Fiber 8g / Sugars 6g / Total Fat 4g

KITCHEN STRATEGY

Make-Ahead Falafel
Falafel is a great make-ahead option. Just bake them and freeze on a sheet pan until semi-hard, then transfer them to a freezer-safe resealable bag. Defrost in the oven or in the microwave and slide into a pita or serve with rice or couscous.

PASTA

One of my favorite pantry staples is whole-grain pasta. It's shelf stable, economical, and so versatile, allowing me to pull together a healthy dinner in no time. Pasta recipes tend to be pretty flexible too, so you can swap like ingredients. For example, if I don't have chicken, I can amp up the vegetables, or add cooked beans, or shredded meat from last night's roast. If I don't have bell peppers in the house, perhaps there is broccoli lingering in the crisper, or asparagus or fennel or roasted squash.

When one of my daughters was diagnosed with a gluten intolerance, my eyes became truly opened to the gluten-free pasta options in the market—from quinoa and rice-based pastas to ones made with buckwheat and even seaweed. Because pasta is so friendly and willing to please, you can easily substitute whatever type of pasta you want for the traditional semolina kind. Word to the wise, though: watch the noodles as they cook, since gluten-free varieties have a tendency to overcook in a heartbeat!

SLOW-ROASTED TOMATO SPAGHETTINI

SERVES 4   **PREPARATION TIME** 30 MINUTES   **COOKING TIME** 2 HOURS, 15 MINUTES

10 plum tomatoes, halved lengthwise

2 tablespoons olive oil

1 teaspoon kosher salt

½ teaspoon ground black pepper

¼ cup dry white wine

2 shallots, halved lengthwise and thinly sliced

2 garlic cloves, thinly sliced

12 ounces whole-grain spaghettini (thin spaghetti)

¼ cup finely grated Parmesan cheese

¼ cup finely chopped fresh basil leaves

It's easy to create incredible pasta sauces when tomatoes are ripe and at their juicy best. However, for the other half of the year (or longer, depending on where you live), it can be tricky to squeeze big tomato flavor from a pale and hard tomato. The solution? Slow-roasting in the oven to concentrate the flavor and to tenderize. Bonus: your house will smell wonderful!

1 Preheat the oven to 275°F. In a large bowl, toss the halved tomatoes with 1 tablespoon of the olive oil, ½ teaspoon of the salt, and ¼ teaspoon of the pepper. Arrange the tomatoes cut side down on a parchment paper–lined rimmed baking sheet. Drizzle with the wine and cook the tomatoes until their skins start to shrivel, about 1 hour. Remove the baking sheet from the oven and peel away the skins. Turn over the tomatoes and continue to bake until the tomatoes are shriveled but not dried out, 40 to 50 minutes longer. Set the baking sheet aside. Once the tomatoes are cool, roughly chop them.

2 In a large, deep skillet heat the remaining 2 tablespoons oil over medium-high heat. Add the shallots, reduce the heat to medium, and cook, stirring often, until they are very soft, about 8 minutes. Stir in the sliced garlic and remaining ½ teaspoon salt, and cook until the garlic is fragrant, about 1 minute. Stir in the chopped tomatoes along with any accumulated juices. Turn off the heat.

3 Bring a large pot of salted water to a boil. Add the pasta and cook according to the package instructions until al dente. Use tongs or a pasta scoop to transfer the spaghettini to the skillet with the tomato-shallot mixture. Set the skillet over medium-low heat and toss the pasta with the tomatoes, adding up to ¼ cup of the pasta water to thin out the sauce, if needed.

4 Divide the pasta among 4 bowls and serve sprinkled with Parmesan cheese, fresh basil, and the remaining ¼ teaspoon black pepper.

PER SERVING: Calories 464 / Protein 16g / Dietary Fiber 9g / Sugars 8g / Total Fat 14g

---

SUPERMARKET STRATEGY

When to Double Down

If plum tomatoes are on sale, buy twice as many and roast two sheet pans at the same time, one on the upper-middle rack and one on the lower-middle rack (rotate them from top to bottom and back-to-front midway through roasting). Store the roasted tomatoes in the fridge or freeze them for up to 6 months.

CARAMELIZED BRUSSELS SPROUTS, PINE NUTS, AND PENNE

SERVES 4   **PREPARATION TIME 15 MINUTES**   **COOKING TIME 40 MINUTES**

3 tablespoons pine nuts

½ pound whole-grain penne

2 slices center-cut bacon, finely chopped

1 teaspoon olive oil

1 medium yellow onion, halved and thinly sliced

3 cups sliced Brussels sprouts

¼ cup low-sodium chicken broth

Juice of ½ lemon

¼ teaspoon kosher salt

½ teaspoon ground black pepper

2 tablespoons finely chopped fresh thyme

¼ cup finely grated Parmesan cheese

Lemon wedges

My husband grew up disliking Brussels sprouts because he always had them boiled, which brings out the cruciferous flavor. Sautéing and roasting the sprouts, however, brings out their natural earthy sweetness, which pairs perfectly with smoky bacon—even a little bit imparts so much flavor. And here's another clever twist: I include lemon as the garnish instead of extra Parmesan cheese.

1 Toast the pine nuts in a small skillet set over medium heat until they become golden brown, shaking the skillet often, 4 to 5 minutes. Transfer the pine nuts to a plate and set aside.

2 Bring a large pot of salted water to a boil. Add the pasta and cook according to the package instructions until al dente. Set ½ cup of the pasta water aside, then drain the pasta and return it to the pot.

3 Cook the bacon in a large skillet over medium heat until it is browned and crisp, 5 to 6 minutes. Use a slotted spoon to transfer it to a paper towel–lined plate and set aside.

4 Add the olive oil to the bacon fat, then add the onion and cook until it is soft, about 3 minutes. Add the Brussels sprouts, raise the heat to medium-high, and cook until the sprouts begin to turn golden, about 7 minutes.

5 Pour in the chicken broth and lemon juice, stir in the cooked bacon, and season with the salt and pepper. Toss the drained pasta into the Brussels sprout mixture. Add the thyme, toasted pine nuts, and Parmesan cheese, along with a few spoonfuls of pasta water (if the pasta looks dry). Divide the pasta among 4 plates and serve with lemon wedges.

PER SERVING: **Calories 322** / **Protein 16g** / **Dietary Fiber 11g** / **Sugars 6g** / **Total Fat 8g**

RIGATONI WITH TURKEY MEATBALLS

SERVES 6   **PREPARATION TIME** 15 MINUTES (plus 30 minutes to chill)
COOKING TIME 25 MINUTES

¼ cup finely chopped fresh flat-leaf parsley, plus extra for serving

¼ cup finely chopped fresh basil leaves, plus extra for serving

3 tablespoons finely chopped fresh chives

1 pound lean ground turkey

1 large egg, lightly beaten

4 garlic cloves, very finely chopped or pressed through a garlic press

⅓ cup panko-style bread crumbs (preferably whole wheat)

1 teaspoon kosher salt

½ teaspoon ground black pepper

¼ cup grated Parmesan cheese

3 tablespoons olive oil

12 ounces whole-grain rigatoni

Herbs steal the thunder usually reserved for tomatoes in this incredibly fresh and aromatic twist on spaghetti and meatballs. Ground turkey stands in for beef, and a generous amount of chopped parsley, basil, and chives gives the turkey meatballs a wonderfully bright taste. If I'm in the mood for sweet-and-savory Middle Eastern–style meatballs, I'll add some sautéed onions and chopped dried apricots or currants.

1 In a small bowl, combine the parsley, basil, and chives. In a large bowl, combine the turkey, egg, chopped garlic, half the herb mixture, the bread crumbs, ¾ teaspoon of the salt, and ¼ teaspoon of the pepper. Cover the bowl with plastic wrap and refrigerate for 30 minutes.

2 Adjust an oven rack to the upper-middle position and preheat the oven to 400°F. Line a baking sheet with parchment paper or aluminum foil. Remove the meatball mixture from the refrigerator and form the mixture into 36 balls, each about 1 inch in diameter. Space the meatballs ½ inch apart on the prepared baking sheet and bake until the meatballs are almost cooked through, about 15 minutes.

3 Remove the baking sheet from the oven and sprinkle the meatballs with 2 tablespoons of the Parmesan. Turn the broiler to high and broil the meatballs until the Parmesan is melted and browned, 3 to 4 minutes (watch the meatballs closely, as broiler intensities vary).

4 While the meatballs cook, make the sauce. Heat the olive oil in a large skillet over medium-high heat. Add the remaining garlic cloves, the remaining herb mixture, the

remaining ¼ teaspoon salt, and the remaining ¼ teaspoon pepper. Stir until the garlic is fragrant, 2 to 3 minutes, then turn off the heat and set aside.

5 Bring a large pot of salted water to a boil. Add the pasta and cook according to the package instructions until al dente. Set 1 cup of the pasta water aside, then drain the pasta and return it to the pot.

6 Pour the sauce over the pasta and toss to coat. Add ½ cup of the reserved pasta water and stir to combine, adding more pasta water as needed. Taste for seasoning, sprinkle with the remaining 2 tablespoons Parmesan, and serve the rigatoni with the turkey meatballs and extra chopped parsley and basil.

PER SERVING: Calories 417 / Protein 31g / Dietary Fiber 8g / Sugars 3g / Total Fat 13g

---

KITCHEN STRATEGY

Big-Batch Meatballs

When making meatballs, I rarely ever make just enough for one meal. Instead, I triple or even quadruple the recipe to make loads of meatballs—either regular-size ones or cute minis to turn a simple soup dinner into a bulkier meal. You can also pat the meatball mixture into herby burger patties, or even press it into a loaf pan for meatloaf.

meatballs

Everyone loves meatballs—they are quick to make, extremely economical, can feed a crowd, and can be prepared in advance (and stocked in the freezer for at-the-ready dinners). Which is why it's useful to know how to change the flavoring every time you make them to suit your mood. You can even make a big batch of the "base mix," divide it into two or three smaller bowls, and add different ingredients to each for varied flavor profiles.

STEP 1: CHOOSE MEAT AND BUILD YOUR BASE.

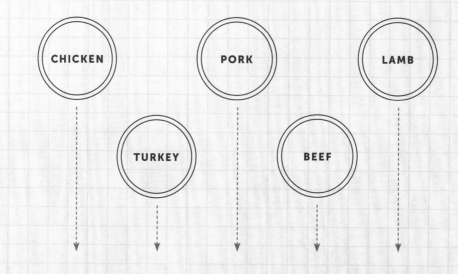

CHICKEN   PORK   LAMB

TURKEY   BEEF

TO EACH POUND OF GROUND MEAT, ADD:

1 EGG

⅔ CUP BREAD CRUMBS

1 TEASPOON KOSHER SALT

1 TEASPOON GROUND BLACK PEPPER

STEP 2: CHOOSE MEATBALL STYLE,
add preferred ingredients, and gently combine.

TRADITIONAL

Herbs (fresh basil, parsley, rosemary)

Garlic (finely chopped fresh or powder)

Grated cheese (Parmesan, Grana Padano, pecorino)

EXOTIC

Herbs (fresh cilantro, tarragon, sage)

Spices (Moroccan ras el hanout, curry powder, herbes de Provence)

Sautéed vegetables (onions, bell peppers, fennel, scallions)

Dried fruit (apricots, currants, raisins, cherries)

Grated cheese (Gouda, Fontina, smoked mozzarella)

STEP 3: GET ROLLING AND COOK.

Roll into 1-inch balls, place on a prepared baking sheet, and cook at 375°F. for 20 minutes. For extra flavor, brown the meatballs on one side in an oven-safe skillet and then transfer the skillet to the oven to finish cooking.

ROTINI WITH SMOKY EGGPLANT, MINT, AND FETA

SERVES 4   **PREPARATION TIME** 15 MINUTES   **COOKING TIME** 25 MINUTES

2 medium Japanese or Chinese eggplants, cut into ½-inch pieces

2 tablespoons olive oil

1½ teaspoons kosher salt

½ teaspoon smoked paprika

8 ounces rotini pasta

1½ cups gently packed fresh mint leaves, plus extra roughly chopped for serving

Zest and juice of 1 lemon

2 medium garlic cloves, very finely chopped or pressed through a garlic press

½ cup crumbled feta cheese

To make this mint sauce, I blend a lot of fresh mint with still-hot pasta cooking water. The water semi-blanches and softens the mint, making it easier to blend in and bringing out its flavor-driving essential oils. Paired with smoked paprika–roasted eggplant and creamy-salty feta cheese, it's a really nice dish to eat when you're craving something a little different.

1 Preheat the oven to 400°F. Line a baking sheet with parchment paper. In a medium bowl, toss together the eggplant, 1 tablespoon of the olive oil, 1 teaspoon of the salt, and the smoked paprika. Turn the eggplant out onto the prepared baking sheet and roast until golden brown and tender, about 20 minutes.

2 While the eggplant roasts, cook the pasta. Bring a large pot of salted water to a boil. Add the pasta and cook according to the package instructions until al dente. Reserve ¾ cup of the pasta water, then drain the pasta.

3 Add the mint leaves to a blender jar and pour the hot pasta water over the top. Add the remaining ½ teaspoon salt and the lemon zest, and blend until puréed.

4 To the pot used for cooking the pasta add the remaining 1 tablespoon olive oil and the garlic. Cook until the garlic is fragrant, about 1 minute, then return the pasta to the pot. Add the eggplant, lemon juice, and mint sauce and stir to combine.

5 Divide the pasta among 4 bowls. Sprinkle each with some mint and the feta, then serve.

PER SERVING: Calories 447 / Protein 16g / Dietary Fiber 6g / Sugars 6g / Total Fat 12g

STIR-FRIED BEEF
OVER SEAWEED NOODLES

SERVES 4   **PREPARATION TIME 15 MINUTES** (plus 30 minutes to marinate)
COOKING TIME 15 MINUTES

FOR THE BEEF

12 ounces flank steak, halved lengthwise, then sliced crosswise into ¼-inch-wide strips

1½ tablespoons tamari sauce (or soy sauce, if gluten isn't a problem), plus more if needed

2 garlic cloves, very finely chopped or pressed through a garlic press

FOR THE NOODLES

1 tablespoon sesame seeds

1 12-ounce package kelp noodles (or other cooked long thin noodles)

2 teaspoons canola oil

8 scallions, ends trimmed and sliced into long strips lengthwise

1 small red bell pepper, seeded and thinly sliced into long strips

¼ teaspoon kosher salt

1 teaspoon toasted sesame oil

Not only is kelp a wonderfully sustainable and renewable resource (it can grow up to a foot a day!), but kelp noodles are incredibly healthy, they're gluten-free, and they require only a quick rinse under water before tossing into a skillet with some beef stir-fry fixings. The thin strands have an unusual crunch to them that works really well with al dente vegetables like scallions and peppers.

1 To marinate the beef: Add the beef to a medium bowl along with the tamari and garlic. Stir, cover the bowl with plastic wrap, and refrigerate for up to 8 hours or leave at room temperature for 30 minutes.

2 To make the noodles: Toast the sesame seeds in a large skillet over medium heat, shaking the pan often, until they are browned, about 2 minutes. Transfer the seeds to a plate, turn off the heat, and wipe the pan.

3 Place the kelp noodles in a colander or fine-mesh sieve and rinse under cold water, then set aside. Set the skillet over high heat and add the canola oil. Once the oil shimmers, add the beef and stir for a second, then cook the meat until lightly browned on both sides and still pink in the middle, 5 to 6 minutes. Transfer the meat to a large bowl.

4 To the skillet add the scallions, red pepper, and salt, and cook until the vegetables wilt, 2 to 3 minutes. Add the noodles to the skillet along with the beef, drizzle with the sesame oil, and toss together. Once the noodles are warmed through, taste and add more tamari, if needed. Divide among 4 plates and serve sprinkled with the sesame seeds.

PER SERVING: Calories 186 / Protein 16g / Dietary Fiber 2g / Sugars 1g / Total Fat 11g

If you don't already have a section of your pantry devoted to Asian ingredients, then I suggest you do this! Ingredients like soy sauce, rice vinegar, and ginger are kid-friendly, and are a great way to bring a new flavor profile to your kitchen table. All the ingredients listed below can be found in the international-foods aisle of your supermarket.

Miso

This fermented paste is most often made from soybeans, but it can also be made with rice or barley. Miso comes in several varieties, most often white and varying shades of red and brown. Generally, the lighter the color of the paste, the less intense the flavor.

Soy Sauce and Tamari

Made from soybeans, soy sauce is a fermented seasoning that adds umami and depth to dishes (it's a great vegan substitute for Worcestershire sauce). Look at the label before buying to make sure there aren't any artificial colors or flavors added. Some people with gluten sensitivities opt for tamari sauce, which is typically made with a higher concentration of soybeans and little to no wheat. Be sure to read the nutrition label before purchasing and buy only brands labeled as "gluten-free" if you are especially sensitive or allergic.

Chili-Garlic Sauce

Similar to its cousin, tangy Sriracha sauce, chili-garlic sauce is a potent blend of dried red chiles, lots of garlic, salt, sugar, and white vinegar. It's great stirred into sauces, marinades, or soups when you're interested in adding flavor as well as heat to a dish.

Sriracha Sauce

Smooth Sriracha sauce is similar to chili-garlic sauce and is even made with many of the same ingredients: chiles, garlic, vinegar, salt, and sugar. The main difference is that it is smooth rather than chunky, giving it more of the feel of a condiment (like ketchup) rather than an ingredient (like tomato paste).

Mirin Rice Wine

Sweet rice wine is similar to sake; however, it has a high sugar content (since the sugar occurs naturally, it counts as a complex carb). It is great for adding to sauces since it has a tendency to cook down into a nice glaze.

Rice Vinegar

Mild rice vinegar (often called rice wine vinegar because the vinegar is sometimes made from fermented rice wine) is a subtly acidic addition to salad dressings, sauces, and marinades. Try to buy unseasoned if you can—seasoned rice vinegar contains added sugar, salt, and sake.

Fresh Ginger

Like fresh garlic, fresh ginger is an absolute cooking must! It gives an acidic, tingly heat to everything from salad dressing to scones. Sold in "fingers," ginger that is freshest looks taut and isn't leathery or shriveled. Use the edge of a teaspoon to scrape away the thin skin before grating, chopping, or slicing. In fact, I even keep a peeled hunk of ginger in a plastic bag in my freezer—it grates without any trouble, and its pungent flavor is just as bracing as if it were fresh from the fridge.

PENNE with BEET-POBLANO PESTO and CHICKPEAS

SERVES 4   PREPARATION TIME 30 MINUTES   COOKING TIME 35 MINUTES

FOR THE PESTO

2 poblano peppers

2 small beets with green tops, beets peeled and cut into ½-inch pieces, greens chopped and reserved

¼ cup vegetable or low-sodium chicken broth

¼ cup olive oil

2 tablespoons fresh lemon juice

⅓ cup Parmesan cheese

2 garlic cloves, roughly chopped

½ teaspoon ground chipotle chile (or chili powder, for less heat)

FOR THE PASTA

2 tablespoons pecan halves

8 ounces whole-grain penne pasta

1 cup cooked chickpeas (homemade, page 81; or canned, rinsed)

This smoky, spicy pesto is made by blending raw beet greens (or any raw leafy greens, such as spinach or arugula) with roasted poblano peppers and Parmesan cheese. I boil the chopped beets with the pasta in the same pot—how's that for efficient? The sweetness of the beets rounds out the charred, roasted flavor of the peppers and the heat of the chipotle chile powder. Toasted pecans add a nice texture and crunch to the finished dish.

1 To make the pesto: Place the poblanos on an aluminum foil–lined rimmed baking sheet and preheat the broiler to high. Roast the poblanos using tongs to turn them every 3 to 5 minutes, until all sides are blackened and charred, 15 to 18 minutes total. Transfer the peppers to a medium bowl and cover the bowl with plastic wrap. Set aside for 15 minutes. Once the peppers are cool enough to handle, remove the stems, peel away the skins, and seed them. Place the poblanos in a food processor.

2 Add the beet greens to the poblanos in the food processor, then add the vegetable broth, olive oil, lemon juice, Parmesan cheese, garlic, and ground chile. Process the mixture until it is nearly smooth, scraping down the sides of the bowl as needed, about 1 minute.

3 To make the pasta: Preheat the oven to 350°F. Place the pecans on a clean rimmed baking sheet and cook until toasted, about 8 minutes. Transfer the pecans to a cutting board and once cool, roughly chop.

(recipe continues)

4 Bring a large pot of salted water to a boil. Add the pasta and the beets, and cook the pasta according to the package instructions until al dente (the beets will tint the pasta slightly; if using preroasted beets, add them in step 5). Add the chickpeas, cook for 10 seconds, then drain the pasta, beets, and chickpeas in a colander, reserving ¼ cup of the pasta water.

5 To a large bowl add the pasta mixture along with the pesto and stir to combine. If you want the consistency of the pesto to be looser, add the reserved water. Serve sprinkled with the toasted pecans.

PER SERVING: Calories 536 / Protein 18g / Dietary Fiber 11g / Sugars 6g / Total Fat 26g

KITCHEN STRATEGY

Pesto Pronto
Make a double batch of the pesto and use it throughout the week as a spread for sandwiches and wraps, a bruschetta topping, or a dip for raw vegetables. You can even freeze cubes of pesto in an ice cube tray, then transfer the cubes to a freezer bag and store in the freezer for up to 3 months.

SUPERMARKET STRATEGY

Vacuum-Sealed Roasted Beets
Most supermarkets now carry already roasted and vacuum-sealed beets, saving cooks about an hour of roasting time. You can usually find them in the produce area. Simply open the package and use them at room temperature or warm them in the microwave or in a hot oven before serving.

DECONSTRUCTED LASAGNA

SERVES 4   **PREPARATION TIME** 15 MINUTES   **COOKING TIME** 35 MINUTES

8 ounces lasagna noodles, broken into smaller pieces

2 teaspoons olive oil

1 medium yellow onion, halved and very finely chopped

3 garlic cloves, very finely chopped or pressed through a garlic press

2 teaspoons kosher salt

½ teaspoon ground black pepper

2 tablespoons roughly chopped fresh marjoram

Pinch of red pepper flakes

½ pound lean ground beef

2 cups canned whole tomatoes, chopped (or canned chopped tomatoes)

½ cup quartered bocconcini (mozzarella balls) or ½-inch pieces of fresh mozzarella

2 tablespoons finely grated Parmesan cheese

In this case, "deconstructed" is really just a trendy way of saying easy! Instead of taking the time to layer the pasta, sauce, and several kinds of cheeses, I toss everything together to make a lasagna bowl that satisfies, with all of the same, indulgent components but far fewer calories and effort. Fresh marjoram has a minty, oregano-like flavor that is a nice change of pace from basil or dried Italian herbs—but really, any kind of fresh herb is delicious in tomato sauce, so use what's handy.

1 Bring a large pot of salted water to a boil. Add the lasagna noodles and cook according to the package instructions until al dente. Drain in a colander and set aside.

2 To a large, deep skillet or pot set over medium heat add the olive oil, onion, garlic, 1 teaspoon of the salt, and the black pepper, and cook until the onion is soft and sticky, stirring often, for 6 to 7 minutes. Stir in the marjoram and red pepper flakes, and once they are fragrant, after 30 seconds, stir in the beef, using a wooden spoon to break it into small pieces. Cook, stirring often, until the beef is no longer pink, about 5 minutes.

3 Add the chopped tomatoes and remaining 1 teaspoon salt, reduce the heat to medium-low, and simmer the sauce until it reduces slightly, about 10 minutes.

4 Divide half of the cooked lasagna noodles among 4 bowls. Top each with some mozzarella and sauce, then divide the remaining noodles over the top. Add some more mozzarella and sauce, and serve sprinkled with Parmesan cheese.

PER SERVING: Calories 567 / Protein 31g / Dietary Fiber 5g / Sugars 8g / Total Fat 18g

SHELLS AND SHRIMP WITH LEMONY BREAD CRUMBS

SERVES 4   PREPARATION TIME 15 MINUTES   COOKING TIME 20 MINUTES

⅓ cup panko-style bread crumbs (preferably whole wheat)

Zest and juice of 1 lemon

1 tablespoon finely chopped fresh flat-leaf parsley

½ teaspoon kosher salt

¼ teaspoon ground black pepper

8 ounces small pasta shells

8 ounces rock shrimp (or peeled and deveined small shrimp, chopped into ¼-inch pieces)

2 teaspoons olive oil

2 garlic cloves, thinly sliced

1 small fresh red chile (such as Fresno), halved, seeded, and thinly sliced crosswise

¼ teaspoon red pepper flakes

5 cups loosely packed baby spinach leaves, coarsely chopped

Tiny rock shrimp offer a taste of luxurious shellfish at a lower cost, but if you can't find them, buy small shrimp and just chop them up even smaller. The toasted panko bread crumbs are crispy and crunchy, and the lemon zest gives them a great citrusy taste. Fresno chiles add moderate heat. For a vegan adaptation, leave out the shrimp and add cooked white beans (for protein) when you add the spinach.

1 Set a large nonstick skillet over medium-high heat, add the bread crumbs, and cook, stirring often, until they are toasted and fragrant, 3 to 5 minutes. Transfer the bread crumbs to a medium bowl and wipe out the skillet. To the toasted bread crumbs stir in the lemon zest, parsley, ¼ teaspoon of the salt, and ⅛ teaspoon of the pepper.

2 Bring a large pot of salted water to a boil. Add the pasta and cook according to the package instructions until al dente. Reserve 1 cup of the pasta water, then drain the pasta.

3 Season the shrimp with the remaining ¼ teaspoon salt and ⅛ teaspoon pepper. Heat the olive oil in the cleaned skillet over medium-high heat. Add the garlic and chile, and cook, stirring, until the garlic is fragrant and soft, about 2 minutes. Add the shrimp and the red pepper flakes, and cook, stirring often, until the shrimp turn pink, 3 to 4 minutes.

4 Stir the spinach into the shrimp mixture and continue to cook, stirring often, until.the spinach wilts, about 1 minute. Stir in ¼ cup of the reserved pasta water, the lemon juice, and the cooked shells, and toss to combine, adding more pasta water as needed. Serve the pasta sprinkled with the seasoned bread crumbs.

PER SERVING: Calories 434 / Protein 25g / Dietary Fiber 5g / Sugars 4g / Total Fat 5g

TUNA NOODLE BOWLS

SERVES 4   PREPARATION TIME 20 MINUTES   COOKING TIME 30 MINUTES

8 ounces bite-size whole-grain pasta (such as farfalle or elbows)

2 teaspoons olive oil

1 medium shallot, very finely chopped

1 large leek (white and light green parts only), halved lengthwise, then thinly sliced crosswise

½ cup reduced-fat cream cheese (Neufchâtel)

Zest and juice of ½ lemon

2 6-ounce cans water-packed albacore tuna, drained and flaked

½ cup frozen peas

½ teaspoon kosher salt

½ teaspoon ground black pepper

2 tablespoons finely chopped fresh chives

1 cup (about 2 ounces) baked potato chips, lightly crushed

A smart combination of reduced-fat cream cheese and baked potato chips slims one of my favorite one-pot meals, tuna noodle casserole. Serving the pasta in individual bowls rather than from a casserole dish also means that you don't have to worry about the pasta drying out as it bakes in the oven. Honestly, the baked potato chips crumbled on top are my favorite part!

1   Bring a large pot of salted water to a boil. Add the pasta and cook according to the package instructions until al dente. Reserve 2 cups of the pasta water, then drain the pasta.

2   Heat the olive oil over medium-high heat in a medium skillet. Add the shallot and leek and cook until soft, stirring often, 10 to 12 minutes. Stir in the cream cheese, lemon zest and juice, and ½ cup of the reserved pasta water, stirring until smooth.

3   Add the tuna and peas and simmer briefly, just to warm the tuna and thaw the peas, adding more water as needed, about 4 minutes longer. Stir in the salt and half the pepper, then stir in the drained pasta and chives.

4   Divide the pasta among 4 bowls, sprinkle with the crushed potato chips and remaining black pepper, and serve.

PER SERVING: Calories 499 / Protein 33g / Dietary Fiber 4g / Sugars 6g / Total Fat 13g

---

KITCHEN STRATEGY

DIY Bread Crumbs
Instead of crumbled potato chips, brown freshly pulverized bread in some olive oil in a skillet. Season with salt and fresh herbs if you like, then sprinkle the crunchy seasoned crumbs over the pasta before serving.

SOBA NOODLES WITH GARLICKY CLAMS AND FENNEL

SERVES 4   **PREPARATION TIME** 10 MINUTES   **COOKING TIME** 20 MINUTES

1 tablespoon unsalted butter

1 medium fennel bulb, cored and thinly sliced lengthwise (finely chop some fennel fronds and save for serving)

4 garlic cloves, very finely chopped or pressed through a garlic press

½ cup low-sodium chicken broth

¼ cup dry white wine

1 tablespoon low-sodium soy sauce (or tamari, if making gluten-free)

20 small (littleneck) clams, scrubbed

1 package soba noodles (about 8.8 ounces)

Hearty, nutty buckwheat soba noodles pair nicely with light sauces, like this one made with lots of garlic and clams. If you're not a soba noodle lover, substitute whatever noodle you like— be it udon, quinoa pasta, or linguini.

1 Melt the butter in a large pot over medium-high heat. Add the fennel and garlic and cook, stirring often, until the fennel is soft, about 5 minutes.

2 Add the chicken broth, wine, and soy sauce, bring to a simmer, then add the clams. Cover the pot and cook until the clams open, 3 to 4 minutes. Turn off the heat (discard any clams that don't open).

3 Bring a large pot of salted water to a boil. Add the noodles and cook according to the package instructions. Drain the noodles, then rinse them under cold running water to cool (if using linguini, skip this step). Turn the cooled noodles out into a large serving dish.

4 Use a slotted spoon to arrange the clams over the noodles. Pour the sauce over the clams and noodles, sprinkle with chopped fennel fronds, and serve.

PER SERVING: Calories 332 / Protein 23g / Dietary Fiber 2g / Sugars 1g / Total Fat 4g

---

KITCHEN STRATEGY

Cooking Wine

A little wine (or sake or vermouth) added to a sauce or broth can lend a lot of complexity. In the recipe above, I sometimes substitute ¼ cup sake for half the chicken broth, giving this pasta dish a delicate sweetness.

KITCHEN STRATEGY

Dress Up Your Pasta
A simple bowl of noodles becomes so much
more when you add thoughtful extras like pan-
seared shrimp, Parmesan shavings, homemade
bread crumbs (see page 157), or roasted vegetables. I've even been known to toss leftover
soup with plain pasta for an instant veggie-rich
and perfectly seasoned sauce!

BROCCOLI-RIBBON FETTUCCINE
WITH PARMESAN

SERVES 4 **PREPARATION TIME** 15 MINUTES **COOKING TIME** 15 MINUTES

2 medium heads of broccoli, florets removed (save for another time) and stems reserved

8 ounces fettuccine (whole-grain, if available)

3 tablespoons olive oil

3 garlic cloves, very finely chopped or pressed through a garlic press

¼ teaspoon red pepper flakes

Zest and juice of ½ lemon

¼ cup low-sodium chicken or vegetable broth

1 cup halved grape or cherry tomatoes (quartered, if very large)

1 teaspoon kosher salt

½ cup grated Parmesan cheese

Buying broccoli bunches, or "trees" as my girls call them, will save you money compared with buying broccoli crowns. There is no reason to toss the stems—just peel away the tough skin and get ready for a pleasant, sweet, and tender broccoli-stalk surprise! I like to shave the stalks into thin ribbons and toss them with fettuccine. It adds vitamin-rich volume and bulk. For another way to use broccoli stems, see the broccoli slaw recipe on page 261.

1 Set the broccoli stems on a cutting board. Use a vegetable peeler to peel away the tough outer layer of skin, then use the peeler to shave long, thin ribbons from the stalks (about 2 cups total).

2 Bring a large pot of salted water to a boil. Add the pasta and cook according to the package instructions until al dente. Drain the pasta in a colander and reserve ¼ cup of the pasta water.

3 Heat the olive oil in a large, deep skillet over medium-high heat. Add the garlic and red pepper flakes and cook, stirring often, until they are fragrant, about 1 minute. Stir in the lemon zest and broccoli ribbons and cook, stirring occasionally, until the ribbons are tender, 1 to 2 minutes.

4 Reduce the heat to low and stir in the chicken broth, lemon juice, tomatoes, and salt. Add the fettuccine and toss to combine, stirring in some pasta water to loosen the sauce if needed. Stir in ¼ cup of the Parmesan cheese. Divide the pasta among 4 bowls and serve sprinkled with the remaining ¼ cup cheese.

PER SERVING: Calories 400 / Protein 17g / Dietary Fiber 7g / Sugars 5g / Total Fat 16g

— *Chapter 7* —

FISH AND SEAFOOD

The more I learn about fish and seafood, the more I find the research compelling. The bottom line is this: if you eat fish a few times a week, both your heart and your brain will be the better for it. So, I make eating fish two to three times a week a priority for my family.

You can get a good deal on fish when you buy it fresh. In fact, the fish on sale at your grocery store is usually cheaper than frozen fish. You need to eat the fish within a day of purchasing, but if you can commit to it, the reciprocal health benefits are invaluable. Fish can be purchased at a variety of price points; you'll find recipes in this chapter that meet all of them. Flounder, tilapia, and trout are usually quite affordable, while higher-priced fish like wild salmon, tuna, and shrimp go on sale often enough that they can be a part of your meal plan without breaking the bank. Keep in mind that when there's a lot of fish available—like during salmon season—you can typically find great deals.

GRILLED ORANGE-GLAZED TUNA

SERVES 4   **PREPARATION TIME** 10 MINUTES   **COOKING TIME** 12 MINUTES

1 cup fresh orange juice

2 teaspoons low-sodium soy sauce

½-inch piece of fresh ginger, peeled and halved crosswise

1 garlic clove, smashed

4 5-ounce, 1¼-inch-thick tuna steaks (yellowtail or albacore are good options)

½ teaspoon kosher salt

½ teaspoon ground black pepper

1 teaspoon canola oil, plus extra for grilling

2 scallions (white and light green parts only), finely chopped

1 small bunch fresh cilantro, finely chopped

Tuna is the perfect fish when you are craving something meaty and substantial. It is best served seared or grilled, rare (red) or medium rare (reddish-pink) in the middle. While tuna can be pricey, when I see it on sale I seize the opportunity and change my dinner plans so I can serve tuna that night.

1   Heat a charcoal or gas grill to high. Add the orange juice, soy sauce, ginger, and garlic to a small saucepan and set over medium-low heat. Let the sauce simmer until it begins to reduce and thicken, about 5 minutes. Turn off the heat and use a slotted spoon to remove and discard the garlic and ginger.

2   Season both sides of each tuna steak with the salt and pepper and then rub with the canola oil. Use tongs to dip a folded paper towel into some oil, then use it to grease the grill grates. Set the tuna on the grill and cook without moving until grill-marked, about 3 minutes. Use a metal spatula to flip the tuna steaks and cook on the other side until also grill-marked, about 3 minutes more (this will yield a medium-rare tuna steak; if you prefer your tuna cooked more or less, adjust the cooking time).

3   Transfer each tuna steak to a plate and pour over some of the glaze. Finish with scallions and cilantro and serve.

PER SERVING: Calories 224 / Protein 40g / Dietary Fiber 1g / Sugars 7g / Total Fat 3g

SCALLOPS WITH GRUYÈRE-HERB CRUMBS

SERVES 4   **PREPARATION TIME** 15 MINUTES   **COOKING TIME** 15 MINUTES

12 large sea scallops, blotted dry

¾ teaspoon kosher salt

½ teaspoon ground black pepper

1 tablespoon olive oil

1 medium shallot, finely chopped

1 garlic clove, very finely chopped or pressed through a garlic press

¼ cup dry white wine

Zest and juice of ½ lemon

¼ cup panko-style bread crumbs (preferably whole wheat)

1 tablespoon finely grated Gruyère cheese

1 tablespoon finely chopped fresh flat-leaf parsley

1 teaspoon finely chopped fresh tarragon leaves (optional)

Cheesy coquilles St. Jacques *are one of my husband's child-hood favorites, so I created a scallop recipe that hints at the nutty Gruyère while staying on the healthier side. The bread crumbs add perfect crunch to top the creamy scallops.*

1 Adjust an oven rack to the upper-middle position and preheat the broiler to high. Season the scallops with ½ teaspoon of the salt and ¼ teaspoon of the pepper. Heat the olive oil in a large oven-safe skillet over medium heat. Add the shallot and garlic and cook, stirring often, until the shallot is tender, about 3 minutes.

2 Pour in the wine and simmer until it is reduced by half, about 3 minutes. Add the scallops and cook until they are opaque and feel firm to light pressure, 3 to 4 minutes (cook the scallops in two batches if they don't all fit in the skillet). Stir in the lemon juice and season with the remaining ¼ teaspoon salt. Turn off the heat.

3 In a small bowl, stir together the bread crumbs, lemon zest, grated cheese, parsley, and tarragon (if using). Sprinkle the mixture over the scallops in the skillet and set the skillet under the broiler. Broil until the crumbs are golden brown, 2 to 3 minutes (watch the scallops closely, as broiler intensities vary). Sprinkle with the remaining ¼ teaspoon pepper and serve immediately.

PER SERVING: Calories 109 / Protein 9g / Dietary Fiber 1g / Sugars 0g / Total Fat 5g

SESAME-CRUSTED SALMON
WITH MISO SAUCE

SERVES 4   **PREPARATION TIME 15 MINUTES**   **COOKING TIME 25 MINUTES**

FOR THE SALMON

2 10-ounce salmon fillets, any pin bones removed

¼ teaspoon kosher salt

¼ teaspoon ground black pepper

2 tablespoons sesame seeds (white, black, or mixed)

FOR THE SAUCE

½ cup low-sodium chicken broth

2 tablespoons mirin (rice wine) or dry white wine

1 tablespoon rice vinegar

1 tablespoon miso paste (preferably white)

1 ¼-inch-thick crosswise slice of yellow or white onion

2 garlic cloves, smashed

FOR COOKING AND SERVING

1 teaspoon canola oil

1 tablespoon unsalted butter

1 tablespoon finely chopped fresh chives

Salmon is probably the fish I serve the most to my family. It's full of omega-3 fatty acids, and the rich flavor is satisfying. To make a creamy sauce—without the cream—I rely on mild white miso paste and just a wink of butter.

1 To prepare the salmon: Preheat the oven to 375°F. Halve each fillet crosswise so you end up with 4 pieces. Season the salmon with the salt and pepper. Place the sesame seeds on a small plate and press the top side of each piece of salmon into the sesame seeds, lightly patting the seeds on to encourage them to stick. Set the salmon aside.

2 To make the sauce: Whisk together the broth, ¼ cup of water, the mirin, vinegar, and miso paste in a small saucepan. Add the onion and garlic and cook over medium heat until the mixture thickens and gets creamy, stirring often, for about 5 minutes. Turn off the heat.

3 Heat a large oven-safe nonstick skillet over medium heat. Add the canola oil, and once it shimmers, add the salmon fillets, sesame side down. Cook until the sesame seeds are golden, about 3 minutes, then flip the fillets over. Transfer the skillet to the oven and bake until the fillets resist light pressure and are nearly opaque all the way through, 11 to 13 minutes.

4 Remove the salmon from the oven and set aside while finishing the sauce. Remove the onion and garlic from the sauce and set the saucepan over low heat. Whisk in the butter until the sauce is creamy.

5 Serve the salmon sesame side up, drizzled with the miso sauce and sprinkled with the chives.

PER SERVING: Calories 319 / Protein 34g / Dietary Fiber 0g / Sugars 1g / Total Fat 17g

HORSERADISH-CRUSTED SALMON WITH BEETS AND SWEET POTATO

SERVES 4   PREPARATION TIME 20 MINUTES   COOKING TIME 1 HOUR

4 small beets, peeled and halved

1 small sweet potato, peeled and cut into 2-inch cubes (about the same size as the beets)

2 teaspoons olive oil

2 garlic cloves, very finely chopped or pressed through a garlic press

½ medium yellow onion, finely chopped

½ teaspoon kosher salt

½ teaspoon ground black pepper

2 10-ounce salmon fillets

2 tablespoons light mayonnaise

1½ tablespoons prepared horseradish (not sauce)

⅓ cup panko-style bread crumbs (preferably whole wheat)

1 teaspoon dried thyme

1 teaspoon finely grated lemon zest

Stunning beets and sweet potatoes make a pretty bed for roasting salmon. The horseradish adds just a touch of warmth and encourages crunchy flecks of panko bread crumbs to stick to the surface of the fish. Feel free to try other root vegetables, such as carrots, parsnips, and new potatoes (you may have to reduce the cooking time a little).

1 Preheat the oven to 375°F. Place the beets and sweet potato in two separate small bowls (so the beets don't stain the potato) and toss each with 1 teaspoon olive oil, 1 garlic clove, and half the chopped onion. Divide ¼ teaspoon salt between the bowls, then divide ¼ teaspoon pepper between the bowls and toss to combine. Place the beets and sweet potatoes in a baking dish big enough to hold the salmon too, cover with aluminum foil, and bake until they are just tender, stirring halfway through baking, about 45 minutes.

2 Slice the salmon in half crosswise into 4 equally sized pieces. Season the salmon with the remaining ¼ teaspoon salt and remaining ¼ teaspoon pepper and set aside. In a small bowl, mix the mayonnaise and horseradish. Smear the mixture over the top of the salmon fillets.

3 On a small plate, mix the bread crumbs, thyme, and lemon zest. Press the crumbs into the horseradish-mayonnaise mixture on the fish, then place the fillets on top of the beets and sweet potatoes. Bake until the salmon is opaque and the center resists light pressure, 10 to 12 minutes.

4 Divide the salmon among 4 plates and serve alongside the roasted beets and sweet potato.

PER SERVING: Calories 376 / Protein 35g / Dietary Fiber 5g / Sugars 9g / Total Fat 15g

COD AND COCONUT CURRY OVER CILANTRO RICE

SERVES 4   **PREPARATION TIME 20 MINUTES**   **COOKING TIME 1 HOUR, 10 MINUTES**

FOR THE RICE

1 cup short-grain brown rice

½ teaspoon kosher salt

2 tablespoons finely chopped fresh cilantro leaves

FOR THE CURRY

1 pound fresh cod fillet, cut into 1-inch chunks

1 teaspoon kosher salt

1 lime

2 teaspoons canola oil

1 small yellow onion, grated on the medium holes of a box grater

1 1-inch piece of fresh ginger, peeled and grated on the medium holes of a box grater

1 garlic clove, peeled and grated with a Microplane-style grater

2 tablespoons prepared Thai green curry paste

1 14-ounce can unsweetened light coconut milk

2 tablespoons finely chopped fresh cilantro leaves

I went to graduate school in Washington, D.C., where my standby takeout favorite was Thai coconut curry, a dish ubiquitous in Georgetown, where I lived. Here is my healthy, budget-friendly version featuring unsweetened light coconut milk and fresh cod. You can use a variety of proteins in your curry, from chicken to shrimp, pork, and beef, but I like mild cod and its incredible health benefits, like the omega-3s and vitamins B_{12} and B_6.

1 To make the rice: Place the rice in a large bowl and rinse under cold water, agitating the rice often. Drain and repeat until the water in the bowl is clear. Place the drained rice in a medium saucepan with 2¼ cups water and the salt. Bring the water to a boil, reduce the heat to low, cover the pot, and cook until the rice is tender and all the liquid is evaporated, about 45 minutes. Turn off the heat and leave the pan covered for 10 minutes, then fluff the rice with a fork and stir in the cilantro.

2 To make the curry: Season the cod with the salt and set aside. Use a Microplane-style grater to zest 1 teaspoon of lime and set aside. Then juice the lime and set aside.

3 Heat the canola oil in a large skillet over medium-high heat. Add the grated onion, ginger, and garlic, and cook, stirring, for 30 seconds. Stir in the curry paste and cook for 1 minute more, then pour in the coconut milk, ½ cup water, and the lime zest. Bring the sauce to a simmer and cook, whisking frequently, until it is reduced by one-quarter, 10 to 12 minutes.

4 Add the cod, reduce the heat to medium-low, and cook until the fish is opaque and flakes easily, about 5 minutes. Add the lime juice and the chopped cilantro. Divide the rice among 4 plates and serve the curry on top.

PER SERVING: Calories 372 / Protein 22g / Dietary Fiber 4g / Sugars 5g / Total Fat 14g

TILAPIA IN CAPER-TOMATO SAUCE

SERVES 4   **PREPARATION TIME 10 MINUTES**   **COOKING TIME 15 MINUTES**

Zest and juice of 1 lemon

1 teaspoon kosher salt

2 tilapia fillets, sliced down the middle to yield 4 long strips

1 tablespoon olive oil

½ teaspoon ground black pepper

¼ teaspoon red pepper flakes (optional)

1 tablespoon tomato paste

1½ cups finely chopped or hand-shredded canned tomatoes

2 tablespoons capers, rinsed

Gently cooking fish fillets in a fragrant sauce is a deliciously dependable way to eat healthfully on short notice. I always have tilapia fillets in the freezer—they keep well and defrost quickly. Paired with pantry staples like canned tomatoes, lemon, and capers, the tilapia becomes an easy and healthy pantry meal.

1   Place half the lemon juice and ½ teaspoon of the salt in a medium bowl. Add the tilapia fillets and turn to coat in the seasoned lemon juice. Set aside.

2   Add the olive oil, black pepper, and red pepper flakes (if using) to a large skillet. Set the heat to medium-high and cook, stirring often, until the spices are fragrant, about 1 minute. Stir in the lemon zest and once it sizzles, stir in the tomato paste. Cook, stirring often, until the tomato paste deepens in color, 1½ to 2 minutes.

3   Add the tomatoes and remaining ½ teaspoon salt and cook, stirring often, until the tomatoes break down and become jam-like, 3 to 4 minutes. Add the remaining lemon juice and the capers to the skillet and bring the mixture to a simmer.

4   Nestle the tilapia fillets in the tomato mixture, cover the pan, reduce the heat to medium-low, and cook until the fillets feel firm to slight pressure and they flake easily, 6 to 8 minutes. Divide the fillet strips among 4 plates and serve with the sauce.

PER SERVING: Calories 173 / Protein 27g / Dietary Fiber 2g / Sugars 3g / Total Fat 5g

SNAPPER WITH BROCCOLI "PESTO" AND WHITE BEAN SALSA

SERVES 4   PREPARATION TIME 20 MINUTES   COOKING TIME 12 MINUTES

FOR THE PESTO

1 cup roughly chopped broccoli (florets and tender parts of stalk; about ½ small head)

1 small bunch fresh basil leaves (about 25 leaves)

4 garlic cloves, roughly chopped

2 tablespoons fresh lemon juice

2 tablespoons olive oil

¼ teaspoon kosher salt

¼ teaspoon ground black pepper

FOR THE BEAN SALSA

½ cup cooked white beans (homemade, page 81; or canned, rinsed)

1 small tomato, finely chopped

1 medium shallot, finely chopped

¼ teaspoon kosher salt

¼ teaspoon ground black pepper

FOR THE FISH

4 5-ounce red snapper fillets

¼ teaspoon kosher salt

¼ teaspoon ground black pepper

Cooking fish enclosed in parchment paper is an excellent way to ensure that the fish doesn't dry out. In this preparation, I top the fish with a nutless "pesto" and take the liberty of adding nutrient-rich broccoli to the mixture, which adds a touch of flavor and heft. If you don't have parchment paper, aluminum foil will work in a pinch.

1 To make the pesto: Preheat the oven to 400°F.: Use a food processor to combine the broccoli, basil, garlic, lemon juice, olive oil, salt, and pepper until the mixture becomes a chunky paste, about 20 seconds.

2 To make the bean salsa: Stir the beans, tomato, shallot, salt, and pepper together in a medium bowl.

3 To cook the fish: Season the fish with the salt and pepper. Tear off 4 large sheets of parchment paper (large enough to easily enclose the fish in a roomy packet). Set each fillet in the center of a sheet and cover with a spoonful of the pesto, gently pressing it on the fish to cover.

4 Divide the bean salsa over the pesto. Fold one side of the parchment over to meet the other side, then tightly fold up the edges, beginning at the bottom corner and moving around to the upper corner, to seal the paper shut so it creates a half-moon shape.

5 Bake the packages on a rimmed baking sheet for 12 minutes. Slide each packet onto a plate and let everyone rip open their own packet so they can experience the wonderful fragrance of the steam. Eat the fish right out of the packet, or slide onto the plate and discard the parchment.

PER SERVING: Calories 316 / Protein 31g / Dietary Fiber 4g / Sugars 2g / Total Fat 16g

SHRIMP, QUINOA, AND ANDOUILLE JAMBALAYA

SERVES 4   **PREPARATION TIME** 30 MINUTES   **COOKING TIME** 35 MINUTES

FOR THE JAMBALAYA

2 teaspoons canola oil

2 chicken or turkey andouille sausages, finely chopped (Italian sausage works, too)

1 medium red onion, finely chopped

1 celery stalk, finely chopped

1 large green bell pepper, finely chopped

½ teaspoon kosher salt

2 garlic cloves, very finely chopped or pressed through a garlic press

1 tablespoon finely chopped fresh thyme leaves

1½ teaspoons smoked paprika

1 dried bay leaf

½ teaspoon ground black pepper

1 cup diced canned tomatoes

1½ cups quinoa, rinsed well under cold water

A New Orleans classic, jambalaya has smoky, garlicky, spicy flavors that meld in a perfect casserole, made from rice, sausage, ham, and either shrimp or chicken (or sometimes both!). In my version, I replace the smoky traditional tasso ham with calorie- and fat-free smoked paprika. I also use quinoa instead of white rice, for a protein and fiber boost.

1 To make the jambalaya: Heat the canola oil in a large heavy-bottomed pot set over medium-high heat. Add the sausage and cook, stirring often, until browned, about 5 minutes. Use a slotted spoon to transfer the sausage to a bowl.

2 To the pot add the onion, celery, bell pepper, and salt. Reduce the heat to medium and cook, stirring often, until the vegetables are soft but not browned, about 6 minutes.

3 Stir in the garlic, thyme, paprika, bay leaf, and black pepper and once again cook until the garlic is fragrant, about 1 minute. Add ¾ cup water and the tomatoes, bring the liquid to a boil over high heat, then add the quinoa and the sausage. Let it return to a boil, reduce the heat to low, cover, and cook until the quinoa is tender, 15 to 18 minutes. Use a fork to fluff and stir the quinoa, then place a paper towel on top of the pot and put the cover back on. Let the quinoa stand for 10 minutes.

4 To make the shrimp: Add the lemon juice to a medium bowl along with the garlic and salt. Add the shrimp and toss to coat. Heat the canola oil in a medium skillet over medium-high heat. Add the shrimp and cook until they are golden and just start to curl, 2 to 3 minutes.

FOR THE SHRIMP

Juice of ½ lemon

1 garlic clove, very finely chopped or pressed through a garlic press

½ teaspoon kosher salt

½ pound peeled and deveined medium shrimp (20–24 per pound)

1 teaspoon canola oil

FOR FINISHING AND SERVING

1 tablespoon chopped fresh flat-leaf parsley (optional)

½ lemon, cut into quarters

5 To finish and serve: Divide the jambalaya among 4 bowls and top with some shrimp. Sprinkle with the parsley (if using) and serve with a lemon wedge on the side.

PER SERVING: Calories 416 / Protein 25g / Dietary Fiber 7g / Sugars 6g / Total Fat 11g

SUPERMARKET STRATEGY

If You Can't Find Andouille

Andouille sausage is a Louisiana-style smoked pork sausage seasoned with paprika, garlic, and oregano, among other herbs and spices. If you can't find it in your supermarket, kielbasa or Italian sausage is a great and readily available substitute. Or, leave out the sausage completely and substitute pulled chicken (left over from last night's dinner or shredded off a rotisserie chicken) that you stir into the simmering liquid with the uncooked quinoa.

SHELLFISH BOUILLABAISSE

SERVES 6   PREPARATION TIME 30 MINUTES   COOKING TIME 50 MINUTES

FOR THE STOCK

12 ounces jumbo shell-on shrimp (16–20 per pound)

1 small fennel bulb, core removed and bulb roughly chopped (reserve fronds for serving)

1 medium yellow onion, roughly chopped

1 celery stalk, roughly chopped (reserve leaves for serving)

1 medium carrot, roughly chopped

3 garlic cloves, smashed

3 large fresh thyme sprigs

1 dried bay leaf

2 teaspoons kosher salt

1 teaspoon whole black peppercorns

1 8-ounce bottle clam juice

FOR THE BOUILLABAISSE

3 tablespoons olive oil

1 garlic clove, very finely chopped or pressed through a garlic press, plus 2 cloves, smashed

2 1-inch-wide strips orange peel

½ teaspoon ground black pepper

(ingredients continue)

The taste of bouillabaisse, with its accents of saffron, fennel, thyme, and its main component, the freshest seafood, brings me right back to my time living in France and settling in to a corner café for a warming bowl on a cool autumn day. It's easy for the cost of this fish soup to become quite high, so feel free to take some liberties by changing the seafood according to what you find on sale and saving "free" herbs like fennel fronds and celery leaves to finish the soup.

1 To make the stock: Peel and devein the shrimp, saving the shells. Set the shrimp in a medium bowl and refrigerate. Place the shells in a large pot with the chopped fennel, onion, celery, carrot, garlic, thyme, bay leaf, salt, and peppercorns. Add 7 cups water and the clam juice, and bring to a boil over medium-high heat. Reduce the heat to medium and simmer until the vegetables are soft, about 20 minutes. Strain the stock through a fine-mesh sieve into a large bowl, pressing on the solids to extract as much liquid and flavor as possible. Discard the solids.

2 To make the bouillabaisse: Heat 1 tablespoon of the olive oil in a large, clean pot over medium heat. Add the finely chopped garlic, the orange strips, black pepper, and saffron, and cook until the garlic and saffron are fragrant, about 1 minute. Add the tomato and salt, raise the heat to medium-high, and cook until the tomato releases its liquid and becomes thick, stirring often, 5 to 8 minutes. Add the vermouth and cook until it is reduced by half, then add the strained stock. Bring to a boil, reduce the heat to medium, and gently simmer for 10 minutes.

(recipe continues)

Large pinch of saffron threads

1 large tomato, finely chopped

½ teaspoon kosher salt

½ cup dry vermouth or white wine

1 baguette, sliced on the bias into long, thin pieces

12 ounces cod fillet, cut into 1-inch chunks

8 ounces small (littleneck) clams, scrubbed

8 ounces mussels, scrubbed and beards removed if present

1 lemon, cut into wedges

3 Adjust an oven rack to the upper-middle position and preheat the broiler to high. Rub each baguette slice with the smashed garlic, then place on a wire rack set over a rimmed baking sheet. Brush the baguette slices with some of the remaining olive oil and broil until charred around the edges, 3 to 5 minutes (watch the bread closely, as broiler intensities vary). Remove from the oven and set aside.

4 Add the cod to the pot and simmer for 3 minutes. Add the clams, mussels, and shrimp, cover, and cook until the clams and mussels begin to open and the shrimp become opaque, 2 to 3 minutes.

5 Divide some broth, fish, and shellfish among 6 bowls. Sprinkle each with fennel fronds and celery leaves and serve with a few slices of baguette and a lemon wedge.

PER SERVING: Calories 245 / Protein 27g / Dietary Fiber 1g / Sugars 2g / Total Fat 10g

---

SUPERMARKET STRATEGY

Two Ways to Be Herb Smart

1. Have a recipe that calls for small quantities of different herbs and don't want to buy separate bunches? Check out the "poultry mix" of herbs that most supermarkets offer. It's usually a sprig or two of thyme, rosemary, sage, and sometimes a bay leaf. It's great when you know you won't use the larger bundles, but would still like a variety of herbs.
2. Have a ton of fresh mint, basil, or cilantro? Preserve your herbs in ice cubes. Purée 2 parts fresh herbs with 1 part water (e.g., 2 cups herbs, 1 cup water) and blend until smooth. Divide among ice cube trays and freeze. Add the cubes to sauces, soups, or pasta.

OVEN-BAKED CRAB CAKES WITH TANGY YOGURT SAUCE

SERVES 4 (or 8 as an appetizer)   **PREPARATION TIME 15 MINUTES**
COOKING TIME 20 MINUTES

FOR THE CRAB CAKES

1 large egg, lightly beaten

¼ cup light mayonnaise

1 tablespoon Dijon mustard

½ teaspoon Old Bay seasoning

2 teaspoons Worcestershire sauce

¼ teaspoon Sriracha sauce (or other hot sauce)

1 pound lump crabmeat, picked over for shell fragments

⅔ cup panko-style bread crumbs (preferably whole wheat)

FOR THE SAUCE

⅓ cup plain reduced-fat Greek yogurt

1 tablespoon light mayonnaise

1 tablespoon ketchup

1 tablespoon pickle relish or finely chopped pickles

One of my favorite way to splurge is to make crab cakes packed with lump crabmeat. (I buy mine at the warehouse stores to save at least a couple bucks.) When my dear friend Jen and I had our first babies, she made me her favorite crab cakes. I've adapted her recipe and now it's part of my repertoire. This rendition is baked, not fried, and I use very little breading, which means the delicate crab taste shines through.

1 To make the crab cakes: Line a rimmed baking sheet with parchment paper and preheat the oven to 375°F. Stir together the egg, mayonnaise, mustard, seasoning, Worcestershire, and Sriracha until well combined. Stir in the crabmeat, add the bread crumbs, and gently stir to combine.

2 Divide the crab cake mixture into 16 golf ball–size portions, forming each into a thick patty and placing them on the prepared baking sheet. Bake the crab cakes until golden, about 20 minutes.

3 To make the sauce: Mix the yogurt, mayonnaise, ketchup, and pickle relish in a medium bowl. Serve the crab cakes warm and alongside the dipping sauce.

PER SERVING: Calories 252 / Protein 25g / Dietary Fiber 1g / Sugars 4g / Total Fat 9g

SUPERMARKET STRATEGY

Budget-Kind Salmon Cakes

Try canned salmon as an alternative to crabmeat for making omega-3–loaded cakes. Cook the salmon cakes in a nonstick pan lightly misted with oil for the best flavor.

WHOLE BROILED TROUT
WITH HERBS AND LEMON

SERVES 4   **PREPARATION TIME 10 MINUTES**   **COOKING TIME 15 MINUTES**

¼ cup olive oil

3 fresh thyme sprigs, plus extra for serving

3 fresh sage sprigs, plus extra for serving

2 fresh rosemary sprigs, plus extra for serving

3 garlic cloves, smashed

½ teaspoon ground black pepper

2 whole trout (about 12 ounces each), opened to lay flat

1 teaspoon kosher salt, plus extra for serving

3 lemons, 1 halved and 2 sliced into rounds

This is the kind of dish that is fancy enough for company but fast and easy enough for a midweek family meal. Ask your fishmonger to open the fish for you so it easily lays flat (butterflied) on a baking sheet. Trout is delicious grilled (be sure to grease your grill grates well before laying the fish skin side down on the grill)—and so are lemons!

1 Add the olive oil to a small saucepan. Add the thyme, sage, rosemary, garlic, and pepper. Turn the heat to medium-low and slowly warm the olive oil until the mixture smells fragrant, about 5 minutes. Turn off the heat.

2 Adjust an oven rack to the upper-middle position and heat the broiler to high. Line a rimmed baking sheet with aluminum foil and place the trout on top, open like a book. Season the trout with the salt, then squeeze the halved lemon over the fish. Drizzle each fillet with 1 teaspoon of the herb oil. Place the lemon rounds on the baking sheet alongside the fish.

3 Broil the fish until the flesh is opaque and flakes easily, 5 to 7 minutes (watch the fish closely, as broiler intensities vary) and the lemons are slightly browned and charred around the edges (if the lemons cook faster than the fish, remove them early).

4 Place a few of the extra herb sprigs on a serving platter and surround with the charred lemons. Use a metal spatula to transfer the fish on top of the herbs. Drizzle with the remaining herb oil, sprinkle with salt, and serve.

PER SERVING: Calories 263 / Protein 20g / Dietary Fiber 0g / Sugars 1g / Total Fat 18g

Chapter 8

CHICKEN AND TURKEY

Four-Step Spring Chicken with Orange, Fennel, and Dill

Sesame and Pumpkin Seed–Breaded Chicken

Chicken Braised in Carrot Juice

Garlic and Herb Roast Chicken Thighs with Fingerling Potatoes

Piri-Piri Barbecued Chicken Kebabs

Lemon-Thyme Turkey Pita Burgers

Poached Chicken Puttanesca

Spicy Honey-Mustard Chicken

Sizzling Chicken Cordon Bleu

Beer-Braised Chicken Legs with Bacon and Apricots

Moroccan Slow Cooker Chicken Legs and Chickpeas

Open-Faced Turkey-Chipotle Joe

Turkey Fajitas

There is a reason that poultry is a big player on the dinner-time circuit: it's inexpensive, it's healthy, and it's a blank canvas that takes on just about any flavor or seasoning.

The boneless and skinless chicken breast is just the beginning. Yes, I too rely (a lot!) on this handy supper cut, but there's a myth out there that you have to limit yourself to white meat (i.e., chicken breasts) if you're trying to eat lean and healthy. Dark meat is actually quite lean when you remove the skin; and compared with white breast meat, it is much juicier and richer, which means it lends itself to braises and roasts. So why leave it behind? The key to adopting a healthy lifestyle is not to sacrifice, but to keep the dinner table interesting and inviting.

Another way to get your juicy, rich fix—using either white or dark meat—is to cook chicken still on the bone. The bone in a chicken thigh or breast offers up loads of flavor, and, generally speaking, it will provide a moister end result. Whether you dress it up for company or keep it simple for Tuesday night—however you cook it—a delicious chicken (or turkey!) dinner is always going to be a winner.

FOUR-STEP SPRING CHICKEN
WITH ORANGE, FENNEL, AND DILL

SERVES 4 **PREPARATION TIME 15 MINUTES** **COOKING TIME 20 MINUTES**

1 pound boneless, skinless chicken breasts (about 2 large breasts) or 4 4-ounce chicken cutlets

¾ teaspoon kosher salt

½ teaspoon ground black pepper

¼ cup all-purpose flour

1 tablespoon olive oil

1 fennel bulb, cored and thinly sliced lengthwise

1 sweet onion (Maui or Vidalia), halved and thinly sliced

2 teaspoons finely grated orange zest

¾ cup low-sodium chicken broth

2 tablespoons reduced-fat sour cream

2 tablespoons chopped fresh dill

A recipe for a speedy chicken dish is an absolute must for anyone who aims to get a nutritious and tasty dinner on the table fast. I introduced my four-step chicken piccata in my first book, Ten Dollar Dinners. *Here, I vary the technique with a creamy version that's even lighter than the original.*

1 Rinse the chicken and pat it dry. If using 2 large breasts, place the breasts on a cutting board and halve them horizontally so you end up with 4 pieces of even thickness (if using chicken cutlets, skip this step). Use ½ teaspoon of the salt and ¼ teaspoon of the pepper to season both sides of the chicken pieces. Place the flour in a shallow dish and dredge the chicken, evenly coating both sides. Heat the olive oil in a large skillet over medium-high heat. Place the chicken in the hot skillet and cook until both sides are browned and the chicken is no longer pink in the middle, about 8 minutes total. Transfer the chicken to a plate.

2 Add the fennel and onion to the skillet along with the remaining ¼ teaspoon salt and ¼ teaspoon pepper, reduce the heat to medium, and stir often until they are softened, about 5 minutes, then add the orange zest.

3 Pour the chicken broth into the skillet, using a wooden spoon to stir and scrape up any browned bits from the bottom of the skillet.

4 Stir in the sour cream, turn off the heat, and return the chicken to the skillet to coat with the sauce. Divide the chicken and sauce among plates and serve sprinkled with fresh dill.

PER SERVING: Calories 224 / Protein 25g / Dietary Fiber 3g / Sugars 2g / Total Fat 7g

four-step dinner

I rely on four-step chicken *all the time.* You can make a four-step dinner with any sauté-friendly meat or fish (pork loin, fish fillet, turkey or veal cutlets), which means you can turn almost any recipe into a four-step dish! Bonus: Cleanup's a cinch too since the whole dish is prepared in one pan.

STEP 1: SEASON THE MEAT OR FISH WITH SALT

and pepper and dredge in flour. Brown on both sides in a skillet in a splash of oil and remove. Add dried herbs or spice blends for more flavor if you like (such as Italian seasoning, chili powder, or smoked paprika).

MEAT   FISH

STEP 2: ADD AND BROWN THE AROMATICS.

VEGETABLES
(bell peppers, fennel, leeks, mushrooms, onions, shallots, zucchini)

AROMATICS
(chopped bacon, capers, garlic, ginger, olives, chipotle chiles in adobo sauce)

HERBS AND SPICES
(bay leaves, leeks, red pepper flakes, rosemary, thyme)

STEP 3: DEGLAZE THE PAN WITH LIQUID
to make a sauce.

BROTH
(beef, chicken, fish, vegetable)

SPIRITS
(beer, sake, vermouth, wine)

FRUIT JUICE OR WATER

TOMATOES
(chopped, puréed)

STEP 4: ADD YOUR CHOICE OF FINAL FLAVORINGS,

then return the meat or fish to the pan to coat with the sauce and serve.

FRESH HERBS
(basil, dill, parsley, tarragon)

SPLASH OF ACID
(citrus juice, hot sauce, vinegar)

CONDIMENTS
(Parmesan cheese, Sriracha, soy sauce)

AN ENRICHERER
(pat of butter, spoonful of Greek yogurt or reduced-fat cream cheese, Dijon mustard, pesto, olive oil)

Here are a few examples for how to take recipes in this book and change them into an any-protein four-step dinner.

First, switch the protein to a sauté-friendly meat or fish. Then follow the four-step method below.

RECIPE	SEASON, DREDGE + BROWN THE PROTEIN	SET ASIDE THE PROTEIN AND ADD + BROWN THE AROMATICS	DEGLAZE THE PAN WITH LIQUID	ADD FINISHING TOUCHES
BEER-BRAISED CHICKEN LEGS WITH BACON AND APRICOTS (page 205)	Season with salt and pepper, then dredge and brown	Render the bacon with the onion, then add the apricots and bay leaf	Deglaze with beer, beef broth, and water	Finish the sauce with Dijon and parsley, return the protein to the pan to coat with the sauce, and serve
SNAPPER WITH BROCCOLI "PESTO" AND WHITE BEAN SALSA (page 175)	Season with salt and pepper, then dredge and brown	Quickly cook the shallot and tomatoes, then add the beans	Deglaze with wine or water	Finish with the pesto, return the protein to the pan to coat with the sauce, and serve
POACHED CHICKEN PUTTANESCA (PAGE 201)	Season with salt and pepper, then dredge and brown	Quickly cook the garlic, red pepper flakes, olives, and capers	Deglaze with finely chopped tomatoes and add water if needed	Finish with oregano, return the protein to the pan to coat with the sauce, and serve

SESAME AND PUMPKIN SEED–BREADED CHICKEN

SERVES 4   **PREPARATION TIME 20 MINUTES**   **COOKING TIME 25 MINUTES**

¾ cup fine cornmeal

⅓ cup shelled pumpkin seeds (pepitas)

2 tablespoons untoasted sesame seeds

1½ teaspoons kosher salt

1 large egg white

2 large boneless, skinless chicken breasts (about 1 pound)

2 tablespoons canola oil

1 lemon, sliced into wedges

Seeds are a wonderful source of fiber, antioxidants, and protein. Instead of using the usual flour and bread crumb dusting, I coat these cutlets with a mixture of ground pumpkin and sesame seeds and cornmeal for a sweet, nutty, and crunchy effect.

1 Use a food processor to pulverize the cornmeal, pumpkin seeds, sesame seeds, and ½ teaspoon of the salt. Transfer the mixture to a medium bowl. In another medium bowl, whisk together the egg white and 1 teaspoon water until frothy.

2 Rinse the chicken and pat it dry. Place the breasts on a cutting board and halve them horizontally so you end up with 4 pieces. Place a large sheet of plastic wrap on a cutting board and set 1 piece of chicken on top. Cover with another sheet of plastic wrap and then pound the chicken to a ¼-inch thickness using a meat mallet or a heavy-bottomed pot. Remove the chicken from the plastic wrap and halve on a diagonal. Repeat with the remaining pieces of chicken (it's fine to reuse the same sheets of plastic) so you end up with 8 thin pieces. Season both sides of the chicken with the remaining 1 teaspoon salt.

3 Dip the chicken into the egg white mixture, then dredge through the flour-and-seed mixture. Set aside on a plate.

4 Heat 2 teaspoons of the canola oil in a large nonstick skillet set over medium heat. Add a few pieces of the coated chicken and cook until browned, 3 to 4 minutes. Flip the chicken and brown the other side, about 3 minutes longer. Transfer to a paper towel–lined plate. Repeat, adding 2 teaspoons of the oil before browning each batch. Serve the chicken hot with lemon wedges.

PER SERVING: Calories 271 / Protein 18g / Dietary Fiber 2g / Sugars 0g / Total Fat 13g

CHICKEN BRAISED IN CARROT JUICE

SERVES 4   **PREPARATION TIME** 20 MINUTES   **COOKING TIME** 1 HOUR

1¼ pounds boneless, skinless chicken breasts (about 3 medium breasts)

1¼ teaspoons kosher salt, plus more to taste

2 tablespoons all-purpose flour

4 teaspoons canola oil

1 medium yellow onion, peeled and sliced into sixths

1½ cups carrot juice

1 cup low-sodium chicken broth

4 garlic cloves, halved lengthwise

1 1-inch piece of fresh ginger, peeled and sliced into 3 rounds

2 fresh thyme sprigs

2 teaspoons unsalted butter

Carrot juice and chicken? Yes! Carrot juice in combination with aromatics like onions and ginger tenderizes and sweetens the chicken while it slowly braises in the oven. The cooking liquid left in the pan makes a wonderfully rich and tasty pan sauce, too. For an all-in-one braised chicken meal, add a few small- to medium-size red potatoes to the baking dish before placing it in the oven. Keep on the peel for extra fiber.

1 Preheat the oven to 350°F. Rinse the chicken and pat it dry. Place the chicken on a cutting board and use ¾ teaspoon of the salt to season both sides of the chicken. Add the flour to a medium bowl and dredge the chicken, evenly coating both sides of each breast.

2 Heat 2 teaspoons of the canola oil in a large nonstick skillet set over medium-high heat. Add the onion and season with ¼ teaspoon salt. Cook until both cut sides of each onion wedge are browned, about 4 minutes. Transfer the onion to a baking dish.

3 Add the remaining 2 teaspoons oil to the skillet. Set the chicken breasts in the skillet and brown on both sides, about 6 minutes total. Transfer the chicken to the baking dish with the onion.

4 To the skillet add the carrot juice, broth, garlic, ginger, thyme, and remaining ¼ teaspoon salt. Bring to a simmer, then pour the braising liquid over the chicken. (Don't wash the skillet yet—you'll use it in step 5.) Bake the chicken until an instant-read thermometer inserted into the thickest breast reads 155°F., 35 to 40 minutes. Remove the baking dish

(recipe continues)

from the oven and use a slotted spoon to transfer the chicken and onion to a serving platter. Loosely cover the platter with aluminum foil.

5 Pour the braising liquid through a fine-mesh sieve and into the skillet used to brown the chicken and onion (discard the garlic, thyme, and ginger). Bring the liquid to a simmer, reduce the heat to medium-low, and cook until the liquid is reduced by about one-third, 8 to 10 minutes. Turn off the heat and whisk in the butter.

6 Uncover the chicken and slice it crosswise into thin pieces. Pour the sauce over the chicken and serve with the onion.

PER SERVING: Calories 227 / Protein 26g / Dietary Fiber 0g / Sugars 4g / Total Fat 11g

GARLIC AND HERB ROAST CHICKEN THIGHS WITH FINGERLING POTATOES

SERVES 4   **PREPARATION TIME** 40 MINUTES   **COOKING TIME** 1 HOUR, 10 MINUTES

1½ pounds skinless, bone-in chicken thighs (about 8)

1 teaspoon kosher salt

½ teaspoon ground black pepper

¾ pound fingerling potatoes (or Yukon Gold or russet), sliced into 1-inch-thick rounds)

10 garlic cloves, peeled and lightly smashed

2 tablespoons olive oil

5 large fresh thyme sprigs

2 large fresh rosemary sprigs

2 fresh sage leaves, roughly chopped

Juice of 1 lemon

Herbed roasted chicken with its buttery, crispy skin is an occasional indulgence, not an everyday event. In this version of roasted chicken, I get my fix by pan-searing skinless chicken thighs in a hot skillet to develop a beautiful and tasty crust. The potatoes get a solo head start in the oven and then are topped with the herbs and chicken so both components of the dish are infused with flavor.

1 Preheat the oven to 400°F. Rinse the chicken and pat dry. Season the surface of the chicken thighs with ½ teaspoon of the salt and ¼ teaspoon of the pepper. Set aside.

2 In a large baking dish combine the potatoes, garlic, and 1 tablespoon of the olive oil. Sprinkle the potatoes with the remaining ½ teaspoon salt and ¼ teaspoon pepper and roast until they just barely begin to get golden, about 15 minutes.

3 Meanwhile, place the chicken thighs in a large bowl and toss with the remaining 1 tablespoon olive oil. Heat a large skillet over high heat, add the chicken, and cook on one side until crisp and not sticking to the skillet, 6 to 8 minutes.

4 Remove the potatoes from the oven. Place the thyme, rosemary, and sage on top and then arrange the chicken pieces on top of the herbs. Pour the lemon juice over the chicken, reduce the oven temperature to 325°F., and return the baking dish to the oven. Bake until the chicken is cooked through and its juices run clear, about 45 minutes.

5 Transfer the chicken, potatoes, and garlic to a platter and serve.

PER SERVING: Calories 375 / Protein 38g / Dietary Fiber 1g / Sugars 1g / Total Fat 16g

PIRI-PIRI BARBECUED CHICKEN KEBABS

SERVES 4   **PREPARATION TIME 25 MINUTES** (plus 2 hours to marinate)
COOKING TIME 10 MINUTES

FOR THE PIRI-PIRI SAUCE

5 mild or spicy fresh red chiles (such as Fresno or red jalapeños), stemmed and quartered crosswise

3 garlic cloves, halved

¼ cup fresh cilantro leaves

½ teaspoon dried oregano

Juice of 2 limes, plus 1 lime sliced into wedges

2 tablespoons white vinegar

1 teaspoon kosher salt

FOR THE GRILLED CHICKEN KEBABS

1¼ pounds boneless, skinless chicken thighs, halved lengthwise

2 tablespoons tomato paste

1 tablespoon agave syrup (or honey)

Canola oil, for grilling

When threaded on skewers, chicken thighs enable you to stretch a few dollars into dinner for four. A vinegary and spicy African-Portuguese piri-piri sauce is excellent as a marinade and a basting sauce. Enriched with tomato paste and agave syrup, this piri-piri takes on a familiar barbecue-y flavor. The technique works beautifully with boneless, skinless chicken breasts, too. For a less spicy piri-piri, replace the chiles with a small red bell pepper (or half the chiles with half a bell pepper).

----

1 To make the piri-piri sauce: Use a food processor to blend the chiles, garlic, cilantro, oregano, lime juice, vinegar, and salt until the piri-piri marinade is well combined and semi-smooth, about 1 minute. Pour the marinade into a medium bowl. Transfer 3 tablespoons of the marinade to a small bowl, whisk in the tomato paste and agave syrup, cover with plastic wrap, and refrigerate.

2 To make the chicken kebabs: Rinse the chicken and pat it dry. Add the chicken to the remaining marinade in the bowl and turn the chicken to evenly coat all of the pieces, then cover the bowl with plastic wrap and refrigerate for at least 2 hours and up to overnight.

3 Heat a charcoal or gas grill to medium-high heat. Remove the chicken pieces from the marinade and thread them onto 4 metal or wood skewers (if using wood skewers, soak them in water for 20 minutes before using so they don't burn on the grill). Discard the marinade.

(recipe continues)

4 Add some canola oil to a small bowl. Use tongs to dip a folded paper towel into the oil, then use it to grease the grill grates. Add the skewers to the grill and cook until browned, about 3 minutes. Turn the skewers. Use a grill brush to coat the top, browned side of the chicken with some of the reserved piri-piri sauce. Once the other side of the chicken skewers are browned, after 3 to 4 minutes, turn the skewers and brush the top of the browned chicken with more sauce. Once the chicken is cooked through, 1 to 2 minutes longer, remove from the grill and serve with lime wedges.

PER SERVING: Calories 192 / Protein 28g / Dietary Fiber 0g / Sugars 4g / Total Fat 6g

ENTERTAINING STRATEGY

Turn Burgers into Sliders

Small bite-size sliders are perfect for entertaining. Simply form the turkey burgers into smaller patties and cook for about half as long. Serve in mini pitas or burger buns (if you can't find mini burger buns, use a small round cookie cutter to stamp out slider-size buns from standard buns; save the bun scraps for making bread crumbs) skewered with a small cube of cheese. I like to match the flavor profile of the burger to the cheese, so if lots of herbs are used, I might go for a bocconcini (mozzarella ball), or if the burger has a Mediterranean accent, I find a small cube of feta works nicely.

LEMON-THYME TURKEY PITA BURGERS

SERVES 4   **PREPARATION TIME** 20 MINUTES   **COOKING TIME** 10 MINUTES

1 link uncooked Italian-seasoned turkey sausage (3 to 4 ounces), casing removed

1 large egg white

Zest and juice of ½ lemon

1 tablespoon finely chopped fresh thyme leaves

¼ teaspoon kosher salt

¼ teaspoon ground black pepper

¾ pound lean ground turkey

2 tablespoons fresh or dried whole wheat bread crumbs

Canola oil or nonstick pan spray

¼ cup crumbled feta cheese

2 whole wheat pita bread rounds, cut in half

4 slices roasted red pepper

¼ cup plain reduced-fat Greek yogurt

2 scallions (white and light green parts only), thinly sliced

These turkey burgers are juicy and flavorful, busting the myth that turkey burgers are dry. The key is to combine lean ground turkey with an Italian-flavored turkey sausage, which has just enough fat to keep the burger moist. You can serve the burgers on a standard bun, but I like the fun of sliding them into a pita bread.

1 Stir together the sausage, egg white, lemon zest and juice, thyme, salt, and pepper. Add the turkey and gently mix just until combined. Add just enough bread crumbs to absorb the extra liquid (you may need only 1 tablespoon of the bread crumbs). Form the turkey mixture into 4 patties.

2 Heat a charcoal or gas grill to medium-high heat, or heat a grill pan over medium-high heat. If using a charcoal or gas grill, use tongs to dip a folded paper towel into the canola oil, then use it to grease the grill grates. If using a grill pan, lightly mist with canola oil or nonstick pan spray. Cook the burgers until browned, 4 to 5 minutes. Flip the burgers and cook on the other side until browned and the center of the burger resists light pressure, 4 to 5 minutes longer.

3 Sprinkle a heaping tablespoon of feta cheese over the top of each burger and continue to cook for 30 seconds more. Slide a patty into each pita half. Add a roasted red pepper to each half along with 1 tablespoon yogurt. Sprinkle with the scallions and serve.

PER SERVING: Calories 310 / Protein 25g / Dietary Fiber 3g / Sugars 2g / Total Fat 13g

POACHED CHICKEN PUTTANESCA

SERVES 4 **PREPARATION TIME** 25 MINUTES **COOKING TIME** 30 MINUTES

FOR THE PUTTANESCA

1 pound ripe tomatoes, cored and finely chopped

8 pitted Kalamata olives, very thinly sliced

1 lemon, halved and juiced (save the juiced halves)

1 tablespoon brine-packed capers, rinsed

1 teaspoon kosher salt

1 tablespoon extra-virgin olive oil

1 large garlic clove, very finely chopped

¼ to ½ teaspoon red pepper flakes

2 tablespoons roughly chopped fresh oregano or marjoram

FOR THE POACHED CHICKEN

1¼ pounds boneless, skinless chicken breasts (about 3 medium breasts)

1 cup low-sodium chicken broth

1 large fresh thyme sprig

1 teaspoon kosher salt

¼ teaspoon whole black peppercorns

Chicken may be the protein here, but the ripe and juicy tomatoes are definitely the star. Puttanesca sauce is famous for being a little spicy and a little salty. I make it here with olives, capers, and red pepper flake–infused garlic oil. The mixture is tossed with chopped tomatoes, which macerate while the chicken breasts poach. Save the poaching liquid and use as you would chicken broth.

1 To make the puttanesca: In a medium bowl, stir together the tomatoes, olives, lemon juice, capers, and salt. In a small skillet set over medium heat, add the olive oil, garlic, and red pepper flakes. Cook, swirling often, until the garlic is fragrant and golden, 1 to 1½ minutes. Turn off the heat, pour the seasoned oil over the tomato mixture, and stir to combine. Stir in the oregano and set aside, stirring occasionally, while making the chicken.

2 To poach the chicken: Rinse the chicken and pat it dry. To a medium skillet add the broth, 1 cup water, the reserved lemon halves, the thyme sprig, salt, and peppercorns. Bring the mixture to a simmer over medium heat. Reduce the heat to low and add the chicken breasts. Cover the skillet, leaving the lid slightly askew, and poach the chicken for 10 minutes. Turn over the chicken breasts, re-cover the skillet, and poach until the chicken breasts are cooked through and reach 155°F. on an instant-read thermometer, about 10 minutes longer. Turn off the heat, uncover, and let the chicken breasts rest for 10 minutes before removing them from the skillet.

3 Once the chicken is cool enough to handle, slice it crosswise into thin rounds. Serve covered with the puttanesca sauce.

PER SERVING: Calories 245 / Protein 33g / Dietary Fiber 2g / Sugars 3g / Total Fat 10g

SPICY HONEY-MUSTARD CHICKEN

SERVES 4   PREPARATION TIME 15 MINUTES   COOKING TIME 15 MINUTES

FOR THE HONEY MUSTARD

¼ cup Dijon mustard

2 teaspoons honey

1 tablespoon light mayonnaise

¼ to ½ teaspoon hot sauce (such as Frank's or Tabasco)

FOR THE CHICKEN

1 pound boneless, skinless chicken breasts (about 2 large chicken breasts) or 4 4-ounce chicken cutlets

¾ teaspoon kosher salt

½ teaspoon ground black pepper

1 cup whole wheat bread crumbs

½ teaspoon dried thyme

Olive oil mister or nonstick pan spray

Here's my healthier version of fried chicken tenders. The home-made honey mustard helps the whole wheat bread crumbs stick to the chicken. Make double the amount of the honey mustard if you want some dipping sauce on the side.

1 To make the honey mustard: Whisk the mustard, honey, mayonnaise, and hot sauce together in a medium bowl.

2 To make the chicken: Preheat the oven to 400°F. Rinse the chicken and pat it dry. If using 2 large breasts, then place the chicken breasts on a cutting board and halve them horizontally so you end up with 4 pieces of even thickness (if using chicken cutlets, skip this step). If the chicken pieces are thicker than ½ inch, place a large sheet of plastic wrap on a cutting board and set 1 piece of chicken on top. Cover with another sheet of plastic wrap and then pound the chicken to a ½-inch thickness using a meat mallet or a heavy-bottomed pot. Season the chicken with ½ teaspoon of the salt and ¼ teaspoon of the pepper.

3 Add the chicken to the bowl with the mustard mixture and turn to coat. In a second medium bowl, stir together the bread crumbs, thyme, remaining ¼ teaspoon salt, and remaining ¼ teaspoon pepper.

4 Dredge each piece of chicken through the bread crumbs, gently pressing the crumbs into each side. Place a metal cooling rack on top of a baking sheet, and mist the rack with olive oil or nonstick pan spray. Spray each piece of chicken on both sides and set it on the rack. Bake the chicken until golden brown and cooked through, 25 to 30 minutes. Serve hot.

PER SERVING: Calories 213 / Protein 24g / Dietary Fiber 2g / Sugars 3g / Total Fat 6g

SIZZLING CHICKEN CORDON BLEU

SERVES 4   **PREPARATION TIME 10 MINUTES**   **COOKING TIME 10 MINUTES**

1 tablespoon unsalted butter

3 tablespoons panko-style bread crumbs (preferably whole wheat)

¾ teaspoon kosher salt

1 pound boneless, skinless chicken breasts (about 2 large breasts) or 4 4-ounce chicken cutlets

½ teaspoon ground black pepper

2 teaspoons canola oil

2 slices deli ham (about 1½ ounces), halved

2 slices Swiss cheese (about 1½ ounces), halved

My twist on the classic chicken cordon bleu offers all the same delicious tastes and textures in a trim package. Instead of stuffing an entire chicken breast with the ham and cheese, I layer the ham and cheese on top of a thin chicken cutlet and then broil the chicken to get the cheese melted and bubbling. The browned bread crumbs offer the buttery crunch of the classic, minus the hefty fat and carbs.

1 Melt the butter over medium heat, then add the bread crumbs and ¼ teaspoon of the salt. Cook, stirring often, until the bread crumbs are deeply browned and toasty, about 2 minutes. Transfer to a small bowl and set aside.

2 Adjust an oven rack to the upper-middle position (4 to 5 inches from the heating element) and preheat the broiler to high. Line a rimmed baking sheet with aluminum foil. Rinse the chicken and pat it dry. If using 2 large breasts, place the breasts on a cutting board and halve them horizontally so you end up with 4 pieces of even thickness (if using chicken cutlets, skip this step). Season both sides of the chicken with the remaining ½ teaspoon salt and the pepper.

3 Heat the canola oil in a large nonstick skillet. Add the seasoned chicken pieces and cook until browned, 3 to 4 minutes. Turn off the heat and use a metal spatula to transfer the chicken to the prepared baking sheet, browned side down. On top of each chicken piece add half a slice of ham and cover with half a slice of cheese. Broil the chicken until the cheese is melted and bubbling, 3 to 4 minutes (watch the cheese closely, as broiler intensities vary).

4 Serve the chicken sprinkled with a generous teaspoon of the bread crumbs.

PER SERVING: Calories 228 / Protein 28g / Dietary Fiber 0g / Sugars 0g / Total Fat 11g

BEER-BRAISED CHICKEN LEGS
WITH BACON AND APRICOTS

SERVES 4   **PREPARATION TIME** 25 MINUTES   **COOKING TIME** 1 HOUR, 15 MINUTES

1½ pounds skinless, bone-in chicken drumsticks (about 8)

1 teaspoon kosher salt

½ teaspoon ground black pepper

1½ teaspoons olive oil

2 slices center-cut bacon, finely chopped

1 sweet onion (Maui or Vidalia), halved and thinly sliced

½ cup dried apricots, quartered

1 cup light beer

1 cup low-sodium beef broth

1 dried bay leaf

1 tablespoon Dijon mustard

1 tablespoon finely chopped fresh flat-leaf parsley

I turned to the rich, malt-flavored beer-based beef stews of Belgium as inspiration for these braised chicken drumsticks. A cup of light beer boosted with beef broth and a couple bacon slices add a smoky, savory taste. Serve with some whole-grain noodles or brown rice for a true stick-to-your-ribs meal.

1   Rinse the chicken and pat it dry. Season the chicken with ½ teaspoon of the salt and ¼ teaspoon of the pepper.

2   Heat the olive oil in a large heavy-bottomed pot or Dutch oven over medium-high heat. Add the chicken and brown on all sides, about 12 minutes total. Transfer to a paper towel–lined plate and set aside.

3   Add the bacon to the pot and cook until crisp and browned, about 5 minutes. Use a slotted spoon to transfer the bacon to a paper towel–lined plate and add the onion to the pot. Reduce the heat to medium-low, add the remaining ½ teaspoon salt and ¼ teaspoon pepper, and cook, stirring often, until the onion is golden brown about 15 minutes.

4   Stir the apricots into the onion, cook for 1 minute, then raise the heat to medium-high. Pour in the beer and let it simmer and reduce for 2 minutes. Add the broth, ½ cup water, the bay leaf, chicken, and bacon, and bring the mixture to a simmer. Reduce the heat to low, cover the pot, and simmer gently for 30 minutes. Then uncover the pot and cook until the liquid reduces a little, about 15 minutes longer.

5   Transfer the chicken pieces to a serving platter. Whisk the mustard into the sauce and pour over the chicken. Sprinkle with the parsley and serve.

PER SERVING: Calories 244 / Protein 21g / Dietary Fiber 2g / Sugars 10g / Total Fat 10g

MOROCCAN SLOW COOKER CHICKEN LEGS AND CHICKPEAS

SERVES 4   **PREPARATION TIME 20 MINUTES**   **COOKING TIME 3 HOURS, 30 MINUTES**

1½ pounds skinless, bone-in chicken drumsticks (about 8)

2 teaspoons ras el hanout (Moroccan spice blend)

½ teaspoon kosher salt

¼ teaspoon ground black pepper

1 sweet onion (Maui or Vidalia), halved and thinly sliced

3 garlic cloves, smashed

Zest and juice of 1 lemon

1½ cups cooked chickpeas (homemade, page 81; or canned, rinsed)

1 tablespoon almond butter

1 cup low-sodium tomato sauce

¼ cup low-sodium chicken or beef broth

1 dried bay leaf

Finely chopped fresh flat-leaf parsley

This is a super-easy "forget about it" slow cooker meal that boasts a boldness thanks to ras el hanout, a Moroccan spice blend that is similar to curry powder, but more floral and less pungent. While it is available in most supermarkets, if you can't find it in yours, use a blend of cardamom, cumin, cinnamon, and turmeric. You might find the almond butter surprising here, but it adds a wonderful rich creaminess along with its protein and healthy fat. This is so good served over whole wheat couscous.

1 Rinse the chicken and pat it dry. Stir the ras el hanout, salt, and pepper together in a small bowl. Rub the seasoning into the chicken.

2 To the bowl of a slow cooker add the onion, garlic, and lemon zest. Arrange the chicken drumsticks on top, then pour the lemon juice over the chicken.

3 Add the chickpeas, almond butter, and tomato sauce, making sure the almond butter is covered in liquid. Pour in the broth, add the bay leaf, and cook for 3½ hours on high heat or 7 hours on low heat. Serve sprinkled with parsley.

PER SERVING: Calories 320 / Protein 27g / Dietary Fiber 8g / Sugars 15g / Total Fat 7g

KITCHEN STRATEGY

Tip for Removing Chicken Skin

To easily remove the skin from chicken drumsticks or thighs, use a paper towel to grab the slippery skin and pull it down toward the end of the chicken bone. It will come right off.

FLEXIBLE

slow cooker dinner

The slow cooker can be a huge time-saver and the perfect way to create just about any type of dinner. And because you're typically cooking a large amount of food at once, you often get built-in leftovers. Just pile your ingredients into the slow cooker (you can even do this the night before and store the cooker in the refrigerator), set it to cook, and voilà—a satisfying yet fuss-free weeknight meal, plus a kitchen filled with the amazing aroma of dinnertime.

STEP 1: CHOOSE YOUR DINNER.

SHREDDED MEAT

(such as tacos or pulled meat sandwiches)

MEAT WITH SAUCE

(such as braised short ribs or chicken cacciatore)

STEW

(such as chili or a hearty meat soup)

STEP 2: INTO THE SLOW COOKER,
add 1 chopped onion, 2 chopped garlic cloves, and flavorings (spices and herbs).
THEN ADD:

2 POUNDS BONELESS MEAT
(chicken breast, pork shoulder, brisket)

½ CUP LIQUID

2 POUNDS BONE-IN MEAT
(chicken legs or thighs, pork chops, short ribs)

½ CUP LIQUID

1 TO 2 CUPS CHOPPED HARD VEGETABLES

2 POUNDS CUBED TOUGH-CUT MEAT
(lamb shank, beef chuck, turkey breast)

1 CUP LIQUID

1 TO 2 CUPS CHOPPED HARD VEGETABLES

Liquid Options (choose one or more to yield the necessary amount): stock or broth, beer or wine, puréed tomatoes, fresh fruit juice, water

STEP 3: COOK FOR 3 TO 4 HOURS ON HIGH
or 6 to 8 hours on low—tougher cuts may take longer. Season to taste.

OPEN-FACED TURKEY-CHIPOTLE JOE

SERVES 4   **PREPARATION TIME 20 MINUTES**   **COOKING TIME 30 MINUTES**

1 teaspoon olive oil

1 pound lean ground turkey or crumbled tempeh

1 medium yellow onion, finely chopped

1 red bell pepper, halved, seeded, and finely chopped

1 garlic clove, very finely chopped

1 to 3 tablespoons chopped chipotle chiles in adobo sauce (depending how spicy you want it)

3 tablespoons tomato paste

¼ cup beef broth

1 tablespoon Worcestershire sauce (or vegetarian Worcestershire sauce)

3 tablespoons ketchup

2 tablespoons Dijon mustard

2 tablespoons apple cider vinegar

2 whole wheat burger buns, halved and toasted

When I'm craving comfort and sweetness, this rendition of the sloppy joe always does the trick. I stretch the meat by adding sautéed bell peppers and onions and I introduce a smoky note from chipotle chiles in adobo sauce. I like to eat these fork-and-knife style, served open-faced on whole wheat bun halves. Top with some lightly dressed baby spinach or the Broccoli-Stalk and Cilantro Slaw on page 261 and you'll have quite the meal.

1 Heat the olive oil in a large nonstick skillet over medium-high heat. Add the ground turkey and cook, using a wooden spoon to break it up and stir it often, until the turkey loses its pink color, about 7 minutes. Scoot the turkey to the edges of the skillet, creating a large well in the center. To the center add the onion and bell pepper, cooking until the edges of the pepper and onion start to soften, 1 to 2 minutes.

2 Stir the meat into the vegetables and cook until the vegetables are softened, about 7 minutes more. Mix in the garlic, chipotle with some adobo sauce, and tomato paste and cook, stirring often, until the paste becomes dark red, about 3 minutes.

3 Pour in ½ cup water, the beef broth, and Worcestershire and cook, stirring often, until the liquid has almost evaporated and the mixture is sizzling and bubbling, 6 to 8 minutes. Stir in the ketchup, mustard, and vinegar. Remove from the heat. Place a burger bun half on each of 4 plates and top with the chipotle joe.

PER SERVING: Calories 358 / Protein 24g / Dietary Fiber 3g / Sugars 6g / Total Fat 12g

TURKEY FAJITAS

SERVES 6   **PREPARATION TIME** 45 MINUTES   **COOKING TIME** 25 MINUTES

¼ cup fresh lime juice (from about 3 limes)

3 tablespoons olive oil

4 garlic cloves, very finely chopped or pressed through a garlic press

½ teaspoon smoked paprika

½ teaspoon ground cumin

1 teaspoon kosher salt

¾ teaspoon ground black pepper

1 pound turkey cutlets, cut into 1-inch-wide strips (5 to 6 cutlets)

2 red or yellow bell peppers, halved, seeded, and thinly sliced

1 medium yellow onion, cut into 6 wedges

4 scallions (white and light green parts only)

Twelve 6-inch corn tortillas, warmed

¾ cup plain reduced-fat Greek yogurt

1 cup tomato salsa (homemade or store-bought)

I've loved fajitas since as long as I can remember—they were a mainstay at our dinner table while I was growing up in Tucson, Arizona. My trick to keeping the cost and calorie count under control is to keep the protein lean and load up on veggies. Flour tortillas are most often associated with fajitas, but corn tortillas offer more fiber and less fat.

1 Whisk the lime juice, olive oil, garlic, paprika, cumin, ½ teaspoon of the salt, and ¼ teaspoon of the pepper in a small bowl. Place the turkey strips in a large resealable plastic bag with the remaining ½ teaspoon salt and ½ teaspoon pepper. Add half of the marinade, seal the bag, and massage the bag to distribute the marinade.

2 Place the bell peppers, onion wedges, and scallions in a second large resealable plastic bag. Pour in the remaining marinade, seal the bag, and massage to distribute the marinade. Refrigerate both bags for at least 15 minutes and up to 2 hours.

3 Preheat the oven to 400°F. Line a baking sheet with aluminum foil and add the vegetables (discard the marinade). Roast the vegetables until they are tender and start to lightly char, about 15 minutes, stirring halfway through cooking.

4 Meanwhile, grill the turkey. Heat a grill pan over medium-high heat until very hot, 3 to 4 minutes. Remove the turkey from the bag and set it on a paper towel–lined plate (discard the marinade). Use another paper towel to blot the turkey dry. Add the turkey to the grill pan and cook it until both sides are golden brown and the turkey is cooked through, about 6 minutes total.

5 Serve the roasted vegetables and grilled turkey with warm corn tortillas, yogurt, and salsa.

PER SERVING: Calories 342 / Protein 24g / Dietary Fiber 4g / Sugars 4g / Total Fat 10g

Chapter 9

BEEF, PORK, AND LAMB

Greek Pork Chops with Zucchini and Feta

Cider-Brined Pork Loin with Pine Nut Relish

Braised Pork Paprikash

Slow Cooker Beef and Rice Pockets

Coffee-Rubbed Pork Tenderloin

Crispy Beef Tacos with Pineapple-Avocado Salsa

Flatiron Steaks with Quick Cauliflower Kimchi

Minty Lamb Patties with Cucumber-Radish Salad

Filet Mignon with Creamy Dijon Sauce

Grilled Bison Burgers

Lamb Tagine with Squash and Prunes

I love hearty red meat, and sometimes I just crave the taste and satisfaction of slicing into a grilled steak or indulging in a juicy burger. By choosing lean cuts of meat, I can keep an eye on the amount of saturated fats and calories while still offering beef, pork, and lamb to my family.

When shopping for pork, I go for tenderloin, which actually has fewer calories and less fat than skinless chicken breasts, or pork loin, which is leaner than skinless chicken legs and thighs. Both cuts are versatile and can be cooked whole as roasts or sliced into chops or thin cutlets. When selecting beef, choose cuts with less marbled fat. The leanest cuts come from the chuck (shoulder), the round (hind quarters), and the sirloin (the middle portion just in front of the round). Lamb tends to be richer than most other meats, so I stretch it with a low-fat option such as lots of vegetables or, for lamb burgers, with lean ground turkey.

GREEK PORK CHOPS WITH ZUCCHINI AND FETA

SERVES 4   **PREPARATION TIME** 15 MINUTES   **COOKING TIME** 15 MINUTES

FOR THE PORK CHOPS

1 teaspoon dried oregano

½ teaspoon dried thyme

½ teaspoon sweet paprika

1 teaspoon kosher salt

½ teaspoon ground black pepper

4 ½- to ¾-inch-thick lean bone-in pork rib chops

1 tablespoon canola oil

FOR THE ZUCCHINI

2 medium zucchini, halved lengthwise and sliced crosswise into ¼-inch-thick pieces

¼ teaspoon kosher salt

2 tablespoons finely chopped fresh parsley (basil, mint, or oregano is great, too)

1 medium tomato, finely chopped

1 teaspoon olive oil

Juice of ½ lemon

¼ cup finely crumbled feta cheese (about 2 ounces)

Thin-cut bone-in lean pork rib chops cook in minutes and offer a hearty, meaty richness that can be extra satisfying. A pantry spice blend of dried oregano, thyme, and paprika seasons the chops, and the browned bits left in the pan later flavor the zucchini as it sautés. Choose chops that don't have striations of fat in the meat; if they have a large fat cap, simply trim it off before cooking.

1 To season and cook the pork chops: Stir together the oregano, thyme, paprika, salt, and pepper in a small bowl. Set the pork chops on a cutting board and season both sides of each chop with the spice blend.

2 Heat a large skillet over high heat for 1 minute. Add the canola oil, and once it shimmers, add the chops. Reduce the heat to medium-high and cook, without moving the chops, until they are nicely browned, 3 to 4 minutes. Flip the chops and cook on the other side until browned and the centers resist light pressure, 2 to 3 minutes more. Transfer to a plate and set aside.

3 To cook the zucchini: Add the zucchini to the skillet with the salt and cook, stirring occasionally, until the zucchini softens, 3 to 4 minutes. Stir in the herbs, then transfer the zucchini to a medium bowl. Stir in the tomato, olive oil, and lemon juice, then sprinkle with the feta cheese.

4 Divide the zucchini among 4 plates and serve with the pork chops.

PER SERVING: Calories 252 / Protein 28g / Dietary Fiber 2g / Sugars 3g / Total Fat 13g

CIDER-BRINED PORK LOIN
WITH PINE NUT RELISH

SERVES 6   **PREPARATION TIME 35 MINUTES** (plus 8 hours to marinate)
COOKING TIME 45 MINUTES

FOR THE PORK

1¼ cups apple cider

3 tablespoons maple syrup

2 garlic cloves, peeled and smashed

2 tablespoons kosher salt

3 whole black peppercorns

3 whole cloves

3 allspice berries

1 cinnamon stick

1 dried bay leaf

1 2¼-pound pork loin roast, trimmed of fat and silverskin

FOR THE RELISH

2 medium plum tomatoes, coarsely chopped and juices reserved

2 tablespoons golden raisins

1 tablespoon cider vinegar

¼ teaspoon ground cinnamon

⅛ teaspoon cayenne pepper

¼ teaspoon kosher salt

2 tablespoons pine nuts

1 tablespoon finely chopped fresh flat-leaf parsley

Apple cider, maple syrup, and warm spices like cinnamon, cloves and allspice capture the essence of fall in this hearty centerpiece pork roast. To cool the brine quickly, have about one cup of ice cubes on hand. Make a double or triple batch of the pine nut and raisin chutney—it's excellent with grilled chicken or used to spice up a simple turkey sandwich.

1 To prepare the pork: Stir together the cider, maple syrup, garlic, salt, peppercorns, cloves, allspice, cinnamon stick, and bay leaf in a medium pot. Bring the mixture to a simmer over medium-high heat. Turn off the heat and add 1 cup of ice cubes and ¾ cup of cold water. Transfer the brine to a large container and set aside to cool completely. When it's cool, put the pork loin in the brine, cover, and refrigerate for at least 8 hours or preferably overnight.

2 To make the relish: In a medium pot, stir together the tomatoes, raisins, cider vinegar, cinnamon, cayenne, and salt. Bring the mixture to a simmer over medium-high heat and cook, stirring often, for 2 minutes. Reduce the heat and simmer until the tomatoes are soft and the raisins are plump, about 10 minutes.

3 While the relish simmers, toast the pine nuts in a small skillet set over medium heat. Shake the pan often until the nuts are golden, 3 to 4 minutes. Stir the toasted pine nuts and parsley into the relish.

**FOR COOKING AND
SERVING**

½ teaspoon kosher salt

½ teaspoon ground black
pepper

¼ teaspoon ground
cinnamon

¼ teaspoon ground cloves

⅛ teaspoon cayenne pepper

2 teaspoons canola oil

4 To cook the pork and serve: Preheat the oven to 350°F. Remove the loin from the brine and pat dry with paper towels. In a small bowl, stir together the salt, black pepper, cinnamon, cloves, and cayenne. Rub the spice mixture all over the pork and set aside.

5 Heat the canola oil in a large oven-safe skillet set over high heat. Once the oil shimmers, add the pork and cook, turning occasionally, until browned on all sides, 8 to 10 minutes total. Transfer the skillet to the oven and roast until an instant-read thermometer inserted in the thickest part of the roast reaches 145°F., 20 to 25 minutes.

6 Remove the skillet from the oven and transfer the pork to a cutting board. Loosely tent with aluminum foil and set aside to rest for 10 minutes. Slice crosswise into ½-inch-thick pieces. Serve with the pine nut relish.

PER SERVING: Calories 293 / Protein 35g / Dietary Fiber 1g / Sugars 3g / Total Fat 15g

---

SUPERMARKET STRATEGY

Buy Loins on Sale and Freeze
When I see pork loins or pork tenderloins on sale, I'll buy a few and trim them when I get home, then pop them into the freezer. If you buy a large pork loin, you can cut it into smaller roasts, boneless steaks, or super-thin pork cutlets.

BRAISED PORK PAPRIKASH

SERVES 6   **PREPARATION TIME** 25 MINUTES   **COOKING TIME** 1 HOUR, 15 MINUTES

1 teaspoon caraway seeds

3 tablespoons sweet paprika

1 tablespoon smoked paprika

1 dried bay leaf

1 tablespoon kosher salt

1½ teaspoons ground black pepper

2 tablespoons tomato paste

2 large yellow onions, roughly chopped

3 garlic cloves, roughly chopped

2 medium tomatoes, roughly chopped

1 1½- to 1¾-pound pork loin, trimmed of fat and silverskin

1 tablespoon canola oil

2 cups low-sodium chicken broth

½ cup plain reduced-fat Greek yogurt

¼ cup roughly chopped fresh flat-leaf parsley

This lush and decadent sauce tastes much richer than it is. Two kinds of paprika—sweet and smoked—give it its deep, dark burnished red tint, while tomato paste, fresh tomatoes, and a yellow onion–garlic mash add body and sweetness. Braising the lean pork in the sauce not only adds more flavor to the papri-kash but the acid in the sauce tenderizes the pork, too. This is wonderful served over whole-grain pasta tossed with a small knob of butter and chopped parsley.

1 Set a large heavy-bottomed pot over medium heat. Add the caraway seeds and toast, stirring often, until they are fragrant and golden, 1 to 1½ minutes. Transfer the seeds to a plate (don't wash the pot—you'll use it in step 3) and once they're cool, pulverize the seeds in a spice grinder or coffee grinder. Transfer the ground caraway to a small bowl and add the sweet and smoked paprika, bay leaf, 2 teaspoons of the salt, 1 teaspoon of the pepper, and the tomato paste. Set aside.

2 Use a food processor to combine the onions and garlic until there aren't any large pieces. Transfer to a medium bowl, then add the tomatoes to the food processor and pulver-ize until puréed.

3 Season the pork loin with the remaining 1 teaspoon salt and remaining ½ teaspoon pepper. Heat the oil in the pot used to toast the caraway seeds over medium-high heat until it shimmers, about 1½ minutes. Add the pork loin and cook until it is nicely browned on all sides, 8 to 10 minutes total. Transfer the pork loin to a plate and set aside.

4 Reduce the heat to medium, add the onion-garlic mix-ture to the pot, and cook, stirring often, until the liquid is evaporated and the onion mixture starts to stick and brown, about 10 minutes.

5 Stir the paprika mixture into the pot and cook until the mixture darkens slightly, about 1 minute. Stir in the pulverized tomatoes and cook until the tomatoes reduce slightly, 3 to 5 minutes, then add the chicken broth and 2 cups water. Once the liquid comes to a boil, reduce the heat to medium-low and simmer gently for 15 minutes. Return the pork loin to the pot, cover, and cook until the internal temperature of the pork loin reads 145°F., 20 to 25 minutes.

6 Use tongs to transfer the pork loin to a cutting board. Loosely tent the loin with aluminum foil and let it rest for 10 minutes. Meanwhile, continue to cook the sauce over medium heat until it thickens slightly, about 10 minutes. Stir the yogurt into the sauce.

7 Carve the pork loin crosswise against the grain into thin slices and transfer to a platter. Drizzle about half of the sauce over the pork and serve the rest on the side. Sprinkle with the parsley and serve.

PER SERVING: Calories 323 / Protein 31g / Dietary Fiber 3g / Sugars 5g / Total Fat 17g

SUPERMARKET STRATEGY

Reduced-Fat vs. Nonfat Greek Yogurt
Full-fat Greek yogurt has upward of 10 grams of fat per serving! Reduced-fat Greek yogurt will typically save you more than 50 percent of the fat without sacrificing richness or texture. Unlike nonfat Greek yogurt, which is prone to separate or curdle when puréed into soups or added to sauces, reduced-fat Greek yogurt is generally heat stable (if using nonfat yogurt, be sure to read the ingredients label to make sure no fillers were added). For cold preparations (salad dressings, dips, etc.), nonfat Greek yogurt is fine if that's your preference.

SLOW COOKER BEEF AND RICE POCKETS

SERVES 8 (with 1 pound of barbecued beef left over)   **PREPARATION TIME TK**

COOKING TIME 4 HOURS, 30 MINUTES

FOR THE BARBECUED BEEF

2 pounds lean chuck roast, trimmed of extra fat

½ teaspoon kosher salt

½ teaspoon ground black pepper

½ cup low-sodium or sodium-free tomato sauce

3 tablespoons apple cider vinegar

Zest and juice of 1 orange

1 teaspoon Worcestershire sauce

3 tablespoons lightly packed light or dark brown sugar

2 teaspoons dried oregano

1 teaspoon sweet paprika

¼ teaspoon red pepper flakes

(ingredients continue)

Omusube are a common Japanese "to-go" food—compressed rice balls stuffed with a variety of savory meats or vegetarian fillings and wrapped in seaweed. My family loves to try just about anything in them, from cream cheese and salmon to tuna salad or a spicy chicken curry. One of our all-time favorites is this tangy orange-barbecued beef. (By the way—the shredded beef is delicious simply served alongside steamed white rice for a more straightforward meal.) Here's more good news: you'll have about a pound of barbecued beef left over for making sandwiches tomorrow!

1 To make the barbecued beef: Season the chuck roast with the salt and pepper and set it into the insert of a slow cooker. Whisk together the tomato sauce, vinegar, orange zest and juice, Worcestershire, brown sugar, oregano, paprika, and red pepper flakes in a medium bowl. Pour the mixture over the beef, cover the slow cooker, and cook until a fork easily pierces the center of the beef, 4 to 5 hours on high, or 8 to 10 hours on low.

2 Transfer the roast to a cutting board and let it rest for 5 minutes. Use a spoon to skim the fat from the top of the sauce. Then use 2 forks to shred the meat, discarding any extra fat. Return the beef to the defatted sauce and return the insert to the slow cooker, cooking the sauce on high until it has reduced slightly, about 30 minutes longer. Keep warm.

(recipe continues)

FOR THE PICKLED CUCUMBERS AND SESAME SEEDS

1 cucumber, peeled, halved, seeded, and thinly sliced crosswise

½ red onion, finely chopped

¼ cup apple cider vinegar

¼ cup sugar

1 tablespoon kosher salt

Pinch of red pepper flakes (optional)

1 tablespoon white or black sesame seeds

FOR THE RICE POCKETS

4 cups cooked short-grain rice (white generally works better than brown)

4 large nori (seaweed) sheets (8 by 11 inches), cut into quarters

6 medium carrots, grated on the medium holes of a box grater (about 1½ cups)

3 To make the pickled cucumbers: Place the cucumber and onion in a small bowl. Heat the vinegar, sugar, salt, red pepper flakes (if using), and ½ cup water in a small saucepan over medium-high heat until the liquid simmers and the salt and sugar are dissolved. Pour the hot vinegar mixture over the cucumbers and set aside for 15 minutes. Drain most of the liquid from the cucumbers, then cover the bowl with plastic wrap and refrigerate to chill slightly.

4 Add the sesame seeds to a small skillet set over medium heat and toast the seeds, shaking the pan often, 2 to 3 minutes. Transfer to a plate to cool.

5 To assemble the rice pockets: Place the rice in a serving bowl and set it on the table. Sprinkle the chilled pickled cucumbers with the toasted sesame seeds and place on the table along with the nori sheets. Transfer the barbecued beef and sauce to a bowl. Place some rice in the center of a nori wrapper; top with some beef, cucumbers, and carrots, then roll and eat.

PER SERVING: Calories 289 / Protein 15g / Dietary Fiber 3g / Sugars 10g / Total Fat 7g

---

STUFF, WRAP, EAT, REPEAT!

One of my favorite approaches for a DIY dinner party is to invite a crowd over to make *omusube* rice pockets. Here are some more ideas for filling them:

Roasted vegetables from the Summer Squash and Mushroom Tacos (page 115)

Smashed Black Beans with Peppers (page 260)

Grilled Orange-Glazed Tuna (page 164)

Sesame-Crusted Salmon with Miso Sauce (page 166)

Chopped chile shrimp from the Garlic-Chili Shrimp and Miso Garden Salad (page 96)

Shredded chicken from the Garlic and Herb Roast Chicken with Fingerling Potatoes (page 195)

Lamb Tagine with Squash and Prunes (page 236)

COFFEE-RUBBED PORK TENDERLOIN

SERVES 6   **PREPARATION TIME 25 MINUTES** (plus overnight to marinate)
COOKING TIME 50 MINUTES

FOR THE PORK

2 tablespoons packed light brown sugar

2 tablespoons kosher salt

2 dried bay leaves

2 1½-pound pork tenderloins, fat trimmed

FOR THE RUB AND COOKING

Nonstick pan spray

1 tablespoon instant coffee granules

1 tablespoon garlic powder

1 tablespoon packed light brown sugar

1 tablespoon dried oregano

Kosher salt

½ teaspoon onion powder

1 tablespoon olive oil

FOR THE SAUCE

2 tablespoons reduced-fat cream cheese (Neufchâtel)

1 tablespoon olive oil

1 shallot, halved and thinly sliced

½ cup red wine

Kosher salt and ground black pepper

Pork tenderloin hits all the sweet spots: it's wonderfully tender, extra-lean, and very flavorful, and it goes on sale often enough to make it a smart buy. The rub for the meat gets a huge boost of flavor here from a surprise ingredient: instant coffee. The coffee adds depth to both the roast's crust and the drippings used to make the sauce. This recipe is the perfect choice when you are craving hearty comfort food, but want to keep a lean protein on the menu.

1 To brine the pork: Add the brown sugar, salt, and bay leaves to a large bowl. Pour 1 cup warm water over the sugar-salt mixture, whisking until the sugar and salt are dissolved. Whisk in 3 cups cold water and then add the pork (it should be completely submerged—a medium plate can be placed on top to help weight it down). Cover the bowl with plastic wrap and refrigerate overnight.

2 To make the rub and cook the pork: Preheat the oven to 350°F. Line a baking dish with aluminum foil and lightly coat with nonstick pan spray. In a small bowl, stir together the instant coffee, garlic powder, brown sugar, oregano, ½ teaspoon salt, and onion powder. Remove the pork from the refrigerator (discard the brine) and use paper towels to pat the tenderloin dry. Rub the coffee mixture all over the tenderloin.

3 Heat a medium skillet over high heat for 1 minute. Add the olive oil and the pork, and cook until browned, about 4 minutes. Use tongs to turn over the pork and cook on the other side until browned, about 4 minutes more. Transfer the pork to the prepared baking dish and roast until barely pink in the middle and an instant-read thermometer registers 150°F.

(recipe continues)

at the thickest part of the tenderloin, 30 to 35 minutes. (Don't wash the skillet—you'll use it in step 4.) Remove the baking dish from the oven and transfer the pork to a cutting board. Loosely tent with aluminum foil and rest for 10 minutes.

4 To make the sauce: Microwave the cream cheese in a medium bowl in 10-second increments until it warms up. Whisk in ¾ cup warm water and set aside. Set the pan used to brown the pork over medium heat, add the oil and shallot, and cook, stirring often, until soft, about 3 minutes. Add the wine, stirring and scraping up any browned bits from the bottom of the pan. Stir in the cream cheese mixture and simmer until slightly thickened, about 2 minutes. Taste the sauce and season with ½ teaspoon salt and ¼ teaspoon pepper.

5 Slice the rested pork crosswise against the grain into ¼- to ½-inch-thick pieces and serve with the shallot pan sauce.

PER SERVING: Calories 349 / Protein 46g / Dietary Fiber 1g / Sugars 2g / Total Fat 14g

---

THREE TRICKS FOR THE TASTIEST PORK

Pork chops, loin, and tenderloin (the leanest of the three, even leaner than chicken breasts!) are tender cuts of meat that offer low-fat protein. Because the meat can be so lean, you need to pay special mind to how you cook it so it doesn't dry out. Here are a few pointers.

1 Add a marinade, spice rub, or other flavoring so the tenderloin tastes rich and robust.

2 Use a thermometer to ensure you don't overcook the pork. Pull it out of the oven right when its temperature (taken at the thickest part of the roast or chop) reaches 145°F (the temperature will rise slightly as the meat rests).

3 Rest the pork. Once it's finished cooking, let it rest for 5 to 15 minutes (less time for thin chops, more time for a loin roast) so the juices stay in the meat rather than stream onto the cutting board when the meat is sliced.

CRISPY BEEF TACOS WITH PINEAPPLE-AVOCADO SALSA

SERVES 4   **PREPARATION TIME** 30 MINUTES   **COOKING TIME** 35 MINUTES

FOR THE SALSA

½ medium avocado, cut into small pieces

Juice of 1 lime

1 cup chopped pineapple (canned or fresh)

⅓ cup plain reduced-fat Greek yogurt

½ red bell pepper, seeded and finely chopped

¼ medium red onion, finely chopped

1 tablespoon very finely chopped fresh cilantro leaves

1 tablespoon olive oil

¼ teaspoon kosher salt

¼ teaspoon ground black pepper

FOR THE TACO FILLING

2 teaspoons olive oil

1 red bell pepper, halved, seeded, and finely chopped

½ medium yellow onion, cut into ½-inch pieces

2 garlic cloves, very finely chopped or pressed through a garlic press

8 ounces 90 to 93% lean ground beef

I grew up in a household where taco night was a weekly event. Mom stuffed a corn tortilla with a ground beef filling, clasped it shut with her bent-up metal tongs, and gingerly lowered each taco, one by one, into a shallow frying pan filled with hot vegetable oil that transformed the tortillas into curved shells. I've updated Mom's approach with my secret strategy for making my crunchy taco shells: dry oven heat. By skipping the oil altogether you get a healthier taco in which the flavor of the corn tortilla really comes through. If you don't have a large enough skillet to cook the vegetables and brown the meat at the same time, cook them in two separate skillets.

1 To make the salsa: Toss the avocado with the lime juice in a small bowl and set aside. Stir the pineapple, yogurt, bell pepper, onion, cilantro, olive oil, salt, and pepper together in a medium bowl. Add the avocado and gently stir to combine. Cover the bowl with plastic wrap and refrigerate for at least 15 minutes or up to several hours before serving.

2 To make the taco filling: Heat the olive oil in a large skillet over medium heat. Once it shimmers, add the bell pepper and onion and cook until the onion is soft, about 5 minutes. Stir in the garlic, then scoot the vegetables to one side of the pan.

3 Add the beef to the skillet next to the vegetables, crumbling it in and using a wooden spoon to break it up as it cooks. Once the beef is about halfway cooked through and browned, after 3 to 4 minutes, stir in the paprika, chipotle powder, cumin, and salt. Place the tomato on top of the vegetables and cook, stirring the vegetables and beef separately until the beef is completely browned, about 6 minutes longer.

1½ teaspoons sweet paprika

½ to 1 teaspoon ground chipotle chile (or chili powder, for less heat)

¾ teaspoon ground cumin

½ teaspoon kosher salt

1 large tomato, cored and finely chopped

¾ cup low-sodium beef broth

FOR SERVING THE TACOS

8 6-inch yellow or white corn tortillas

Plain reduced-fat Greek yogurt or reduced-fat sour cream

Mix the vegetables into the beef, then pour in the broth and let it bubble and cook down until the liquid is evaporated, 8 to 10 minutes. Turn off the heat and set the meat mixture aside.

4 To make the tacos: Preheat the oven to 350°F. Place a wire rack on top of a large baking sheet. Wrap 4 corn tortillas in two damp paper towels, set on a microwave-safe plate, and microwave for 10 to 15 seconds to soften (repeat if the tortillas become dry and break when you make the shells).

5 Holding one tortilla, fill it with a couple tablespoons filling. Gently fold the tortilla in half and secure with a toothpick (as if sewing a stitch). Place the filled taco on the rack. Fill the remaining 3 warmed tortillas, then microwave and fill the next 4 tortillas.

6 Bake the tacos until the outer shell is dry, crisp, and golden, about 10 minutes. Serve with the salsa and 1 or 2 teaspoons of the Greek yogurt.

PER SERVING: Calories 360 / Protein 18g / Dietary Fiber 6g / Sugars 9g / Total Fat 16g

FLATIRON STEAKS WITH QUICK CAULIFLOWER KIMCHI

SERVES 4 **PREPARATION TIME 30 MINUTES** (plus 1 hour, 10 minutes to marinate)
COOKING TIME 15 MINUTES

FOR THE CAULIFLOWER KIMCHI

1 1½-pound head of cauliflower, cored, quartered, and sliced into ⅛-inch-thick slices

2 tablespoons sesame seeds

4 garlic cloves, peeled

1 4-inch piece of fresh ginger, peeled and grated

¼ cup fish sauce

¼ cup low-sodium soy sauce

2 tablespoons rice vinegar

1 tablespoon sugar

8 scallions (white and light green parts only), thinly sliced

1 to 2 teaspoons red pepper flakes

FOR THE STEAK

¼ cup low-sodium soy sauce

¼ teaspoon ground coriander

1 1-pound flatiron steak (about 1 inch thick), trimmed of fat

½ teaspoon kosher salt

¼ teaspoon ground black pepper

2 teaspoons canola oil

Kimchi is a traditional Korean condiment made from heavily pickled vegetables (often napa cabbage). When I was filming The Next Food Network Star *years ago, one of my fellow contestants was Korean, and she made an amazing marinated steak with kimchi. I immediately fell in love with the tangy, sour kimchi served alongside the steak. This quick kimchi doesn't have the same punch as a kimchi that ferments for months, but I still love its robust flavor.*

1 To make the cauliflower kimchi: Place the cauliflower in a large bowl. Toast the sesame seeds in a small skillet over medium heat, shaking the pan often, until the seeds are golden brown, about 2 minutes.

2 In a blender, combine the garlic, half the ginger (reserve the remainder for the meat marinade), the fish sauce, soy sauce, rice vinegar, and sugar. Purée until smooth, then pour over the cauliflower. Add the scallions, toasted sesame seeds, and red pepper flakes and stir to combine. Cover the bowl with plastic wrap and set aside at room temperature to marinate for at least 1 hour or up to several days (the longer it sits, the stronger the kimchi).

3 To prepare the steak: In a small bowl, whisk together the reserved grated ginger, the soy sauce, and ground coriander. Put the steak in a shallow dish, cover with the marinade, and turn so both sides get coated. Set aside at room temperature for at least 10 minutes, or refrigerate for up to 1 hour.

(recipe continues)

4 Remove the steak from the marinade, pat dry with paper towels, and season both sides with the salt and pepper. Heat a grill pan or heavy skillet over medium-high heat for 2 minutes. Add the canola oil, tilt the pan to coat, then add the steak and cook on both sides until browned, about 10 minutes total for medium-rare (or longer for a more well-done steak). Transfer the steak to a cutting board and let rest for 10 minutes before slicing crosswise against the grain into thin pieces. Divide the steak among 4 plates and serve with the cauliflower kimchi.

PER SERVING: Calories 277 / Protein 26g / Dietary Fiber 3g / Sugars 6g / Total Fat 13g

SUPERMARKET STRATEGY

Shopping for Lean Steaks

While I certainly appreciate a rib-eye or porterhouse, when I'm cooking steak for my family I generally go for more affordable and less fatty cuts. Since lean steaks aren't marbled with fat like a rich sirloin or skirt steak is, marinating helps tenderize the steak. Of course, steaks that don't *need* marinating can be marinated for extra flavor.

MINTY LAMB PATTIES WITH CUCUMBER-RADISH SALAD

SERVES 4   **PREPARATION TIME** 20 MINUTES   **COOKING TIME** 10 MINUTES

FOR THE PATTIES

¾ pound lean ground turkey

½ pound ground lamb

2 garlic cloves, very finely chopped or pressed through a garlic press

2 tablespoons finely chopped fresh mint leaves

1 tablespoon finely chopped fresh flat-leaf parsley

Zest of ½ lemon

1 teaspoon kosher salt

¼ teaspoon ground black pepper

Olive oil mister or nonstick pan spray

FOR THE SALAD

3 medium radishes, chopped into ¼-inch pieces

1 medium cucumber, chopped into ¼-inch pieces

2 tablespoons roughly chopped fresh flat-leaf parsley

Juice of 1 lemon

½ teaspoon kosher salt

¼ teaspoon ground black pepper

1 tablespoon olive oil

Lamb can be quite expensive; however, ground lamb is a budget-friendly way to enjoy its hearty flavor. Since ground lamb tends toward the rich side, I like to cut it with mild and lean ground turkey (I can stretch my more expensive lamb!). With some fresh herbs and lemon zest added to the blend, I can make these Mediterranean-style patties in minutes. My daughter Valentine loves them on a bun burger-style, while Philippe and I prefer them served breadless, topped with a simple radish and cucumber salad. The juices from the salad are excellent drizzled over the burgers regardless of how you serve them.

1. To make the patties: Add the turkey, lamb, garlic, mint, parsley, lemon zest, salt, and pepper to a medium bowl and mix to combine, then shape into four ½-inch-thick patties.

2. To make the salad: Stir together the radishes, cucumber, parsley, lemon juice, salt, and pepper. Add the olive oil and stir to combine.

3. Lightly mist a large nonstick skillet with olive oil or nonstick pan spray. Set the skillet over medium-high heat, then add the patties, cooking until they are browned on both sides, 8 to 10 minutes total.

4. Divide the patties among 4 plates. Drizzle with some of the juices from the bowl with the salad, then top with the salad and serve.

PER SERVING: Calories 274 / Protein 27g / Dietary Fiber 1g / Sugars 2g / Total Fat 16g

FILET MIGNON WITH CREAMY DIJON SAUCE

SERVES 4   **PREPARATION TIME 10 MINUTES** (plus 15 minutes for the steaks to rest)
COOKING TIME 35 MINUTES

FOR THE STEAKS

4 5-ounce beef filets

½ teaspoon kosher salt

¼ teaspoon ground black pepper

2 teaspoons olive oil

1 slice center-cut bacon, roughly chopped

FOR THE SAUCE

½ medium yellow onion, finely chopped

2 garlic cloves, very finely chopped or pressed through a garlic press

1 tablespoon all-purpose flour

½ cup dry white wine

¾ cup low-sodium beef broth

1 tablespoon Dijon mustard

2 tablespoons finely chopped fresh tarragon leaves

Steak is a favorite in our family, as it is for so many others. Filet mignon is among the leanest beef options out there, and one of the most tender, so it's a great way to scratch the steak itch while minimizing the saturated fats that typically come along with a juicy steak. I won't sugarcoat it: filet isn't cheap! My strategy for affording the splurge is to save the filet nights for special occasions, which avoids a restaurant trip (and certainly home-made filet is cheaper than a medium-priced restaurant dinner). Or, if I see filet on sale for a good price (it happens every few months), I buy it and put it on the menu. But keep in mind, you can serve this sauce with cheaper cuts, too.

1 To season and cook the steaks: Set the filets on a cutting board and season both sides with the salt and pepper. Let them sit out at room temperature for at least 15 and up to 30 minutes. Preheat the oven to 400°F.

2 Heat the olive oil over medium-high heat in a large oven-safe skillet for 30 seconds. Add the bacon and cook until crisp, stirring often, about 7 minutes. Use a slotted spoon to transfer the bacon to a paper towel–lined plate and set aside. Raise the heat to high and add the steaks. Sear the steaks on both sides until a light crust forms, about 2 minutes on each side.

3 Transfer the skillet to the oven and roast the steaks until cooked to your preferred degree of doneness (between 125° and 130°F. for rare to medium-rare), about 10 minutes. Remove the skillet from the oven and transfer the steaks to a large plate to rest for 10 minutes (don't wash the pan—you'll use it to make the sauce).

4 To make the sauce: Set the same pan used to cook the steaks over medium heat. Add the onion and cook until soft, about 4 minutes. Stir in the garlic and cook until fragrant, about 1 minute, then sprinkle in the flour and stir constantly for 1 minute. Raise the heat to high and pour in the wine and then the broth. Return the bacon to the skillet and let the mixture simmer until it is reduced by one-third and thickened slightly, about 4 minutes.

5 Strain the sauce into a small bowl (discard the solids), and whisk in the Dijon mustard. Set a steak on each of 4 plates, drizzle with the sauce, and serve sprinkled with the tarragon.

PER SERVING: Calories 314 / Protein 29g / Dietary Fiber 0g / Sugars 9g / Total Fat 18g

ENTERTAINING STRATEGY

Practice Makes Perfect

If you prepare a particular dish regularly for your family you will be far more confident (and less stressed) when you cook the same dish for the "important" dinners. Building your arsenal of "everyday" recipes that can be transformed into elegant dinner party showstoppers is an excellent way to boost your hosting prowess.

GRILLED BISON BURGERS

SERVES 4   **PREPARATION TIME** 10 MINUTES   **COOKING TIME** 20 MINUTES

FOR THE UMAMI GLAZE

3 tablespoons Dijon mustard

3 tablespoons low-sodium soy sauce

½ teaspoon sugar

FOR THE BURGERS

1 pound ground bison

½ teaspoon kosher salt

½ teaspoon ground black pepper

2 teaspoons olive oil

8 ounces cremini mushrooms, stems trimmed and caps finely chopped

2 garlic cloves, very finely chopped or pressed through a garlic press

2 teaspoons fresh thyme leaves or 1 teaspoon dried

Canola oil, for grilling

4 burger buns (preferably whole-grain)

1½ cups arugula

Bison is lower in fat than beef, which is excellent health news, but it means you have to take extra care when cooking it so it doesn't dry out. This burger has a savory glaze to seal in extra juiciness and bring out the umami savory-salty notes of the meat. Silky sautéed mushrooms are a great stand-in for cheese.

1 To make the umami glaze: Mix the mustard, soy sauce, and sugar together in a small bowl.

2 To make the burgers: Divide the bison into four ¾-inch-thick patties. Season the tops of the patties with ¼ teaspoon of the salt and ¼ teaspoon of the pepper.

3 Heat the olive oil in a large skillet over medium-high heat. Add the mushrooms and cook, stirring often, until they give off liquid, about 5 minutes. Stir in the garlic and thyme and cook until the mushrooms are soft, about 3 minutes more. Season with the remaining ¼ teaspoon salt and ¼ teaspoon pepper.

4 Heat a grill pan or gas or charcoal grill over medium-high heat. Dip a folded paper towel into the canola oil and use tongs to grease the grill pan or grates. Grill the burgers until nicely marked, about 4 minutes. Flip the burgers and brush with the glaze. Grill on the other side until the burgers are grill-marked and the center of the burger gives to medium pressure, about 4 minutes longer for a medium-rare to medium burger. Transfer the burgers to a platter.

5 Set the buns cut side down on the grill and cook until lightly toasted. Set a bun on each plate and top the bottom half with the burger, followed by the mushrooms and some arugula. Set the top bun over the arugula and serve.

PER SERVING: Calories 286 / Protein 31g / Dietary Fiber 4g / Sugars 3g / Total Fat 7g

LAMB TAGINE WITH SQUASH AND PRUNES

SERVES 6   **PREPARATION TIME** 20 MINUTES   **COOKING TIME** 2 HOURS

2 teaspoons canola oil

1 medium yellow onion, halved and thinly sliced

2 garlic cloves, very finely chopped or pressed through a garlic press

2 cinnamon sticks

¾ teaspoon ground coriander

½ teaspoon ground ginger

1½ pounds boneless lamb shoulder, trimmed and cut into 2-inch pieces

1 2-pound butternut squash, peeled, seeded, and chopped into 1-inch pieces

¾ teaspoon kosher salt

¼ teaspoon ground black pepper

2 cups (about 12 ounces) pitted prunes

2 tablespoons date syrup or honey

2 tablespoons finely chopped fresh cilantro, plus extra for serving

This rich Moroccan stew is a slow-cooked affair, almost always made with an inexpensive cut of meat (here, lamb shoulder), dried fruit (prunes), and lots of spices (coriander, ginger, cinnamon). Traditionally it is cooked in an earthenware clay dish that has a funnel-shaped lid, but a heavy-bottomed soup pot or Dutch oven does the job just fine. This is wonderful served over the Jeweled Wild Rice Pilaf (page 256) or even over plain, fluffy steamed rice. Think of date syrup as the maple syrup of the Middle East—it's a fun alternative to honey. You can find it in gourmet markets, health food stores, and Middle Eastern grocery stores.

1 Heat the canola oil in a large pot over medium heat. Add the onion and cook, stirring occasionally, until tender, about 10 minutes. Add the garlic, cinnamon sticks, coriander, and ginger and cook, stirring often, until fragrant, about 1 minute.

2 Add the lamb, squash, and 5 cups of water. Season with the salt and pepper and bring to a boil over high heat. Reduce the heat to medium-low and cook, occasionally skimming the surface with a spoon, until the lamb is very tender, about 1½ hours.

3 Remove and discard the cinnamon sticks. Add the prunes and honey and stir to combine. Cook until the sauce thickens slightly, about 15 minutes.

4 Stir the cilantro into the tagine and serve it sprinkled with more cilantro.

PER SERVING: Calories 490 / Protein 28g / Dietary Fiber 8g / Sugars 10g / Total Fat 19g

— *Chapter 10* —

SIDES

Roasted Whole
Cauliflower with
Brown Butter

Cauliflower Steaks with
Garlic-Parmesan Crust

Rosemary Sweet
Potatoes with
Almond Butter

Citrus-Roast Broccoli
with Quick-Pickled
Chiles

Curry-Glazed Carrots

Roasted Zucchini and
Carrots with Herbs

Creamy Brown Rice
"Risotto"

Jeweled Wild Rice Pilaf

Roast Chickpeas with
Fennel

Smashed Black Beans
with Peppers

Broccoli-Stalk and
Cilantro Slaw

Enlightened Potato-
Bacon Torte

The humble side dish is perhaps one of the most overlooked opportunities on the dinner table. Side dishes are a great place to deliver important nutrients with little saturated fat—from antioxidants, vitamins, and minerals to complex carbs and heart-smart fiber. Sides are also a great way to save on your dinner budget, since grains and beans are smart meal-stretchers.

When I'm feeling like my family needs a little dinnertime shake-up, I often prepare a sure-bet main course like chicken and I pair it with a curveball side dish such as roasted chickpeas or cauliflower with a seasoned butter or creamy, cheesy brown rice. I *know* they're going to eat the chicken, and will be ecstatic when they try (and I hope love!) the side. Or, I prepare an old-faithful side like green beans or a pilaf, then pair it with a more challenging side like vegetables glazed with curry or wild rice fragranced with saffron. That way everyone gets to be in charge of his or her own plate, and it puts less emphasis (and pressure) on trying the newbie dish.

ROASTED WHOLE CAULIFLOWER WITH BROWN BUTTER

SERVES 4   **PREPARATION TIME** 10 MINUTES   **COOKING TIME** 45 MINUTES

FOR THE CAULIFLOWER

1 small head of cauliflower (about 1¼ pounds)

Olive oil mister

½ teaspoon kosher salt

¼ teaspoon ground black pepper

FOR THE BROWNED BUTTER

2 tablespoons unsalted butter

2 tablespoons brine-packed capers, rinsed

1 garlic clove, very finely chopped or pressed through a garlic press

Juice of ½ lemon

3 tablespoons finely chopped fresh flat-leaf parsley

My daughter Valentine and I love just about any veggie dipped in a little butter—except the one veg I could never get her to eat: cauliflower. I took this on as a challenge and tried cauliflower prepared every which way, finally finding success in a whole roasted head that sweetens and takes on an earthy flavor. Our ritual is to let the roasted cauliflower cool just enough so we can rip off florets without burning our fingers, and then dip the cauliflower into a bit of melted butter. Here, I brown the butter to give it a nutty dimension, then add capers, lemon juice, and parsley for a salty-tangy freshness that is so tasty with the buttery quality of the florets. The key to getting the cauliflower to cook all the way through is to cut out the core, leaving an inverted cone shape.

1   To roast the cauliflower: Preheat the oven to 350°F. Trim the green leaves and stem from the cauliflower head. Flip it over and use a small paring knife to gently separate the core from the head, creating an inverted cone shape in the bottom of the cauliflower. Turn the cauliflower right side up and set it on a rimmed baking sheet.

2   Mist the cauliflower with olive oil, rubbing the oil all over the surface. Season the cauliflower with the salt and pepper, then turn it upside down (so the cored part faces up).

3   Roast the cauliflower for 30 minutes, then flip the head right side up and continue to roast until it is golden and tender, about 15 minutes more (leave it in longer if you want a deeper brown color).

(recipe continues)

4 To make the browned butter: Place the butter in a small saucepan set over medium heat. The butter will get foamy, then the foam will disappear and you'll see little golden-brown specks in the bottom of the saucepan, about 5 minutes after melting.

5 Add the capers and garlic, give the saucepan a swirl, then remove the saucepan from the heat. Add the lemon juice and parsley, give the saucepan another swirl, and either pour the brown butter over the top of the cauliflower for a gorgeous presentation, or serve it in a small bowl alongside the cauliflower for dipping.

PER SERVING: Calories 93 / Protein 2g / Dietary Fiber 2g / Sugars 2g / Total Fat 8g

SUPERMARKET STRATEGY

Stock Up on Long-Lasting Vegetables
Cauliflower, broccoli, cabbage, and Brussels sprouts: these vegetables are a busy person's best friend because they can be bought in bulk, and they keep in the crisper for up to a week (or sometimes a little longer). When I plan my week of dinners, I always try to use up the more perishable vegetables first—spinach, peppers, tender salad greens—and save these cruciferous veggies for later in the week. Throwing away less food equals more savings.

CAULIFLOWER STEAKS WITH GARLIC-PARMESAN CRUST

SERVES 4   **PREPARATION TIME 10 MINUTES**   **COOKING TIME 15 MINUTES**

1 large head of cauliflower (about 2 pounds)

½ teaspoon kosher salt

¼ teaspoon ground black pepper

⅓ cup panko-style bread crumbs (preferably whole wheat)

1 garlic clove, very finely chopped or pressed through a garlic press

2 tablespoons grated Parmesan cheese

2 teaspoons olive oil

Olive oil mister or nonstick pan spray

1 tablespoon finely chopped fresh flat-leaf parsley

1 lemon, cut into wedges

Treated right, cauliflower is actually quite mild, a bit sweet, and even a little buttery. Slicing the cauliflower head into thin steaks highlights how beautiful and intricate the shape is, while garlicky bread crumbs and Parmesan cheese add just a little crunch. If you are trying to sell your kids on an über-healthy vegetable, up the cheese amount a bit to get them to fall in love and then you can slowly reduce it over time.

1 Preheat the oven to 350°F. Slice the cauliflower (don't core it first) into four ½-inch-thick slices (break the remaining cauliflower into florets and save for another time) and season with half the salt and pepper (reserve the smaller florets that crumble when slicing for another use).

2 In a small bowl, mix the bread crumbs, garlic, Parmesan cheese, and the remaining salt and pepper.

3 Heat the olive oil in a large oven-safe skillet over medium-high heat. Add the cauliflower steaks (you may need to brown them in batches and finish them on a baking sheet, depending on the size of your skillet) and cook until they are browned, about 2 minutes. Use a spatula to turn over the steaks and sprinkle the bread crumb mixture evenly over each steak. Lightly mist the bread crumbs with spray.

4 Place the skillet with the steaks in the oven and bake until the bread crumbs are golden and a paring knife easily slips into the cauliflower, about 12 minutes. Transfer the steaks to a serving platter. Sprinkle with the parsley and serve with lemon wedges.

PER SERVING: Calories 76 / Protein 5g / Dietary Fiber 5g / Sugars 4g / Total Fat 1g

ROSEMARY SWEET POTATOES
WITH ALMOND BUTTER

SERVES 4   **PREPARATION TIME** 15 MINUTES   **COOKING TIME** 1 HOUR

4 medium sweet potatoes

8 fresh rosemary sprigs

2 tablespoons sliced almonds

2 tablespoons almond butter

2 tablespoons plain reduced-fat Greek yogurt

1 teaspoon kosher salt

2 tablespoons honey

I'm not sure if there is any more palate-friendly vegetable than the sweet potato. Here, I serve it baked potato–style, loaded with almond butter made extra light and creamy by stirring in a little Greek yogurt. I love how the honey sticks to the nuts and the salt counters the sweetness of the potato and the honey. This is a combo that should be as loved as peanut butter and chocolate.

1 Preheat the oven to 350°F. Prick each sweet potato twice with a fork. Place 2 rosemary sprigs on 4 sheets of aluminum foil. Set a sweet potato on top of the rosemary, wrap in the foil, and set on a baking sheet. Bake the sweet potatoes until a paring knife easily slips into the middle of the largest one, 50 minutes to 1 hour.

2 While the potatoes bake, toast the almonds. Place the almonds on a square of aluminum foil and set on the baking sheet with the potatoes. Once they are browned, after 5 to 7 minutes, remove the almonds from the baking sheet and transfer to a plate to cool (leave the potatoes in the oven until they are done cooking).

3 Combine the almond butter, yogurt, and ½ teaspoon of the salt in a medium bowl.

4 Remove the potatoes from the oven, carefully open the foil, and let the potatoes cool for 10 minutes. Make a slit in the top, then push the ends toward the middle to open the slit. Top each potato with a spoonful of the almond butter–yogurt mixture. Sprinkle with the toasted almonds and the remaining ½ teaspoon salt. Serve drizzled with honey.

PER SERVING: Calories 281 / Protein 6g / Dietary Fiber 5g / Sugars 22g / Total Fat 12g

CITRUS-ROAST BROCCOLI WITH QUICK-PICKLED CHILES

SERVES 4   PREPARATION TIME 10 MINUTES   COOKING TIME 20 MINUTES

FOR THE PICKLED CHILES

⅓ cup white wine vinegar

1 teaspoon kosher salt

1 garlic clove, thinly sliced

2 fresh red chiles (such as Fresno or red jalapeño), sliced into thin rings

FOR THE BROCCOLI

1 large head of broccoli

1 tablespoon olive oil

1 tablespoon orange marmalade

½ teaspoon kosher salt

1 lemon, halved

Preheating your baking sheet while the oven comes up to temperature is key for this vegetable: when the broccoli hits the pan, it immediately starts to caramelize and sweeten. Quick pickled chiles add heat and color, but if you're not a fan of heat and spice, substitute red bell peppers.

1 Set a rimmed baking sheet on the middle oven rack and preheat the oven to 400°F.

2 To pickle the chiles: Bring the vinegar, salt, and garlic to a simmer in a small saucepan over medium-high heat. Add the chiles and turn off the heat. Set aside.

3 To roast the broccoli: Place the broccoli on a cutting board. Use a vegetable peeler to peel away the tough outer skin of the stalk, then halve the broccoli lengthwise. Slice each broccoli half into 3 or 4 long "trees," keeping the florets attached to the stalks.

4 Whisk the olive oil, marmalade, and salt together in a large bowl. Squeeze in the juice from ½ lemon, then add the broccoli and toss to coat with the vinaigrette. Turn the broccoli out onto the preheated baking sheet and return it to the oven. Roast the broccoli until it browns, 12 to 15 minutes.

5 Transfer the broccoli to a platter. Squeeze the remaining lemon half over the top. Drain the pickled chiles and serve the broccoli sprinkled with the chiles.

PER SERVING: Calories 118 / Protein 5g / Dietary Fiber 5g / Sugars 6g / Total Fat 7g

Pantry Swaps for Pickles

Almost anything can be pickled, from peeled hard-boiled eggs to watermelon rind, Kirby cucumbers, green beans, beets, radishes—even apples! Sliced red onions will make the brine a pretty pink color, while jalapeños and red pepper flakes will add spice. Different vinegars will affect a pickle differently—sherry vinegar adds nuance while apple cider vinegar offers a sweet-tang, and rice vinegar brings on a soft, mellow note.

CURRY-GLAZED CARROTS

SERVES 4   **PREPARATION TIME** 5 MINUTES   **COOKING TIME** 10 MINUTES

2 teaspoons coconut oil

1 large bunch young carrots (about 12 ounces or 8 to 12 slim carrots), preferably multicolored, peeled

2 teaspoons red curry paste

¼ cup low-sodium chicken broth

½ teaspoon kosher salt

¼ teaspoon ground black pepper

Juice of 1 lime

2 tablespoons finely chopped fresh basil leaves

I love taking my kids to the farmers' market, where we all compete to find the coolest vegetable or fruit to bring home. (The extra few bucks I spend during an hour or two at the market still makes the outing cheaper than going to a movie!). Ever since Océane discovered purple and yellow carrots at the market, they have been her favorite vegetable. So, whenever I can I get the beautiful heirloom rainbow variety, mostly just to see the joy that they bring to my family.

1 Heat the coconut oil in a large skillet over medium-high heat. Add the carrots and cook until they barely start to get golden, shaking the skillet often, for about 4 minutes.

2 Add the curry paste and shake the pan to roll the carrots in the paste until they are well coated. Pour in the chicken broth, cover the skillet, and reduce the heat to medium-low. Steam the carrots until a paring knife easily slides into the center of the largest one, 1 to 2 minutes for firm carrots or a few minutes longer if you prefer the carrots softer.

3 Uncover the skillet, add the salt and pepper, and let the sauce bubble down into a glaze, 1 or 2 minutes. Transfer the carrots to a plate.

4 Add the lime juice to the skillet, stirring it into the sauce, then immediately pour it over the carrots. Serve the carrots sprinkled with the basil.

PER SERVING: Calories 64 / Protein 1g / Dietary Fiber 3g / Sugars 6g / Total Fat 4g

skillet-glazed vegetables

Skillet-glazed vegetables are my go-to for getting vegetables on the table quickly. Using this plug-and-play strategy will turn week-night vegetables into restaurant-quality side dishes with minimal effort.

STEP 1: CHOOSE AND PREP YOUR VEGETABLE,

HARD VEGE-TABLES

SOFT VEGE-TABLES

(broccoli, Brussels sprouts, carrots, cauliflower, green beans)

(asparagus, peas, zucchini)

then sauté in a splash of oil until they take on some color.

STEP 2: ADD THE AROMATICS AND
cook until fragrant.

FRESH
(chopped fresh chiles, garlic, ginger, lemongrass)

PANTRY
(capers, chipotle chiles in adobo sauce, curry paste, dried herbs, miso paste, tomato paste, whole spices)

STEP 3: DEGLAZE THE PAN WITH A LIQUID,
then cover and steam the vegetables until tender.

BROTH
(beef, chicken, fish, vegetable)

SPIRITS
(sake, vermouth, wine)

FRUIT JUICE, WATER, OR COCONUT MILK

TOMATOES
(chopped, puréed)

STEP 4: REMOVE THE COVER,
reduce the sauce until it becomes thick like a glaze, and finish with your desired combination of:

SPLASH OF ACID
(fish sauce, citrus juice, vinegar)

FRESH, TENDER HERBS

TOASTED NUTS OR SEEDS

Here are a few combinations for inspiration:

VEGETABLES	AROMATICS	LIQUID	FINISH
CARROTS	Fresh Ginger	Orange Juice	Soy Sauce + Sesame Seeds
CAULIFLOWER	Garlic + Mustard	Water	Lemon Juice + Tarragon
BRUSSELS SPROUTS	Red Onion + Bacon	Apple Cider	Lemon Juice + Parsley
GREEN BEANS	Lemongrass +Garlic	Miso + Water	Lime Juice + Toasted Coconut

ROASTED ZUCCHINI AND CARROTS WITH HERBS

SERVES 4   **PREPARATION TIME 10 MINUTES**   **COOKING TIME 30 MINUTES**

FOR THE VEGETABLES

3 large carrots, peeled and cut into sticks 1½ inches long and ½ inch thick

1 large or 2 small zucchini, sliced into ½-inch-thick rounds

1 teaspoon olive oil

¼ teaspoon kosher salt

⅛ teaspoon ground black pepper

FOR THE DRIZZLE

½ cup fresh flat-leaf parsley leaves

2 tablespoons fresh oregano leaves

1 tablespoon finely chopped sweet onion (Maui or Vidalia)

1 garlic clove, very finely chopped or pressed through a garlic press

Pinch of red pepper flakes

Juice of ½ lemon

2 teaspoons white wine vinegar

1 tablespoon olive oil

¼ teaspoon kosher salt

⅛ teaspoon ground black pepper

Almost any veggie can be roasted, and will be tastier for the time spent in the hot oven to coax out its natural sweetness. Adding a tangy herb drizzle takes only an extra minute or two and introduces a fresh and bright counterpoint that I just love. You can swap out the herbs, acid, and aromatics in the sauce to come up with a version that suits whatever you have on hand (see suggestions on page 253). Zucchini and carrots are fantastic sweet companions, but experiment with whatever vegetable is in your crisper drawer.

1. To roast the vegetables: Line a rimmed baking sheet with aluminum foil or parchment paper and heat the oven to 375°F.

2. Toss the carrots and zucchini with the olive oil, salt, and pepper. Place them on the prepared baking sheet and roast until golden and tender, but still firm, about 30 minutes, turning the vegetables over about midway through roasting.

3. To make the drizzle: While the vegetables are roasting, place the parsley, oregano, onion, garlic, red pepper flakes, lemon juice, vinegar, olive oil, salt, black pepper, and 2 tablespoons water in a food processor. Pulse until well blended but not entirely smooth, about five 1-second pulses.

4. Pour the drizzle into a small bowl and set aside. Transfer the roasted vegetables to a shallow serving dish and add half of the drizzle. Use tongs to gently toss to coat. Serve the remaining drizzle on the side.

PER SERVING: Calories 85 / Protein 2g / Dietary Fiber 3g / Sugars 5g / Total Fat 5g

SHAKE UP A HOMEMADE DRESSING

A quick homemade oil-based dressing really gives vegetables a boost, whether they are raw in a salad or have been roasted or steamed. Homemade dressing usually has less sodium and fat than the store-bought ones, but the real benefit is that it just tastes so fresh! In the drizzle opposite, I pair parsley and oregano with sweet onion and garlic, and then add lemon juice and white wine vinegar for acid. Here are some other combinations to get you started. Make a few kinds and refrigerate them in mason jars, then simply shake before drizzling.

HERBS	AROMATICS	ACIDS
Cilantro + Mint	Ginger + Garlic	Lime Juice + Rice Vinegar
Basil	Shallot	Balsamic Vinegar
Tarragon + Dill	Horseradish	White Vinegar
Fennel Fronds	Red Onion	Orange Juice + Champagne Vinegar
Basil + Cilantro	Scallions	Bottled Yuzu Juice + Soy Sauce

CREAMY BROWN RICE "RISOTTO"

SERVES 4   **PREPARATION TIME** 5 MINUTES   **COOKING TIME** 20 MINUTES

2 teaspoons unsalted butter or canola oil

1 medium yellow onion, finely chopped

1 teaspoon kosher salt

1⅓ cups instant whole-grain brown rice

2 cups low-sodium chicken broth

2 tablespoons reduced-fat cream cheese (Neufchâtel)

¼ cup grated Cheddar or Monterey Jack cheese

Using instant whole-grain brown rice to make a creamy risotto reduces by at least half the time it takes to make the dish. Brown rice brings fiber to this picture; plus, it's delicious, thanks to some reduced-fat cream cheese stirred in at the end. The cream cheese gives the rice a fantastic richness and tangy quality without the extra calories of cream or butter. Stir in rotisserie chicken or browned ham to turn this side dish into a main course.

1 Melt the butter in a large skillet over medium-high heat. Add the onion and salt and reduce the heat to medium. Cook, stirring occasionally, until the onion is soft, 4 to 5 minutes.

2 Stir in the brown rice, reduce the heat to medium-low, then add the broth ½ cup at a time, stirring between each addition and waiting to add the next addition until most of the liquid is absorbed (but the skillet is not dry—when you drag a spoon through the rice and liquid, the spoon should leave a trail that doesn't fill in immediately). Once all the liquid is added, after about 12 minutes, taste the rice. If it is still very al dente, add ¼ cup water and continue to cook until the rice is just al dente in the center, 2 to 3 minutes.

3 Turn off the heat and stir in the cream cheese and 2 tablespoons grated cheese. Transfer the rice to a bowl and serve sprinkled with the remaining 2 tablespoons cheese.

PER SERVING: Calories 205 / Protein 6g / Dietary Fiber 2g / Sugars 2g / Total Fat 9g

JEWELED WILD RICE PILAF

SERVES 6   PREPARATION TIME 10 MINUTES
COOKING TIME 1 HOUR (plus 20 minutes to rest)

¼ teaspoon saffron threads, crushed with the back of a metal spoon

¼ cup boiling water

2 cups wild rice and long-grain white rice blend, rinsed

1 tablespoon canola oil

1 medium shallot, finely chopped

½ teaspoon ground cumin

½ teaspoon ground cinnamon

¼ teaspoon kosher salt

¼ teaspoon ground black pepper

⅛ teaspoon ground cardamom

⅓ cup mixed dried fruit, finely chopped (such as apricots, cherries, cranberries, currants, figs, raisins)

⅓ cup roughly chopped roasted pistachios (or almonds or cashews)

Borrowing a page from the Persian rice playbook, I use a wild rice and long-grain white rice blend in this beautifully fragrant classic. I chop the dried fruits into small pieces so they get nicely dispersed throughout the rice, giving extra bang for each calorie. Saffron is pricey, but its flavor here is absolutely worth the few dollars you'll spend. The real plus to this preparation is the crusty, crispy browned rice at the bottom of the pot.

1 Add the saffron to a small bowl, cover with the boiling water, and set aside to soak.

2 Bring a large pot of salted water to a boil over high heat. Add the rinsed wild rice and boil, stirring occasionally, until the rice is tender, 15 to 20 minutes. Drain the rice through a fine-mesh sieve.

3 Heat ½ tablespoon of the canola oil in a small skillet over medium heat. Add the shallot and cook, stirring often, until soft, 5 to 7 minutes. Stir in the cumin, cinnamon, salt, pepper, and cardamom. Stir in the dried fruit.

4 Add the remaining ½ tablespoon canola oil to the bottom of a medium nonstick pot and heat over medium-high heat. Add half the wild rice, top with the shallot–dried fruit mixture, and cover with the remaining rice. Let the rice cook, without stirring, until browned and toasty smelling, about 7 minutes.

5 Drizzle the saffron water over the rice and reduce the heat to low. Use the round long end of a wooden spoon to make five holes in the rice down to the bottom of the pot, then cover the pot with a kitchen towel and a heavy lid (folding the edges of the towel up over the lid to make sure it doesn't catch fire) and cook for 30 minutes. Remove the pan from the heat and set aside for 20 minutes (this is critical—don't skip or shorten this step if you want to be able to serve the nice, crusty rice at the bottom of the pot).

6 To serve, transfer the rice to a serving bowl and top with pieces of the bottom crust. Sprinkle with pistachios and serve.

PER SERVING: Calories 276 / Protein 10g / Dietary Fiber 5g / Sugars 5g / Total Fat 6g

ROAST CHICKPEAS WITH FENNEL

SERVES 4   **PREPARATION TIME 10 MINUTES**   **COOKING TIME 25 MINUTES**

1½ cups cooked chickpeas (homemade, page 81; or canned, rinsed)

1 small fennel bulb, fronds reserved, bulb halved, cored, and thinly sliced lengthwise

1 teaspoon roughly chopped fresh thyme leaves

Olive oil mister

½ teaspoon kosher salt

½ teaspoon ground black pepper

2 teaspoons fresh lemon juice

Chickpeas, also called garbanzo beans, are a fantastic source of lean protein, fiber, and complex carbs. They are firmer than their legume siblings (such as lentils) and even hold their shape better than many beans. Here, I roast them with flavorful fresh fennel that adds the slightest hint of licorice, without being overpowering (fresh fennel is so much milder than fennel seeds). The chickpeas take on a totally different texture that is tender, slightly crisp, and altogether delicious. Serve alongside steamed brown rice or quinoa for a complete meat-free meal.

1   Preheat the oven to 400°F. Transfer the chickpeas to a paper towel–lined baking sheet and shake the baking sheet to dry them. Once the chickpeas are no longer wet, remove the towel and add the fennel to the baking sheet. Sprinkle the thyme over the chickpeas and fennel, then spray liberally with olive oil. Season with the salt and pepper.

2   Roast the chickpeas and fennel until the fennel is tender and lightly browned, 20 to 25 minutes.

3   Remove the baking sheet from the oven and sprinkle the hot chickpeas and fennel with the lemon juice, using a spatula to toss together. Transfer the chickpeas and fennel to a serving dish. Finely chop 2 tablespoons of the fennel fronds and sprinkle over the top before serving.

PER SERVING: Calories 186 / Protein 8g / Dietary Fiber 8g / Sugars 1g / Total Fat 6g

SMASHED BLACK BEANS
WITH PEPPERS

SERVES 4   **PREPARATION TIME 10 MINUTES**   **COOKING TIME 10 MINUTES**

1 tablespoon olive oil

1 garlic clove, very finely chopped or pressed through a garlic press

2 cups cooked black beans (homemade, page 81; or canned, rinsed)

Zest and juice of 1 lime

¼ teaspoon ground cumin

¼ teaspoon sweet paprika

⅛ teaspoon cayenne pepper

½ teaspoon kosher salt

½ teaspoon ground black pepper

1 cup thinly sliced roasted red peppers

3 tablespoons coarsely chopped fresh cilantro leaves

As I grew up in Tucson, my family ate frijoles *(cooked beans "refried" in oil and smashed into a semi-smooth consistency) several times a week. So for me, there is tremendous comfort in that mashed-up goodness. Restaurant-style* frijoles *can often be full of fat. Here, I achieve the creaminess that I crave by smashing the beans with equal parts water and lime juice for a great, bright flavor as well as a nice texture. The roasted peppers are cooked just enough to warm them through, then are served over the beans, offering a smoky flavor that completes the picture. Serve this as an excellent low-fat, high-fiber, and high-protein side dish or alongside brown rice to make it a full meal.*

1 Heat 2 teaspoons of the olive oil in a medium skillet set over medium heat. Add the garlic and cook, stirring, until the garlic is fragrant, about 30 seconds.

2 Stir in the black beans, lime zest and juice, 2 tablespoons water, the cumin, paprika, cayenne, ¼ teaspoon of the salt, and ¼ teaspoon of the black pepper and cook, gently mashing the beans with a potato masher while cooking, until the beans are warmed through, about 5 minutes. Transfer the beans to a serving bowl and wipe out the skillet.

3 Return the skillet to medium heat and add the remaining 1 teaspoon olive oil. Add the roasted red peppers and cook, stirring occasionally, until the peppers are warmed through, 3 to 5 minutes. Season with the remaining ¼ teaspoon salt and remaining ¼ teaspoon black pepper. Stir in the cilantro and serve the peppers over the smashed black beans.

PER SERVING: Calories 162 / Protein 8g / Dietary Fiber 8g / Sugars 2g / Total Fat 4g

BROCCOLI-STALK AND CILANTRO SLAW

SERVES 6   **PREPARATION TIME** 10 MINUTES   **COOKING TIME** NONE

8 ounces broccoli stems (3 to 4 large stems, florets reserved for another time)

2 scallions (white and light green parts only), finely chopped

¼ cup golden raisins

2 tablespoons plain reduced-fat Greek yogurt

1 tablespoon light mayonnaise

1 tablespoon apple cider vinegar

¼ teaspoon kosher salt

¼ teaspoon ground black pepper

3 tablespoons finely chopped fresh cilantro leaves

Raw broccoli is probably one of the healthiest foods on the planet, and I try to include it on our dinner table as often as possible. This means not just the florets but the stalk too, which, when the tough outer skin is peeled away, becomes incredibly tender and sweet—almost like an introduction to asparagus or artichoke hearts. Cilantro, scallions, and apple cider vinegar add lots of flavor to this slaw, tempering the already mild stalk even more, and making it a smart choice for anyone who shies away from the fuller-flavored florets. This broccoli slaw is great on its own, but one of my favorite ways to eat it is piled on top of a barbecue beef sandwich (see page 220) or even sloppy joes (see page 209).

1 Place the broccoli stems on a cutting board. Use a vegetable peeler to remove the tough skin, then thinly slice the stems lengthwise. Halve the pieces crosswise and stack them, then thinly slice them into matchsticks (you should get about 3 cups). Place the broccoli matchsticks in a medium bowl. Add the scallions and raisins.

2 Mix the yogurt, mayonnaise, vinegar, salt, and pepper in a small bowl and drizzle it over the broccoli. Stir to combine and transfer the slaw to a serving bowl. Serve sprinkled with the cilantro.

PER SERVING: Calories 40 / Protein 2g / Dietary Fiber 2g / Sugars 5g / Total Fat 1g

ENLIGHTENED POTATO-BACON TORTE

SERVES 8   **PREPARATION TIME 20 MINUTES**   **COOKING TIME 1 HOUR, 15 MINUTES**

1 teaspoon olive oil

2 slices lean center-cut bacon, finely chopped (optional)

1 shallot, finely chopped

Olive oil mister or nonstick pan spray

3 medium russet potatoes, peeled, halved lengthwise, and sliced crosswise into ¼-inch-thick pieces

1 teaspoon kosher salt

¼ teaspoon ground black pepper

2 tablespoons finely chopped fresh thyme leaves

1¼ cups 2% milk (or unsweetened soy milk)

1 tablespoon cornstarch

⅓ sheet puff pastry, thawed if frozen

1 large egg white

We all have that one recipe that everyone always asks you to bring or make. Mine is my potato-bacon torte, a recipe I shared in my first cookbook, Ten Dollar Dinners, *and the recipe I made on* The Next Food Network Star *that quite possibly won me my own cooking show! The original recipe certainly doesn't skimp on the bacon, cream, or butter. So in this enlightened version, I turn that indulgent recipe into something I can put on my table more frequently. Here, I chop up the bacon into small pieces so I use less while still getting that smoky bacon flavor in each bite, and I top the torte with small pieces of puff pastry rather than using a blanket of pie dough. To make this dish vegetarian, leave out the bacon.*

----

1 Preheat the oven to 375°F. Set a medium nonstick skillet over medium heat and add the olive oil and bacon, cooking until the bacon is almost crisp, 4 to 5 minutes. Stir in the shallot and cook until soft, about 2 minutes longer. Turn off the heat and set the skillet aside.

2 Lightly coat a 9-inch pie plate with olive oil or nonstick pan spray and place half the potato slices in the pie plate, arranging them close together and in a single layer. Season the potatoes with ½ teaspoon of the salt and all the pepper. Sprinkle the bacon-shallot mixture over the potatoes, followed by the chopped thyme. Arrange the remaining potatoes on top, placing them in a nice circular arrangement, then sprinkle with the remaining ½ teaspoon salt.

3 In a medium bowl, whisk 2 tablespoons of the milk with cornstarch until the cornstarch is completely dissolved. Whisk in the remaining milk, then pour the milk mixture over the potatoes until the milk reaches the top of the potatoes (you may not end up using all the milk).

4 Set the pastry dough on a cutting board and use a small cookie or biscuit cutter to cut out shapes from the dough. Arrange the pastry over the potatoes. Whisk the egg white with a pinch of salt, then brush the egg wash over the pastry. Bake until the crust is golden and a paring knife easily slips through the potato layers, about 1 hour (if the pastry starts to get too dark, tent the top of the pie with a piece of aluminum foil). Cool at least 20 minutes before serving.

PER SERVING: Calories 184 / Protein 5g / Dietary Fiber 1g / Sugars 3g / Total Fat 9g

— Chapter 11 —

DESSERT

Lemon-Coconut
Haystacks

Chocolate Chip–
Almond Biscotti

Flourless Fudgy Dream
Cookies

Butterscotch Banana
Crêpes

Stracciatella Meringues

Roasted Fruit and
Homemade Ricotta

Banana-Mango Tofu
Pudding

Dulce de Leche
Brown Rice Pudding

Vanilla and Blueberry
Cheesecake Pudding

Pomegranate-
Apple Gelatin with
Raspberries

Mango-Raspberry
Frozen Yogurt

At our house, dessert is a time to relax around the table, to let the girls hop on our laps, to laugh and share silly stories that somehow didn't make it into our dinner conversation. The fact that we're all eating something sweet is almost secondary to the happiness that surrounds us. For these reasons (and the fact that I have a major sweet tooth), it's really hard for me to imagine a family meal that doesn't end with dessert. The trick is that I want dessert to taste like a treat, but also not be a plate of empty calories and pure sugar.

To this end, I choose ingredients like reduced-fat milk and cream cheese, tofu, whole-grain flour, and a modest amount of sugar when making dessert. Pairing dessert with fruit is an easy strategy, too. I often serve a large bowl of clementines or peaches (which doubles as a centerpiece during the day!) with a small plate of cookies or biscotti, as a great compromise between an "all-fruit" dessert and a big plateful of sweets. For a more grown-up crowd, even just a tiny square of top-quality chocolate set on an espresso saucer is all anyone needs to satisfy a sweet tooth. Arranging fruit in a pretty way and perhaps pairing it with honey or homemade ricotta is a great and classic tactic to end a meal, too.

LEMON-COCONUT HAYSTACKS

MAKES 15 COOKIES   **PREPARATION TIME 10 MINUTES** (plus 15 minutes to chill)
COOKING TIME NONE

1 cup unsweetened
shredded coconut

½ cup almond flour

3 tablespoons coconut oil
(if solid, microwaved until
melted)

Zest and juice of ½ lemon

1 to 2 tablespoons maple
syrup

½ teaspoon vanilla extract

¼ teaspoon kosher salt

*Just one of these little raw gems (pictured here with the
Chocolate Chip–Almond Biscotti, page 268, and the Flourless
Fudgy Dream Cookies, page 270) satisfies a sweet craving without giving me a sugar rush—and that inevitable crash. In fact,
you can even expect an energy boost from the coconut oil and
almond flour. After the rounds are formed, and as the coconut
oil firms up (the fridge speeds this up), they set into cookies, just
like magic.*

1 Place the coconut in the bowl of a food processor and
pulse until semi-fine. Transfer ¼ cup of the pulverized
coconut to a small plate and set aside.

2 To the coconut in the food processor add the almond
flour, coconut oil, lemon zest and juice, 1 tablespoon of
the maple syrup, the vanilla, and salt, and process until well
combined. Taste and pulse in the extra tablespoon of maple
syrup, if needed.

3 Transfer the mixture to a cutting board and shape it into
a 7-inch-long and 1½-inch-wide log. Divide the log into
12 equal pieces, press them into cookie-shaped rounds, and
press them into the reserved pulverized coconut.

4 Set the cookies on a large plate, loosely cover with plastic
wrap, and chill for 15 minutes before serving.

PER SERVING (1 cookie): Calories 108 / Protein 1g / Dietary Fiber 1g / Sugars 2g /
Total Fat 10g

CHOCOLATE CHIP–ALMOND BISCOTTI

MAKES 16 BISCOTTI   **PREPARATION TIME** 35 MINUTES   **COOKING TIME** 55 MINUTES

½ cup sliced almonds

1½ cups white whole wheat flour

1 teaspoon baking powder

¼ teaspoon kosher salt

4 tablespoons (½ stick) unsalted butter, at room temperature

½ cup sugar

2 large eggs

1 tablespoon finely grated orange zest

1 cup semisweet chocolate chips

I love the European tradition of serving a small cookie or biscuit with coffee. Biscotti are the ideal coffee companion, equally delighted to be a little nibble on the side of a richer dessert or as a not-too-sweet dessert themselves. That they are surprisingly easy to make is a happy bonus. These biscotti are soft enough that they can be eaten without dunking into coffee or tea, which makes them a great option for kids.

1 Preheat the oven to 350°F. Place the sliced almonds on a rimmed baking sheet and toast in the oven until golden brown, 4 to 5 minutes. Transfer to a medium plate and set aside. Line the baking sheet with parchment paper and set aside.

2 In a medium bowl, whisk together the flour, baking powder, and salt. Using a stand mixer or a hand mixer, combine the butter and sugar on medium-high speed until light and airy, about 2 minutes. Add the eggs, one at a time, making sure to incorporate the first egg before adding the second. Add the orange zest, reduce the speed to low, and blend for 30 seconds. Add the flour mixture and mix until combined. Turn off the mixer and use a rubber spatula to fold in the toasted almonds and the chocolate chips.

3 Lightly flour the work surface and divide the dough in half. Set the 2 pieces on the parchment paper–lined baking sheet and, using floured hands, shape each into a 16-inch-long log, leaving a 5-inch space between the logs. Use a pastry brush to remove the excess flour. Use your hands to flatten each log into a 2-inch-wide strip.

4   Bake the biscotti logs, turning the baking sheet midway through cooking, until golden and set, about 20 minutes. Remove from the oven and place the baking sheet on a rack; let the biscotti logs cool for 15 minutes. Reduce the oven temperature to 300°F.

5   Transfer each biscotti log to a cutting board and use a serrated knife to slice the log on the bias into sixteen ⅓-inch-thick slices. Arrange the slices cut side down on the baking sheet. Bake the biscotti, rotating the baking sheet halfway through cooking, until the cookies are golden and crisp, about 30 minutes. Transfer the baking sheet to a wire rack and let cool completely. (The biscotti can be stored in an airtight container at room temperature for up to 3 days.)

PER SERVING (1 biscotti): Calories 168 / Protein 3g / Dietary Fiber 2g / Sugars 12g / Total Fat 8g

FLOURLESS FUDGY DREAM COOKIES

MAKES 2 DOZEN COOKIES   **PREPARATION TIME 10 MINUTES**
COOKING TIME 10 MINUTES

1 cup cooked chickpeas (homemade, page 81; or canned, rinsed)

¼ cup chocolate-hazelnut spread

⅓ cup almond butter

3 tablespoons unsweetened cocoa powder

2 tablespoons sugar

1 teaspoon baking powder

1 teaspoon vanilla extract

¼ teaspoon kosher salt

⅛ teaspoon almond extract (optional)

These are my husband's favorite chocolate cookies. They are fudgy and decadent, and no one would ever guess that there are chickpeas (!) in the dough. The chickpeas replace both flour and eggs, making this a fantastic gluten-free dessert option. Add 2 tablespoons of flour to give these a cakelike texture.

1   Adjust the oven racks to the upper-middle and lower-middle positions and preheat the oven to 350°F. Line 2 rimmed baking sheets with parchment paper and set aside.

2   Add the chickpeas and chocolate-hazelnut spread to a food processor and pulse until you get a smooth paste, ten to twelve 1-second pulses, stopping the food processor halfway through to scrape down the sides and bottom of the work bowl.

3   Add the almond butter, cocoa, sugar, baking powder, vanilla, salt, and almond extract (if using) and process until the mixture is smooth. (The dough will be very thick and sticky. If too dense for the food processor, turn the dough out onto a work surface and knead by hand until well combined.)

4   Divide the dough into tablespoon-size balls, and place them 2 inches apart on the baking sheets. Press down the tops lightly, then bake until the edges are firm but the centers are still soft to light pressure, about 10 minutes. Rotate the pans top to bottom and front to back halfway through the baking.

5   Remove the baking sheets from the oven and set them aside. Cool the cookies on the baking sheet for 5 minutes, then transfer to a wire rack until they are completely cooled.

PER SERVING (1 cookie): Calories 48 / Protein 1g / Dietary Fiber 1g / Sugars 3g / Total Fat 3g

BUTTERSCOTCH BANANA CRÊPES

SERVES 4   **PREPARATION TIME 15 MINUTES** (plus 20 minutes to rest)
COOKING TIME 30 MINUTES

FOR THE CRÊPES

1¼ cups white whole wheat flour

Pinch of kosher salt

1 cup 2% milk

¼ cup seltzer water

1 large egg

1 tablespoon unsalted butter, melted

Nonstick pan spray

Confectioners' sugar (optional)

FOR THE BANANAS

2 tablespoons unsalted butter

3 medium bananas, peeled and thinly sliced on the bias

3 tablespoons lightly packed dark brown sugar

¼ cup 2% milk

For my French mother-in-law, making beautifully tanned, thin, and lacy crêpes is second nature. Here, I borrow her smart technique of using reduced-fat milk and eau gazeuse (sparkling water) instead of whole milk, giving the crêpe extra lightness. I also use white whole wheat flour to add a little more nutrition.

1 To make the crêpes: Whisk together the flour and salt in a large bowl. In a medium bowl, whisk together the milk, seltzer water, egg, and melted butter. Add the milk mixture to the flour mixture and whisk until smooth. Transfer to a large liquid measuring cup (or pitcher), cover with plastic wrap, and set aside for 20 minutes (or refrigerate overnight).

2 Heat a medium nonstick skillet over medium-high heat and mist with pan spray. Add about 3 tablespoons of batter to the skillet, and tilt the skillet to create a thin, even circle of batter. Cook until the crêpe is browned, about 2 minutes, then use a nonstick spatula to flip it over. Cook the other side until browned, about 1 minute longer. Slide the crêpe out onto a large plate. Repeat to make 8 crêpes.

3 To make the bananas: Melt the butter in a medium skillet over medium-high heat, then add the bananas. Cook until the bananas begin to caramelize around the edges, shaking the pan occasionally, 2 to 3 minutes. Add the brown sugar and shake the skillet to toss the bananas in the sugar. Once the sugar starts to sizzle and melt, add the milk and cook, stirring gently, until the sauce thickens, about 2 minutes.

4 Roll the crêpes into long cylinders and serve with the butterscotch bananas and a dusting of confectioners' sugar, if desired.

PER SERVING: Calories 377 / Protein 10g / Dietary Fiber 7g / Sugars 27g / Total Fat 12g

STRACCIATELLA MERINGUES

MAKES 4 LARGE MERINGUES   **PREPARATION TIME** 10 MINUTES
COOKING TIME 40 MINUTES (plus 1 hour to cool)

2 large egg whites

⅛ teaspoon table salt

⅛ teaspoon cream of tartar

3 tablespoons granulated sugar

¼ teaspoon vanilla extract

2 tablespoons sifted confectioners' sugar

½ ounce dark chocolate, finely grated on a Microplane-style grater

Finely grated chocolate folded into a glossy meringue offers just enough chocolate flavor to give the nearly fat-free cookies a hint of richness. The large meringues are perfectly crisp around the edges and slightly marshmallow-y at the centers, adding to the feeling of decadence.

1   Preheat the oven to 275°F. Line 2 rimmed baking sheets with parchment paper. Use a pencil to make four 4-inch circles on the parchment so they are at least 1 inch apart. Turn over the parchment (and make sure you can see the pencil outline).

2   Using a stand mixer fitted with the whisk attachment (or a large bowl and a hand mixer), beat the egg whites and salt on medium-high speed until frothy, about 30 seconds. Add the cream of tartar and, with the mixer running, begin adding the granulated sugar a little at a time. Add the vanilla, then sprinkle in the confectioners' sugar and continue to whip until the meringue becomes glossy and forms stiff peaks, 3 to 4 minutes.

3   Turn off the mixer and use a rubber spatula to gently fold in the grated chocolate. Gently divide the meringue into the 4 circles on the baking sheets. Use the back of a spoon to softly spread each mound of meringue so it fills the circle.

4   Bake until the meringues are dry and easily separate from the parchment paper, about 40 minutes. Turn off the oven and let the meringues cool completely in the oven, about 1 hour, before removing them from the parchment paper.

PER SERVING (1 meringue): Calories 78 / Protein 2g / Dietary Fiber 0g / Sugars 13g / Total Fat 1g

ROASTED FRUIT
AND HOMEMADE RICOTTA

SERVES 6   **PREPARATION TIME 45 MINUTES**   **COOKING TIME 20 MINUTES**

FOR THE RICOTTA

2 cups 2% milk

1 cup whole milk

1½ tablespoons white vinegar

½ vanilla bean, split lengthwise, seeds scraped out with the tip of a paring knife (reserve the bean for another use or discard)

FOR THE FRUIT

2 peaches, halved, pitted, and quartered

2 pears, seeded and quartered lengthwise

2 plums, pitted and quartered

1 tablespoon unsalted butter, melted

1 tablespoon lightly packed light brown sugar

¼ teaspoon ground cinnamon

¼ cup hazelnuts

Honey of choice

Setting out an assortment of sweet options for dessert, like homemade ricotta, fresh fruit, roasted fruit, toasted hazelnuts, and honey for drizzling, is visually appealing and allows guests to pick and choose how much (or little) dessert they want.

1 To make the ricotta: Set a large fine-mesh sieve over a large bowl. Line the sieve with a dampened piece of cheesecloth. Pour both of the milks into a medium stainless steel or enameled pot and bring to a boil over medium heat, stirring occasionally. Turn off the heat and stir in the vinegar. Let the mixture set for 5 minutes (it will separate into curds and whey).

2 Pour the mixture into the cheesecloth-lined sieve and drain until the ricotta is nice and thick, 20 to 25 minutes. Pour off and discard the water in the bowl occasionally (for thicker ricotta, drain longer).

3 Turn the ricotta out into a bowl and stir in the vanilla seeds. Use immediately or transfer the ricotta to an airtight container and refrigerate for up to 5 days.

4 To roast the fruit: Preheat the oven to 400°F. Add the peaches, pears, and plums to a large bowl and toss with the melted butter, brown sugar, and cinnamon. Place the fruit on a rimmed baking sheet and roast until slightly soft and caramelized, about 10 minutes. Transfer to a bowl and set aside. Roast the hazelnuts on a second rimmed baking sheet until golden, 6 to 8 minutes. Remove from the oven and transfer to a cutting board to cool, then roughly chop.

5 Serve the ricotta alongside the roasted fruit, chopped hazelnuts, and honey for drizzling.

PER SERVING: Calories 191 / Protein 6g / Dietary Fiber 3g / Sugars 20g / Total Fat 9g

KITCHEN STRATEGY

Ricotta Sweet or Savory

Ricotta can easily take to sweet or savory stir-ins. For a savory use in lasagna, stuffed shells, or gnocchi, I swap the vanilla for lemon zest or finely chopped fresh herbs, or just leave the ricotta plain.

BANANA-MANGO TOFU PUDDING

SERVES 6   PREPARATION TIME 10 MINUTES (plus 15 minutes to chill)
COOKING TIME 3 MINUTES

2 teaspoons unsalted butter

2 medium bananas, peeled, halved lengthwise, and sliced crosswise into 8 pieces

½ cup small fresh mango cubes (from 1 small mango) or frozen and thawed mango

1 12-ounce package soft Japanese silken tofu

2 tablespoons confectioners' sugar

1 teaspoon vanilla extract

⅛ teaspoon ground cinnamon, plus more for serving

¼ teaspoon kosher salt

Puddings are a dessert staple in our house, since I always have the ingredients on hand to make them. I tend to veer toward desserts that have their roots in ingredients with a bit of protein in them, so whether I make a milk-based pudding on the stovetop or a no-cook tofu pudding in the food processor, I know I'll end up with something sweet and creamy that won't take us all on that dreaded sugar-fueled roller-coaster ride of highs and lows.

1 Melt the butter in a large nonstick skillet set over medium heat. Add the banana pieces, flat side down, and the mango cubes and cook until golden on both sides, 2 to 3 minutes total. Transfer to a plate to cool.

2 Place the tofu in the bowl of a food processor. Add the confectioners' sugar, vanilla, cinnamon, and salt along with the cooled bananas and mango. Process until smooth and creamy, about 30 seconds.

3 Divide the pudding among 6 small bowls or 6-ounce ramekins. Refrigerate for at least 15 minutes before serving with a sprinkle of cinnamon. (If not serving immediately, cover each serving with plastic wrap and refrigerate for up to 1 day.)

PER SERVING: Calories 93 / Protein 3g / Dietary Fiber 1g / Sugars 10g / Total Fat 3g

KITCHEN STRATEGY

Chocolate-Tofu Pudding Variation
Swap ½ cup melted semisweet chocolate and 2 teaspoons coconut oil for the butter-sautéed fruit, and add 2 tablespoons cocoa powder to the food processor with the tofu. A little grated orange zest is a nice touch, too.

DULCE DE LECHE
BROWN RICE PUDDING

SERVES 4   **PREPARATION TIME** 5 MINUTES (plus 10 minutes to rest)
COOKING TIME 1 HOUR

1 cup instant brown rice

2 cups unsweetened vanilla almond milk

1 cup reduced-fat evaporated milk

⅓ cup maple syrup

Pinch of kosher salt

3 cinnamon sticks

¼ cup toasted sliced almonds

I love desserts that can go in the oven just before guests arrive for dinner, then come out of the oven in time for dessert. When using brown rice to make rice pudding, you usually have to break it up a bit in a food processor to help expose the starches and encourage creaminess. With quick brown rice, however, that's a step you can happily skip. Caramelized sweetened condensed milk is traditionally used to make thick and rich dulce de leche. Here, I use the same idea of low and slow cooking to encourage the evaporated milk to become rich and caramel-y.

1 Preheat the oven to 300°F. Stir together the rice, almond milk, evaporated milk, maple syrup, and salt in a 1½-quart baking dish. Add the cinnamon sticks.

2 Bake the rice for 30 minutes, then stir and loosely cover with a piece of aluminum foil. Continue to bake, stirring every 15 minutes, until the rice is very soft, about 1 hour total. (The pudding will still look loose and milky, but the rice will absorb the liquid as it cools.)

3 Remove the pudding from the oven, stir, and cover with the foil. Set aside for 10 minutes, then divide among bowls and serve sprinkled with toasted almonds.

PER SERVING: Calories 286 / Protein 9g / Dietary Fiber 2g / Sugars 24g / Total Fat 9g

VANILLA AND BLUEBERRY CHEESECAKE PUDDING

SERVES 4   **PREPARATION TIME** 15 MINUTES (plus 4 hours to chill)
COOKING TIME 10 MINUTES

FOR THE BLUEBERRIES

1 tablespoon sugar

2 teaspoons fresh lemon juice

½ cup fresh or frozen blueberries

FOR THE CHEESECAKE PUDDING

3 tablespoons sugar

2 tablespoons cornstarch

Pinch of kosher salt

1½ cups cold 2% milk

1 teaspoon vanilla extract

¼ cup reduced-fat cream cheese (Neufchâtel)

2 graham crackers, crushed

A little reduced-fat cream cheese stirred into a quick stovetop pudding gives it a tangy, creamy, cheesecake-y flavor and texture, with way less fat and fewer calories than a slice of cheesecake. In these parfait-style puddings, I layer the vanilla pudding with a super-fast blueberry sauce accented with a little lemon juice for a bright, fresh taste. A sprinkle of crushed graham crackers over the top really brings home the cheesecake flavor profile.

1 To make the blueberries: In a small saucepan, bring 2 tablespoons water, the sugar, and lemon juice to a simmer over medium heat, stirring occasionally to dissolve the sugar. Add the blueberries and cook, stirring often, until they soften, 1 to 2 minutes (a little longer if using frozen berries). Use a fork to gently mash most of the berries, then turn off the heat.

2 To make the cheesecake pudding: Whisk the sugar, cornstarch, and salt together in a medium saucepan. Whisk in the cold milk and then set the saucepan over medium-high heat. Continue to whisk until a few bubbles pop at the surface and the mixture is thick, 3 to 4 minutes. Turn off the heat and whisk in the vanilla and the cream cheese.

3 Divide half the pudding among 4 ramekins, then divide the blueberries among the ramekins. Top each serving with the remaining pudding. Cover each ramekin with plastic wrap and refrigerate for at least 4 hours or up to 3 days. Serve chilled, sprinkled with graham crumbs.

PER SERVING: Calories 167 / Protein 4g / Dietary Fiber 1g / Sugars 19g / Total Fat 5g

POMEGRANATE-APPLE GELATIN
WITH RASPBERRIES

SERVES 6   **PREPARATION TIME** 1 HOUR, 10 MINUTES   **COOKING TIME** 6 MINUTES

1 cup apple juice

1 cup pomegranate juice

2 1-ounce envelopes unflavored gelatin

1 cup fresh raspberries

Fruit cocktail suspended in Jell-O was a dessert staple during my childhood. It's no wonder that dipping my spoon into a jiggly-wiggly bowl of it gives me instant comfort! I've updated this oldie-but-goodie by using unflavored gelatin to firm up super-tangy pomegranate juice (antioxidants!) and apple juice. Raspberries are a nice fruit upgrade from my mom's canned fruit cocktail (remember the crazy pink cherry?). Be sure to read the juice label to make sure that the product you are buying doesn't have added sweeteners and is 100 percent juice.

1 Pour the apple and pomegranate juices and 1 cup water into a small saucepan. Sprinkle the gelatin over the surface and set aside for 5 minutes (do not stir).

2 Set the saucepan over low heat, stirring to dissolve the gelatin, about 6 minutes. Divide the gelatin mixture among six small bowls. Add a few raspberries to each bowl, cover the bowls with plastic wrap, and refrigerate the gelatin until it is firm, at least 1 hour or overnight. Serve cold.

PER SERVING: Calories 84 / Protein 8g / Dietary Fiber 1g / Sugars 10g / Total Fat 0g

SUPERMARKET STRATEGY

Save with Seasonal Fruits

Most supermarkets offer the best prices on fruit when the fruit is in season and abundant. So follow the calendar, using fruit that is in season and cheap. When peak-season fruit isn't available (and the alternative is rock-hard mangos or peaches shipped in from faraway lands, with prices to reflect it!), I go with frozen fruits. Individually quick-frozen fruits like mangos, raspberries, and peaches can be a tasty and wallet-friendly alternative to fresh fruit.

MANGO-RASPBERRY FROZEN YOGURT

SERVES 6   **PREPARATION TIME 10 MINUTES** (plus 1 hour, 30 minutes to freeze)
COOKING TIME NONE

2 cups plain reduced-fat Greek yogurt

¼ cup 2% milk

2 cups thawed frozen mango pieces

1 ripe banana

¼ cup no-sugar-added spreadable fruit raspberry jam

Homemade frozen yogurt is a family favorite. You can substitute any other frozen fruit, but mango works especially well combined with plain yogurt. Raspberry jam adds a pretty ribbon of color and sweetness swirled through the yellow yogurt.

1 Place the yogurt, milk, mango, and banana in a blender jar and blend until smooth. Place the blender jar in the freezer and chill for at least 30 minutes or up to 1 hour.

2 Remove the blender jar from the freezer and add the raspberry jam. Use the tip of a knife to swirl the jam into the yogurt and re-freeze until firm, about 1 hour. Let the yogurt stand at room temperature for 10 minutes before dividing among small dessert bowls. (The frozen yogurt freezes well for up to 1 week.)

PER SERVING: Calories 172 / Protein 8g / Dietary Fiber 3g / Sugars 26g / Total Fat 3g

KITCHEN STRATEGY

More Fruits for Frozen Yogurt

Just about any fruit—frozen or fresh—can be used to make frozen yogurt. Some combinations I really like are peach yogurt with raspberry jam swirls and nectarine yogurt with blueberry jam swirls.

ACKNOWLEDGMENTS

Creating a book is an act of collaboration by many minds, hearts, and hands.

Thank you to the entire team at Clarkson Potter for guidance, wisdom, and experience. Special thanks to my editor, Emily Takoudes; pinch hitter Amanda Englander; art director Jane Treuhaft; and designer La Tricia Watford. Thank you to Raquel Pelzel for helping shape words into a book. I love having you as my teammate and friend. Thank you to Tina Rupp for the beautiful photography; to Dahlia Warner, who works magical makeup wonders on me; and to Marjorie Livingston for adding her nutritional expertise.

To my entire Food Network family: thank you for letting me grow up on TV with you. Thank you to my agents at William-Morris Endeavor. Josh, Jon, Jeff, and Andy, I am grateful for all you do.

Michelle Betrock, thank you for being as smart as you are, for working on my team, and for being one of my dearest friends. Angela Robles, you changed the way I look at work forever, and Lisa Johnson, thank you for teaching me about the freedom to fail. Leti Sanchez and Kristyna Andraškova, thank you for loving my kids so deeply, and helping them with their homework so I could finish another chapter.

Finally, to Philippe, Valentine, Charlotte, Margaux, and Océane, my gratitude to God for bringing you into my life knows no limits.

INDEX